The Role of the
Augsburg Confession

The Role of the
Augsburg Confession

Catholic and Lutheran Views

edited by
JOSEPH A. BURGESS

in collaboration with
George Lindbeck, Harry McSorley,
Harding Meyer, and Heinze Schütte

1980

FORTRESS PRESS   PHILADELPHIA

PAULIST PRESS   NEW YORK/RAMSEY/TORONTO

Published by
Fortress Press
Philadelphia, Pennsylvania
and
Paulist Press
New York/Ramsey/Toronto

Library of Congress Cataloging in Publication Data

Main entry under title:

The Role of the Augsburg confession.

All but three of these essays were originally published in 1977 in Katholische Anerkennung des Augsburgischen Bekenntnisses?
Includes bibliographical references.
1. Augsburg Confession—Addresses, essays, lectures.
2. Catholic Church—Relations—Lutheran Church—Addresses, essays, lectures. 3. Lutheran Church—Relations—Catholic Church—Addresses, essays, lectures.
I. Burgess, Joseph, 1929–   II. Katholische Anerkennung des Augsburgischen Bekenntnisses?
BX8069.R64   238'.41   79–7373
ISBN 0–8006–0549–7

Paulist Press ISBN 0–8091–0306–0
Printed in the United States of America

Contents

CONTENTS

Foreword
by
Johannes Cardinal Willebrands

On 12 November 1966 Pope Paul VI appealed for more prayer and greater efforts to unite all Christians, especially because we have begun to converge and because through theological dialogue basic agreements seem possible on the important questions. Every proposal which can lead to overcoming our separation and bring us closer to visible unity deserves careful consideration. The suggestion that the *Confessio Augustana* be used as the theme and starting point of an ecumenical dialogue between Catholics and Lutherans takes seriously the fact that the Reformers did not want to found a new church but held to the one, holy, catholic, and apostolic Church which already existed; that the CA still is a valid confession today; and that unity is only possible on the basis of truth, although "freedom in that which is doubtful" continues.

It is gratifying that the Lutheran World Federation has been positive about the discussions "concerning the possibility of accepting the CA as a legitimate expression of Christian truth." We also welcome the fact that through their essays in this volume Catholic and Lutheran theologians continue to dialogue about this question. We hope that unprejudiced historical and theological investigations will clarify the meaning of the CA so that it becomes possible to restore unity in diversity and to further the unity in truth which the Lord wills. It must be understood, of course, that official reaction by the Catholic Church can only take place after a thorough consideration of all aspects of the problem.

JOHANNES CARDINAL WILLEBRANDS
President of the Vatican Secretariat for Christian Unity

Foreword
by
President David Preus

At the Sixth Assembly of the Lutheran World Federation at Dar-es-Salaam, Tanzania, 13–25 June 1977, the Assembly welcomed "endeavors which aim at a Catholic recognition of the *Confessio Augustana*" and expressed "the willingness of the Lutheran World Federation to engage in dialogue with the Roman Catholic Church on this subject." Lutherans can only look with satisfaction on the fact that once again, after four hundred and fifty years, the CA has been used by Roman Catholic and Lutheran theologians in their efforts to discover our common Christian faith. This in itself is ecumenical progress.

At the same time it would be precipitate to imply that difficulties do not remain. More discussion is needed between Lutheran and Roman Catholic theologians in order to clarify the meaning of the CA and to unravel the challenges which each side makes to the other. The practical implications of any future Roman Catholic recognition would also need to be worked out with great care by each church.

It is important that a start has been made and that we have raised our sights. We are confident that our common concern for the truth of the gospel will draw us together, for we have one Lord, one faith, one Church, and one gospel. To use the words of the Sixth Assembly, our hope is that Roman Catholic recognition of the CA will "further the development towards full ecclesial communion as sister churches."

DAVID W. PREUS
President of the American Lutheran Church
Vice-President of the Lutheran World Federation

Introduction

"Recognition of the CA by the Roman Catholic Church" is a recent challenge, and it is helpful to trace its development. Already in 1967 Peter Brunner had expressed the hope that some sort of Catholic recognition of the statements of faith in the CA would be possible.[1] Then in 1974 Vinzenz Pfnür, a Catholic theologian, supported this idea in a paper given at a meeting of the international Lutheran-Catholic dialogue in Rome; he referred to his teacher, Archbishop Joseph Ratzinger, who already in 1958–1959 had introduced his students in a seminar to the CA and its importance.[2] Pfnür's suggestions were published in the journal *Catholica*,[3] and he reported what had happened at the meeting in Rome in *KNA—Ökumenische Information* under the title: "Recognition of the CA by the Catholic Church?"[4] Next the idea was taken up at Münster by the diocesan Ecumenical Commission, to which Pfnür belongs, and they requested that the German Bishops' Conference "examine the possibility of the recognition of the CA by the Catholic Church." In the middle of 1975 and of 1976 Pfnür published a long article in two parts in the *Internationale Katholische Zeitschrift "Communio"*: "Recognition of the CA by the Catholic Church?"[5]

In November 1975 this idea was brought to the attention of the Secretariat for Christian Unity in Rome through a visit by five representatives of the "Coordinating Group Working for Church Unity," which at the instigation of the League for Protestant-Catholic Reunion had been formed for this occasion from its own membership, the High Church Society of the Augsburg Confession, and other groups. Johannes Cardinal Willebrands, President of the Secretariat for Christian Unity, and Msgr. Charles Moeller took part in the discussion. The Lutherans asked whether "it would not be very important for the ecumenical situation if the CA would be clearly shown to be a

Catholic confession?" The Catholic side did not consider it impossible to consider the CA to be a Catholic confession. It was proposed that a Catholic and a Lutheran theologian be asked to write an appraisal of the CA which could then be the basis for further steps. Three lines developed from this discussion. One leads directly to a meeting arranged by the High Church Society at Schloss Schwanberg in September 1976, to which the Society for Church Renewal in Bavaria had also invited its members. Wolfhart Pannenberg lectured on "The CA as a Catholic Confession," and Heinz Schütte lectured on "The Question of the Possibility of Catholic Recognition of the CA by the Catholic Church." The other two lines lead to initiatives by theologians from the Secretariat for Christian Unity. At the consultation on ecumenical methodology sponsored by the Lutheran World Federation in June 1976 in Geneva, Msgr. Charles Moeller repeatedly stressed the importance of a Catholic recognition of the CA. As a consequence, in the report of the consultation a recommendation was made to the Lutheran churches "to show their openness to and interest in the Catholic discussion of the possibility of receiving the CA as a legitimate expression of Christian truth." This report from the consultation was presented in August 1976 to the meeting of the executive committee of the Lutheran World Federation in Uppsala. In his statement to the executive committee, Heinz Schütte, the observer from the Secretariat for Christian Unity, stressed the importance of the "efforts for a Catholic reception of the CA as the basis for confessional unity." Both theologians from the Secretariat for Christian Unity appealed to a lecture given by Ratzinger in January 1976 in Graz.[6] In it Ratzinger took up the idea of a "Catholic recognition of the CA or, more correctly, of recognizing the CA as catholic," explained the motivation for doing so, showed briefly its implications for both the Lutheran as well as the Catholic Church, and fit the idea into a more comprehensive vision of the future of ecumenism. These very important remarks by Cardinal Ratzinger have occupied an important place in the discussions since the time he made them.[7]

A remarkable switch in roles seems to have taken place. During the Reformation the Lutheran side, in spite of opposition both at Augsburg and in the following religious debates, proposed the CA as the basis for unity or at least the basis for discussion. Now primarily

the Catholic side suggested using the CA as a Catholic confession, while at first only small groups of Lutherans accepted this idea, and Lutheran leaders remained very reserved. To be sure, in the meantime an important breakthrough has taken place on the Lutheran side. At the General Assembly of the Lutheran World Federation in Dar-es-Salaam (13–26 June 1977), the question of a Catholic recognition of the CA was discussed, and the following resolution was passed:

> 4. Recognition of the *Confessio Augustana* by the Roman Catholic Church.
> (18) The Assembly takes cognizance of the fact that distinguished Roman Catholic theologians consider it possible for their church to recognize the *Confessio Augustana* as a particular expression of the common Christian faith. They hope that this recognition would open the way toward a form of fellowship between the Roman Catholic Church and the Lutheran Church in which both churches, without abandoning their particularities and identities, would further the development towards full ecclesial communion as sister churches.
> (19) The Assembly—conscious of the importance of this initiative— welcomes endeavours which aim at a Catholic recognition of the *Confessio Augustana,* expresses the willingness of the Lutheran World Federation to engage in dialogue with the Roman Catholic Church on this subject, and requests that the Executive Committee promote and carefully follow the progress of all studies of this matter, its possibilities, its problems, and its wider ecumenical implications.[8]

Lutherans have been surprised and indeed cautious about the possibility of Catholics recognizing the CA, for the *Confutatio* seemed to have closed the door. Yet as they reflect on the intention of the CA and the Reformation in general, they cannot help but realize that Catholics would be recognizing the basic ecumenical conviction of the Reformation. Lutherans have continuously drawn attention to the fact that the CA wants to be a "witness of the whole Church and for the whole Church" and that the CA binds the members of the Lutheran Church "to all other Christians of the world in the one, holy, universal Christian Church," as both the general secretary and the president of the Lutheran World Federation emphasized in their speeches to the executive committee in 1976. Therefore the only appropriate answer can be a concerned interest and an active involvement in the idea of a Catholic recognition of the CA. For such recognition is only then sensible and lasting when it is not a one-sided Catholic act, but occurs through mutual agreement and includes the active participation of the Lutheran partner, even if not necessarily the whole of Lutheranism.

If Lutherans ask what motives on the Catholic side have led to this idea, two reasons stand out. In the first place, it is the desire to identify one's partner clearly. For a long time the Lutheran-Catholic dialogue has had an official character; because of the results of this dialogue, forms of church fellowship need to be realized and thus decisions made which are binding on the churches. Yet from the Catholic side the question arises again and again: To what extent is what has been said, advocated, and subscribed to in such dialogues really supported and affirmed by the total Lutheran Church? That is to say, is a consensus realized in a dialogue not rendered worthless and invalid through the plurality and disparity of theological opinion within the Lutheran Church? The separate statements made to the *Malta Report,* especially those by Heinz Schürmann and Hans Conzelmann, illustrate this problem very clearly.[9] In order to meet this difficulty, Catholics in a certain sense end up adopting the Lutheran frame of reference by accepting the specific Lutheran conviction that the unity of the Church is based primarily not on the office of the Ministry or church order but on the *consensus de doctrina,* and that it shows itself principally in common confession. Here, when the Church confesses, is that which binds and is binding, that by which the Lutheran Church can be most clearly identified and by which it can be bound. A Lutheran-Catholic dialogue which has such a frame of reference will most probably produce results which participate in the binding force of a confession. Just as Peter Brunner tied his hopes for a revised Catholic judgment of the CA to the requirement that any Catholic-Lutheran dialogue which plans to succeed must be oriented to "whatever norms of doctrine are held," so Cardinal Ratzinger now says: "The search for church unity must, by the very nature of the problem itself, be tied to that which is held in common in the Church. . . . That means that the frame of reference for such efforts must be the confessional writings of the Lutheran Church and the individual theologians only to the extent that they point to what is held in common."[10]

In the second place, Catholics are considering precisely the CA for possible recognition because the CA as the central Lutheran confession is also the least polemical and most conciliatory of the Lutheran confessional writings. In contrast to the early Reformation with its often pointed anti-Roman polemics and practice, in contrast to the old Luther with his bitter rejection of all efforts for unity, and in contrast to the more judgmental Lutheran confessional writings which came later, the CA presents, as Cardinal Ratzinger notes, a picture of Lutheranism in a state of repose, not distorted by excitement, distrust, and dispute. It presents, therefore, the most authentic form of the faith of the Reformation, and this is confirmed by its rapid reception in all Lutheran churches.

The meeting of the High Church Society of the Augsburg Confession at Schloss Schwanberg raised those questions which need to be answered in order for Catholics to be able to recognize the CA. The editors of *Ökumenische Information*—published by the Catholic Press Service (Katholische Nachrichtenagentur) and the Johann-Adam-Moehler Institute in Paderborn—selected Lutheran and Catholic theologians to write on these questions in order to further the discussion of a possible Catholic recognition of the CA. The resultant essays, by Hermann Dietzfelbinger, Harding Meyer, H. Döring, Vilmos Vajta, Hans Jorissen, and Walter Kasper, together with the contributions mentioned above by Vinzenz Pfnür, Wolfhart Pannenberg, and Heinz Schütte, plus an article by P. Brunner, were edited by Harding Meyer and Heinz Schütte and published in 1977 in the series *Ökumenische Perspektiven*, no. 9, edited by Harding Meyer and issued by the Institute for Ecumenical Research at Strasbourg. The editors wish to thank the Catholic Theological Society of America and Lutheran World Ministries for generous grants which made it possible to produce an American edition of most of these essays plus the addition of three more by Avery Dulles, Robert Jenson, and Harry McSorley. Thanks are also due to Denis Janz for translating Walter Kasper and Vinzenz Pfnür, to Fred Kramer for translating Hermann Dietzfelbinger, Hans Jorissen, Harding Meyer, and Heinz Schütte, and to George Lindbeck for translating Wolfhart Pannenberg and updating the essay by Vilmos Vajta.

NOTES

1. P. Brunner, "Reform—Reformation, Einst—heute: Elemente eines ökumenischen Dialoges im 450. Gedächtnisjahr von Luthers Ablassthesen," *Kerygma und Dogma* 13(1967): 179.

2. Cf. Vinzenz Pfnür, *Einig in der Rechtfertigungslehre? Die Rechtfertigungslehre der "Confessio Augustana" (1530) und die Stellungnahme der katholischen Kontroverstheologie zwischen 1530 und 1535* (Wiesbaden: Franz Steiner, 1970), Introduction.

3. Vinzenz Pfnür, "Das Problem des Amtes in heutiger lutherisch/katholischer Begegnung," *Catholica* 28(1974): 125–26.

4. *KNA—Ökumenische Information*, no. 6 (1974).

5. See pp. 1–26 below.

6. "Prognosen für die Zukunft des Ökumenismus," *Bausteine* 17, no. 65 (1977): 6–14.

7. See the extensive citations in this volume, pp. 48–50, 63–64, 74–75 below.

8. Arne Sovik, ed., *In Christ—A New Community: The Proceedings of the Sixth Assembly of the Lutheran World Federation, Dar-es-Salaam, Tanzania, June 13–25, 1977* (Geneva: Lutheran World Federation, 1977), p. 175.

9. MR, pp. 272–73.

10. Ratzinger, "Prognosen," p. 12.

Abbreviations

Apology *Apology of the Augsburg Confession* (Ap. in documentation)

BS   *Die Bekenntnisschriften der evangelisch-lutherischen Kirche,*
          6th ed. rev. (Göttingen: Vandenhoeck & Ruprecht, 1967).

CA   *Confessio Augustana* (1530)

CT   *Concilium Tridentinum,* Published by the Görres-Gesell-
          schaft, 12 vols. (Freiburg: Herder, 1901–29).

CR   *Corpus Reformatorum,* ed. C. G. Bretschneider and H. E.
          Bindseil, 28 vols. (Brunsvigae and Halis Saxorum: C. A.
          Schwetschke et Filium, 1834–60).

DS   *Enchiridion Symbolorum,* ed. H. Denzinger and A. Schön-
          metzer, 33d ed. (Freiburg: Herder, 1965).

LThK²   *Lexikon für Theologie und Kirche,* 2d ed., 11 vols. (Frei-
          burg: Herder, 1957–66).

LW   American Edition of *Luther's Works,* ed. Jaroslav Pelikan
          and Helmut T. Lehmann (Philadelphia: Fortress Press; St.
          Louis: Concordia Publishing House, 1955–).

MR   *Malta Report.* "Report of the Joint Lutheran / Roman Catho-
          lic Study Commission on 'The Gospel and the Church',"
          Lutheran World 19(1972): 259–73; also in *Worship* 46
          (1972): 326–51.

RGG³   *Die Religion in Geschichte und Gegenwart,* ed. K. Galling,
          3d ed., 6 vols. (Tübingen: J. C. B. Mohr, 1957–62).

SL   *Constitution on the Sacred Liturgy (Sacrosanctum Con-
          cilium)* of Vatican II.

ST   *Summa Theologica* by Thomas Aquinas.

St. A.   *Melanchthons Werke in Auswahl,* ed. R. Stupperich, 7 vols.
          (Gütersloh: C. Bertelsman, 1951–55).

Tappert *The Book of Concord: The Confessions of the Evangelical Lutheran Church,* trans. and ed. Theodore G. Tappert (Philadelphia: Fortress Press, 1959).

WA *D. Martin Luthers Werke.* Kritische Gesamtausgabe. (Weimar: Böhlau, 1883–).

WA Br *D. Martin Luthers Werke.* Kritische Gesamtausgabe. Briefwechsel. 15 vols. (Weimar: Böhlau, 1930–78).

WA TR *D. Martin Luthers Werke.* Kritische Gesamtausgabe. Tischreden. 6 vols. (Weimar: Böhlau, 1912–21).

Recognition of the Augsburg Confession by the Catholic Church?

VINZENZ PFNÜR

It is clear that in the last five years, ecumenical dialogue has entered a new phase unnoticed by many. Since 1970 there have appeared—in part simultaneously and independently of one another—more than ten important common clarifications of what were until now seemingly insoluble controversial questions concerning Eucharist and Ministry[1] by various interconfessional groups of theologians. This is an unprecedented phenomenon.

It would go beyond the limits of this essay to evaluate the various documents individually. We must mention in particular, however, the documents resulting from the "Commission on Faith and Order" (WCC) because of the universal dimensions of their broad consensus: *Baptism, Eucharist,* and *Ministry* (Accra, 1974).[2] "They contain perspectives which move out from the limited viewpoint of local particularities to the whole world community of churches."[3]

THE CATHOLIC-LUTHERAN DIALOGUE

Within the Catholic-Lutheran dialogue, the dialogue in the United States and the one on the world level have a particular importance.

The Catholic-Lutheran working group, commissioned by the United States National Conference of Catholic Bishops' Commission for Ecumenical and Interreligious Affairs and the United States National Committee of the Lutheran World Federation, has shown itself to be the pacesetter.[4] Already in 1965 it published a joint declaration on *The Status of the Nicene Creed as Dogma of the Church.* In 1967 the third volume of the series *Lutherans and Catholics in Dialogue* ap-

[This study first appeared in *Internationale katholische Zeitschrift "Communio"* 4 (1975): 298–307; 5 (1976): 374–81, 477–78; cf. *Theology Digest* 24 (1976): 65–70.]

peared with reports and position papers on the theme *The Eucharist as Sacrifice*. In 1970 the dialogue published the first joint Catholic-Protestant document on the question of Ministry: *Eucharist and Ministry*. Even with reference to the very difficult question for Catholic-Protestant dialogue, that of papal primacy, the U.S. dialogue has taken the leadership with the publication in March 1974 of the volume *Papal Primacy and the Universal Church*. A citation will perhaps express the tone of this dialogue, which is not yet self-evident throughout the ecumenical dialogue:

> Even given these disagreements and points yet to be examined, it is now proper to ask, in the light of the agreement we have been able to reach, that our respective churches take specific actions toward reconciliation.
>
> Therefore we ask the Lutheran churches:
> —if they are prepared to affirm with us that papal primacy, renewed in the light of the gospel, need not be a barrier to reconciliation;
> —if they are able to acknowledge not only the legitimacy of the papal ministry in the service of the Roman Catholic communion but even the possibility and the desirability of the papal ministry, renewed under the gospel and committed to Christian freedom, in a larger communion which would include the Lutheran churches;
> —if they are willing to open discussion regarding the concrete implications of such a primacy to them.
>
> Likewise, we ask the Roman Catholic Church:
> —if in the light of our findings, it should not give high priority in its ecumenical concerns to the problem of reconciliation with the Lutheran churches;
> —if it is willing to open discussion of possible structures for reconciliation which would protect the legitimate traditions of the Lutheran communities and respect their spiritual heritage;
> —if it is prepared to envisage the possibility of a reconciliation which would recognize the self-government of Lutheran churches within a communion;
> —if, in the expectation of a foreseeable reconciliation, it is ready to acknowledge the Lutheran churches represented in our dialogue as sister churches which are already entitled to some measure of ecclesiastical communion.[5]

Likewise, in 1965 a "joint working group" at the world level was formed by the Lutheran World Federation and the Vatican Secretariat for Christian Unity. This group proposed the formation of a study commission which then met five times between 1967 and 1971. The closing report formulated at the 1971 meeting in Malta, "The Gospel and the Church" (the so-called *Malta Report*), was published on 9 February 1972, with a foreword by A. Appel, the General Secretary of the Lutheran World Federation, and Johannes Cardinal Willebrands, the President of the Secretariat for Christian Unity.[6]

For the continuation of the dialogue, two tasks were suggested: (1) the question of the reception of the consensus reached; and (2) the question of the "lack of clarity concerning a common teaching on ministry" (MR, 73). The international Lutheran-Catholic working group, which was newly constituted in 1973,[7] appointed at its second meeting in Rome (January 1974) two subcommissions for a more intensive study of this complex of questions. The question of Ministry itself was made more specific by focusing on the question of the episcopal Ministry. As a result of the second meeting, this point (among others) was agreed upon: "In the present situation it seems that the question of the episcopal Ministry has particular importance for further progress in the Lutheran-Catholic unity efforts. The question of joint recognition or reconciliation of Ministries and the subsequent question of the possibilities of eucharistic fellowship always leads to the question of the episcopal Ministry."

In the context of the documents of the ecumenical dialogue, two tasks for the immediate future present themselves: (1) to consolidate the gains already made and to increase a broad mutual basis of trust; and (2) to concretize the discussion of the Ministry question in the question of the episcopal Ministry, with a view to the concrete possibilities of the restoration of church fellowship.

In what follows, the first point will be developed somewhat more precisely. The more a reasonable hope for the restoration of unity between communions and churches emerges in the Catholic-Lutheran dialogue, the more pressing is the task of placing this possible communion on a broad mutual foundation.

THE QUESTION OF RECOGNITION OF THE CA
BY THE CATHOLIC CHURCH

As a concrete step to increase trust on both sides and to deepen the common theological foundations, it was suggested by the international Lutheran-Catholic working group in Rome in January 1974 that the Catholic Church recognize the CA as a witness to the

3

Church's faith.[8] The diocesan Ecumenical Commission of Münster took up this question again at its meeting of 19 June 1974 and suggested that

> the German Conference of Bishops might examine the possibility of the Catholic Church recognizing the CA. Such a recognition would, first, take the CA seriously in its historical and contemporary significance as an expression of the Protestant-Lutheran faith; at the same time it would dismantle a Catholic view of Lutheranism which is determined above all by polemically exaggerated Reformation expressions which stem from the period of radical change and disruption between 1520 and 1521 and which are preserved in collections of heretical Reformation statements, even though these, in the meantime, had already been corrected in the CA. Secondly, such a recognition would be an acknowledgment that the CA advocates no church-dividing teachings and that it can be affirmed on the Catholic side as a witness to the faith of the Church universal.

1. THE RECOGNITION OF THE CA AS AN EXPRESSION
   OF THE CORRECTION OF A POLEMICALLY DISTORTED PICTURE
   OF THE REFORMATION AND AS THE KEY TO A COMMON
   CATHOLIC-LUTHERAN EVALUATION OF THE REFORMATION

Since the Lutheran Church even in the present cannot renounce the Reformation as its point of reference, the Catholic-Lutheran dialogue is confronted with the unavoidable question of a common evaluation of the Reformation. For the Catholic side, the recognition of the CA would represent, in the first instance, a long overdue correction of a picture of the Reformation which has prevailed up to the present. Not untypical of the Catholic view is the presentation one finds in the Catholic textbook on church history, *Von Jesus bis Heute*:[9] The two chapters which deal with the Lutheran Reformation (chapter 21: "Martin Luther"; chapter 22: "The Division of the Church in the West"—chapters 23 and 24 deal with John Calvin and the Council of Trent) treat exclusively the young Luther and also the "main Reformation writings," while not a single word in the thirteen pages mentions the CA. These chapters, as foundations for thematic sections on "Problems of Tomorrow's Church," are supposed to contribute to the themes "Unity of the Church—How will it be possible?" "The Reformation Churches—Where are they going?" and "What do the others believe?" If the reduction of the Reformation to the early

Luther is already an inadmissible limitation, the placing of this early Luther in relation to "The Churches of the Reformation" or the "Faith of Others" is an ecumenically unacceptable short circuit. A similarly disastrous distortion is programmed into the curriculum of religious instruction for the fifth to tenth school years. The theme planned for the eighth grade, "The Catholic Church and the Churches of the Reformation," is divided up into the following possible topics: "1. Cathari and heretics: the pure Church; 2. Indulgences, relics, and the word of God; 3. Luther and the Roman Church; 4. A renewed or a new Church."

In the last fifty years, and not least through the work of Joseph Lortz, the Catholic picture of Luther has turned to some extent in a positive direction in contrast to the views of Denifle and Grisar. Yet despite this, and despite all ecumenical openness in the study and presentation of Reformation history, the thesis already propounded by Johannes Cochläus remains almost self-evident: the criterion of what is "Reformation" is to be found in the early Reformation writings of Luther and Melanchthon, and, in opposition to this, the fundamental Protestant confessional document, the CA, is "not a full expression of the Protestant view."

Such a viewpoint is, however, a perversion of the situation when seen by an unprejudiced spectator. It is precisely the meaning and intent of the CA to establish a standard for what the Lutheran Reformation is. In the twentieth year of the sixteenth century, Luther became the symbol of a broad movement in which widely differing groups, most of which were in conflict with the clergy, understood themselves to be followers of the new teaching (humanists, knights, peasants, artisans, imperial cities, princes). In addition to this fusion of Luther's Reformation concerns with the sociopolitical interests of particular groups, the theological spectrum of the followers of the new teaching became continually wider (Karlstadt, Müntzer, enthusiasts, Anabaptists, Zwingli, Agricola). Finally it was no longer sufficient for the first established Reformation congregations to polemicize against particular points; now, on the contrary, that which was essentially Christian in the Reformation view had to be set forth. The CA must be seen against this background of the 1520s. In defining itself over against the broad Reformation movement and in positively pre-

5

senting "a summary of the doctrines that are preached and taught in our churches for proper Christian instruction, the consolation of consciences, and the amendment of believers" (CA, conclusion of part 1:1), the measure of that which is Lutheran was established in the CA. This norm, as well as the literary genre of an official confession approved by authoritative representatives, raises the CA above the multitude of Reformation pamphlets and polemical works written for particular occasions.

The claim of the CA in this regard was pushed aside by Cochläus with the assertion that Melanchthon did not take the CA seriously but used it as a totally insidious and devilishly deceptive maneuver.[10] However, Cochläus could maintain this thesis in 1530 only by putting the CA over against statements by Luther and Melanchthon from the early 1520s and by passing over in silence Melanchthon's Colossians commentary of 1527, even though by 1529 this had appeared in its third edition and even though Melanchthon had recommended it to theology students in place of the *Loci* of 1521, which he regarded as still far too unrefined.[11] From our point of view today, in which we can survey and take into account the whole further development of Melanchthon's theology, Cochläus' thesis can no longer be maintained. On the points that Cochläus enumerates—the evaluation of patristic Christology and the councils of the ancient Church, the question of the freedom of the will, the necessity of penance, the significance of good works, and the distinction between original, actual, and mortal sin—the CA undoubtedly represents a modification or even a correction of Melanchthon's statements of 1520–21. Nor is this feigned, as Cochläus maintains; rather it is the expression of Melanchthon's theological persuasion which shows itself already in the Colossians commentary of 1527 and which is represented in a still more pointed way in the late *Loci* of 1559.

J. Lortz sees in the CA of "Melanchthon the humanist" an "inroad of this trivializing (of dogma) and relativizing (of what is Christian) into Lutheran Christianity." Lortz seeks to substantiate this monstrous assertion by pointing out that "the most important distinctions and essential deviations of the new doctrine from the old were not dealt with at all. The denial of free will was ignored, as was the fundamental attack on the primacy of the pope. The 'power' of the bishops

6

was to be retained, so long as they allowed the gospel to be truly preached."[12]

With regard to the question of the freedom of the will, the starting point of the Reformation teaching on the bondage of the will was the struggle against the position represented by Gabriel Biel, namely, that man by his own power and without the grace of God was capable of and free to love God above all things and thus to fulfill the divine law according to the substance of the act. In the years 1520–21 this theological concern was exaggerated into a philosophical determinism (everything happens of necessity) and into the assertion that God is the cause of evil. The further development led to a recovery of the proper theological concern for the teaching on the bondage of the will and to a rejection of the exaggerations of 1520–21 as unsuitable. In the course of this development, especially in the case of Melanchthon, the recourse to the hidden will of God, through which Luther in *De Servo Arbitrio* had relativized certain scriptural statements, was disavowed. The only aspects which were obligatory and which deserved to be accepted and retained were revelation and the universal promise of salvation given in the revealed word.[13] While Luther in 1525 still invoked the philosopher Laurentius Valla as Melanchthon had done in the *Loci* of 1521, Melanchthon had already in 1522 abandoned the reference to Valla. Later Melanchthon specifically denied the view of Valla and emphasized again and again that in the question of God's will we ought not to form an opinion "outside of the word and apart from the word."[14]

While Luther in the polemic against the papists deliberately translated the *salvos fieri* of 1 Timothy 2:4 as "recover" (*genesen*) or "become well" (*gesund werden*), for Melanchthon the translation "God wills that all men be saved," which has been universally confirmed by exegesis, became evidence for God's universal salvific will.[15] (The compromise translation which Luther used after 1530, "who wills that all men will be helped [*geholfen*]," has to this day not been revised.) Articles 18 and 19 of the CA must be evaluated in the light of this background.

The assertion that the bondage of the will is passed over is based on a misunderstanding of the theological concern of the teaching on the bondage of the will. Article 18 of the CA reads: "But without the grace, help, and activity of the Holy Spirit, man is not capable of making himself acceptable to God, of fearing God and believing in God with his whole heart, or of expelling inborn evil lusts from his heart." Also, that which is essentially Christian is not relativized, but, on the contrary, Melanchthon comes to a correction of his own view by taking Scripture and revelation seriously. This should be the decisive criterion in the evaluation of Melanchthon and not the reproach that he has "ironed out" "the roughness and internal contradiction of Luther's sayings . . . and in the process the indestructible quality, the infinite growing potential, that which cannot be taught in the classroom, in short, the primeval quality had been destroyed also."[16]

Melanchthon's decision to retain the "power" of the bishops does not stem from a humanistic tendency to relativize but, on the contrary, from his concern "that the pure teaching of the gospel would be handed on to the successors, because this is the first requirement of this position," as he also wrote after the negotiations for union had miscarried in 1530.[17] Moreover, this question must be seen against the background of the discussions of the question, found in the documents of the Frankish delegation at the Imperial Diet of Augsburg, whether the secular authority is competent to "regulate the gospel." Georg Amerbacher, a pastor from Blaufelden with Lutheran tendencies, rejected such an option "as an abominable sin."[18] Also, "Melanchthon believed that the destiny of the Church would be better preserved in the long run with the bishops than with the princes."[19]

The much-referred-to "soft-pedaling" (*Leisetreterei*) on the part of Melanchthon is less a pertinent argument than an indication of the widespread distortion of Melanchthon's view. Luther's statement from 15 May 1530 stands in the background here: "I have read over Master Philipp's *Apologia*; it pleases me very much and I don't know how to improve it or change it. Nor would it be suitable, since I cannot tread so gently and lightly. Christ our Lord grant that it will bear much and great fruit, as we hope and ask. Amen."[20] Read in context, this statement is on the whole positive,[21] and the phrase about treading gently and lightly, in the context of contemporaneous statements, is related not so much to the content as to the form.[22]

Luther's evaluation, expressed in a letter shortly after the presentation of the CA[23] and prefacing the éditions of the CA from 1531 on, is substantially more important: "I have spoken of your testimonies in the presence of kings and was not confounded."

On the other hand, the method practiced since the nineteenth century of measuring the CA by the early Luther cannot be substantiated. (1) There is nothing in the self-understanding found in Luther's early writings which compares with the self-understanding of the CA. (2) The unity of Lutheranism would be endangered if one were to make Luther's "tower experience" the criterion of what the Lutheran Reformation is, because at present there is no consensus among Luther scholars on the time and therefore also on the content of the so-called tower experience: what for one scholar is still typically Catholic is for another already essentially the Reformation. (3) Also, no criterion for what the Reformation is can be gained from the occasion on which the Reformation is celebrated, as the more recent results of research on the question of Luther's posting of the theses show. (4) If one derives the standard for what the Reformation is by using the period up until 1522,[24] then one must also take into account the extremely exaggerated position of Luther at this time, namely, his philosophical determinism[25] or his "pessimism about sin."[26] This again would endanger the Lutheran identity.

From this point of view, the Catholic Church's recognition of the CA would at the same time point to a methodological problem which has thus far been neglected.

For the Catholic side, recognition of the CA brings with it a wide-ranging and fundamental correction of its view of Lutheranism. Until the present, the Catholic picture of Lutheranism has been grounded clearly in that period of the Reformation movement between 1520 and 1525. Accordingly, two factors play an important role. On the one hand, there are the polemically exaggerated statements of Luther and other Reformers in this period which were systematically collected in series of catalogues of heretical Reformation statements;[27] these formed the starting point for the Council of Trent's understanding of the Reformation[28] even though in the meantime these exaggerated Reformation positions were extensively revised in the CA. This revised Reformation position found in the CA did not enter into the Catholic picture of the Reformation. The other factor is the experience which Luther's Catholic opponents had with the practical application of the new teaching in particular cities and regions. This factor, little noticed until now, should not be underestimated as having contributed to the Catholic understanding of the Reformation. Those who witnessed attacks on statues and monasteries, those who were stoned out of the pulpit in the name of the new teaching, hunted by a mob, tricked by the magistrate, and banished from the city—experiences which many Catholic opponents of Luther went through—these read the Reformation writings through different spectacles than those of the Luther scholar in his study. Thus Johannes Mensing wrote: "Dear Philipp, these pious teachers do not alarm us because they are above suspicion. You, however, with your countless errors, tumult, and false teaching, have brought it to the point where no one believes you, even if once in a while a truthful word escapes you. . . . And truthfully, as was said, that is the reason why we trust you so little when you say something which otherwise could perhaps be tolerated and benevolently interpreted, just as we also understand many sayings of the holy teachers in the best sense."[29]

A consequence of the recognition of the CA for the Catholic side would be that this positive contribution to the building up of the Lutheran congregations would stand in the forefront rather than the isolated, polemically exaggerated Reformation statements from that agitated era of revolutionary change. This would be almost unprecedented for the Catholic picture of the Reformation. As key points, confession of faith, church order, catechesis, liturgy in the vernacular, preaching, and hymns could be mentioned. J. Ratzinger correctly says:

> Generally the reality of the Church is seen as that which really divides, and in many respects it is. But one must not forget that it is not only the Roman Catholic Church and the various churches of the East which wish to be 'catholic' churches in the sense of the Church of the first centuries. It is also the Reformation churches, especially those of the CA, who sought and still seek genuine and primitive catholicity. This means that despite the differences of theological interpretation and the differences in historical starting points within the individual confessions, an astonishingly similar life exists, positively and negatively. Just as the humanity of man always manifests itself in a similar way under various signs, so, despite all divisions, the essential Christian content has always prevailed with astonishing uniformity.[30]

2. The CA as a Witness to the Faith of the Whole Church

The recognition of the CA by the Catholic Church would, secondly, "be an acknowledgement that the CA advocates no church-dividing teachings and that it can be affirmed on the Catholic side as a witness to the faith of the entire Church." This will now briefly be demonstrated in connection with the most important doctrinal statements of the CA.

The CA is divided into two parts: (1) the "articles on faith and doctrine," arranged in a salvation-historical and christologically accented order (Articles 1–17), together with a closer examination of the individual questions in a supplemental section (Articles 18–21); and (2) the "articles about matters in dispute, in which an account is given of the abuses which have been corrected" (Articles 22–28).

The Trinitarian and Christological Confession

"We unanimously hold and teach, in accordance with the decree of the Council of Nicaea, that there is one divine essence, which is called and which is truly God, and that there are three persons in this one divine essence, equal in power and alike eternal: God the Father, God the Son, God the Holy Spirit" (CA, 1). In what follows, the CA explains the statements on the one essence and the three persons in God in connection with the teaching tradition of the Eastern and Western churches and rejects all ancient and contemporary "heresies which are contrary to this article." The teaching on the natures of Christ is inserted into the christological confession, "as stated in the Apostles' Creed" (CA, 3), in connection with the formulation of the Council of Chalcedon and the *Bulla Unionis Coptorum* of the Council of Florence (1442).[31]

The importance which the CA attaches to the Apostles' Creed and the Council of Nicaea becomes clear against the background of the line of development, which can be outlined with the following statements by Melanchthon: "One does not know whether that which is handed on about the teaching of the Scripture is from the Spirit of God or from the Spirit of Lies" (1521). "One must not depart from (the ancient writers) without certain and clear Scriptural proof" (1528). "Interpretations and judgments should correspond with the

11

foundation, namely, the law, the gospel, and the creeds. To know and to follow this norm is necessary according to Scripture: if anyone teaches another gospel, let him be anathema" (1556).[32] The CA points to a situation in which, as a result of the disputes among the Reformers over infant baptism, the Lord's Supper, and the Trinity, the relationship between Scripture and tradition is seen differently than it was at the beginning of 1520.[33]

Original Sin, Justification

A precise recognition of the rejected positions is crucial for understanding the CA's teaching on justification. In Article 17 of the 1531 edition of the CA, the churches condemn "the Pelagians and others who teach that without the Holy Spirit, by the power of nature alone, we are able to love God above all things and can also keep the commandments of God insofar as the substance of the act is concerned" and that grace is only attached to the meritorious aspect of such acts.[34] This position, thoroughly rejected ever since Luther's lectures on Romans, is the "seven times accursed theology of the moderns," above all Gabriel Biel (d. 1495) and the tradition mediated by him.[35]

Over against these scholastic teachers who "minimize original sin, . . . attribute to human nature unimpaired power" (Ap., 2:7–8), and "hold that natural man is made righteous by his own powers" (CA, 2:3), the churches teach, according to CA, 2:1, "that since the fall of Adam all men who are born according to the course of nature are conceived and born in sin. That is, all men are full of evil lust and inclinations from their mothers' wombs and are unable by nature to have . . . true faith in God." Against Zwingli, who saw in original sin only an infirmity and not the guilt of sin, CA, 2 emphasizes that original sin "is truly sin and condemns to the eternal wrath of God all those who are not born again through Baptism and the Holy Spirit." Luther's way of speaking of the sin which remains after baptism is directed against the view of Duns Scotus and Biel, according to which, "if the act of sin is gone, nothing which stands in the way of forgiveness remains in the soul . . . except the punishment." Luther's formulations, which are misunderstood apart from this background, were objectionable to Catholic polemic theology. At the religious negotiations in Augsburg in 1530 and in Worms in 1541, unity was achieved on this question by appropriating the Thomist view: the *materiale peccati* (substance of sin) remains, while the *formale peccati,* the guilt, is taken away by baptism.[36]

According to Luther's explanation of the Creed in the *Large Cate-chism* and his *Confession Concerning Christ's Supper* (1528), justi-fication is associated with the work of Christ and the Holy Spirit. Christ has "reconciled us to the Father" and "has won the treasure for us." "The Holy Spirit . . . teaches us to recognize the favor of Christ shown to us and helps us receive it"; he "makes us partakers in the treasure. Therefore to sanctify is nothing else than our being brought to Christ, thereby to share in the blessings won by Christ to which we ourselves could never attain."[37] This ordering of justification to Christ's act of reconciliation and to the work of the Holy Spirit is re-lated to the sovereignty of the exalted Lord in CA, 3, and in CA, 5–14 it is explained more precisely as the work of the Spirit in the Church through ministry, word, and sacrament; it shows itself in the plan of the CA, which accentuates the history of salvation and Christology. This is also shown in the placing of CA, 4 within this plan, and also in the understanding of justification, which takes place, according to the CA, "for Christ's sake" and "through Christ" and can be described both as "being saved through the grace of our Lord Jesus Christ" (CA, 26:27) and as "receiving the promise of the Spirit" (CA, 5:3). The "righteousness that avails before God" is equated with the *iustitia spiritualis,* "the inner spiritual righteousness" (CA, 18; CA, 17). Ac-cording to Melanchthon's exposition of Romans (1529–30), "the Scrip-ture, when it speaks of grace, includes both of these: forgiveness of sins and the gift of the Holy Spirit. . . . Therefore, those who argue that man can be in grace and yet not have the Holy Spirit are mis-taken."[38] Justification, which actualizes itself in the forgiveness of sins for Christ's sake and in the gift of the Holy Spirit, encompasses: (1) a "being made righteous" and a "new birth through the Holy Spirit," which comes about above all in baptism and absolution and then manifests itself in a moral renewal; and (2) a "being regarded as righteous" (*iustum reputari*) which prevails as long as man does not lose his justification by mortal sin.[39] CA, 12 rejects those who "teach that persons who have once become godly (*semel iustificatos*) cannot fall again." In contrast to the statements of Luther and

Melanchthon that the baptized person could endanger his salvation only by giving up fiducial faith (*Fiduzialglauben*)—statements which were rejected by Luther's Catholic opponents—the Apology teaches that one loses the Spirit and faith by a failure to love and neglect of works.[40]

Melanchthon does not reject the intention of the Catholic teaching on merit rightly understood; rather good works are assigned a significance for the "differentiating in blessedness among the Saints," though, according to the CA and the Apology, they proceed as the "fruit" of faith, they are the "works of Christ," and they should and must happen "because of the will of God" and "in praise of God"; they are necessary in order that through them faith will be exercised, will grow, and increase.[41]

In the religious negotiations at the Diet of Augsburg in 1530, one finds a consensus on the doctrine of justification. The forgiveness of sins is said to take place "through the *gratia gratum faciens* (grace making graced) and faith formally and actually (*formaliter*) understood, and through word and sacrament as through instrument and tool." Both the formulation "justification through faith alone" (*sola fide*) and "justification by grace formed with love" (*gratia caritate formata*) are avoided because they wished to avoid the opposite misunderstanding. Although Eck recognized the essential correctness of speaking of justification through faith alone, he nevertheless urged the renunciation of this phrase because through it the simple people would be misled to believe that love and works are unnecessary. Melanchthon, on the other hand, polemicizing against the nominalist position, argued: "if one posits charity or something else, one points to us and not to God's grace."[42] Even if this formula of agreement did not with one blow put an end to the mutual mistrust which had been growing for a decade, and even if it still left open questions concerning the relationship of faith and love, this consensus still has significance insofar as here the Reformation concept of faith is coordinated with the Catholic concept of grace. The Apology (4:116) takes over this formula of agreement: "And since this faith alone receives the forgiveness of sins, renders us acceptable to God, and brings the Holy Spirit, it should be called 'grace that makes us acceptable to God' rather than love, which is the effect resulting from it"; it thereby also excludes a one-sided, forensic understanding of justification. The consensus on the doctrine of justification of 1530 was achieved "in the thing itself" (Eck) and not merely on the level of concepts; its legitimacy lies in the fact that the position opposed by Luther and Melanchthon was advocated neither by the *Confutatio* nor by the Council of Trent, while, on the other hand, the Reformation positions found in the catalogues of heretical statements and rejected from the Council of Trent to the present do not occur in the teaching of the CA and Apology.

Church and Ministry

"As Augustine distinguished the *communio sacramentorum* and the *societas sanctorum*, and as subsequent early and high scholasticism distinguished membership in the community of the means of grace and membership in the community of grace,"[43] so the CA and the Apology respectively distinguished the "assembly of all believers and saints" which is "the Christian Church properly speaking" (*proprie*), and the "community of the external marks of the Church, namely, the word, the confessions, and the sacraments," which also in this life is mixed with unexcommunicated hypocrites and evil "members of the Church," who "have a ministry in the Church," dispense the sacraments "in Christ's place" (*Christi vice et loco*), and "represent the person of Christ."[44] "The Donatists and others of their kind" (according to Ap., 7:29, "the Wycliffites"), "who hold the ministry of the wicked to be unprofitable and unreal" (CA, 8:3), are rejected. The Apology rejects the understanding of the Church as a "Platonic republic," as "an imaginary Church which cannot be found everywhere."[45]

The following statement in CA, 7 is disputed: "For it is sufficient for the true unity of the Christian church that the Gospel be preached in conformity with a pure understanding of it and that the sacraments be administered in accordance with the divine Word." This must be interpreted from its negative context: "It is not necessary for the true unity of the Christian church that ceremonies, instituted by men, should be observed uniformly in all places." In the context of the CA, this statement intends to say that our churches also belong to "one holy Christian Church" that "will be and remain forever." They are not "to be cut off as heretics" since there is agreement in teaching with the

Holy Scripture and "the universal Christian Church, or even the Roman Church (insofar as the latter's teaching is reflected in the writings of the Fathers)," and since disunity consists only in changed traditions and abuses.[46] The Ministry, which the Melanchthon of 1530 and the CA understood to be modeled on the Catholic episcopal Ministry,[47] stands in relation to both parts: those things on which there must be agreement within the Church, and those things on which there need be no necessary uniformity, as is clear in CA, 28. With regard to the first area (word and sacrament), the churches must "*necessarily and de iure divino* (by divine law) render obedience to the bishops" (CA, 28:21–22). With regard to the second area "of church order and ceremonies," "it is proper for the Christian assembly to keep such ordinances for the sake of love and peace, to be obedient to the bishops and parish ministers in such matters. . . . However, consciences should not be burdened by contending that such things are necessary for salvation" (CA, 28:53, 55).

CA, 7 does not exclude Ministry,[48] but rather, in the context of the CA, the terms "pure," "in conformity with a pure understanding," "according to the Gospel," "in accordance with the divine word," and "rightly" imply the Ministry; for CA, 28:20–21 says: "According to divine right, therefore, it is the office of the bishop to preach the Gospel, forgive sins, judge doctrine and condemn doctrine that is contrary to the Gospel, and exclude from the Christian community the ungodly whose wicked conduct is manifest." In no case is the Ministry to fall under "ceremonies instituted by men," because, according to CA, 5, "God instituted the office of the Ministry." In the CA, as in all the Lutheran confessional writings, Ministry is not derived from the priesthood of all believers but from the sending and commissioning of God: "He who hears you hears me" (CA, 28:22).[49] The 1540 edition of the CA sees the appointment of presbyters in Titus 1:5 as the model for the "regular call" (*rite vocari*; CA, 14).[50]

Sacraments

The CA specifies three sacraments: baptism, eucharist, and confession.[51] That this enumeration is not to be understood as exclusive is clear from the fact that the Apology and the late Melanchthon preferred also to see ordination regarded as a sacrament.[52] A recognition of the CA, therefore, would not stand in the way of an open discussion of questions which have yet to be clarified (above all, that of a narrow or broad understanding of the institution by Jesus, as well as the concepts of sign and grace).

The Reformation polemic against the *ex opere operato* is not intended to dispute the efficacy of the sacraments; rather it is directed against a very particular understanding of the *opus operatum,* namely, (1) against Gabriel Biel's version of the Scotist teaching on the sacraments in stereotypical conjunction with the expression "without a good movement in the recipient"; and (2) against this concept used with the doctrine of merit, perhaps in the connection: prayer, fasting, alms, and satisfaction *ex opere operato.*[53]

In the same way, the *sola fide* is not directed against the sacraments: "And by the word *sola* we mean to say that faith alone makes one righteous; we do not exclude the gospel and the sacraments so that if faith alone does everything the word and sacrament should become superfluous, as our opponents slanderously understand us; rather we exclude our meriting of it (righteousness)" (Ap., 4:73).

According to the CA, the sacraments are at the same time "instruments" and "means," "offered through grace"; they "give the Holy Spirit," and "effect," "waken, and strengthen" faith, and "dispense its promises." They are "effectual" and "efficacious" even if the priest, through whom they are received, is evil.[54] In the dispute with the Anabaptists and Zwingli, Luther and Melanchthon emphasize that baptism, eucharist, and absolution "do not depend upon man's faith or lack of it." "A king gives you a castle. If you do not take it, the king has neither lied nor failed in this matter. Rather you have cheated yourself . . . the king has truly given."[55]

Baptism

"Baptism is necessary for salvation." Children, too, should be baptized, for in Baptism they are committed to God and become acceptable to him" (CA, 9). "The Baptism of children is not useless but it is necessary and efficacious for salvation" (Ap., 9:1). With this, the statements made prior to the dispute with the Anabaptists are revised or modified (cf. Luther's statement, excerpted by Cochläus and Fabri and condemned by the Council of Trent, that it would be better for

17

the children to withhold baptism than to baptize them without their own faith).[56]

Eucharist

According to CA, 10, "the true body and blood of Christ are really present in the Supper of our Lord under the form of bread and wine." The Apology, in connection with the religious negotiations of 1530, adds the small word *substantialiter* (substantially) and points to the common teaching of the Roman and Greek churches on the "transformation" (*Verwandlung*) of the bread into the body of Christ.[57] The central point of controversy is not the word *sacrifice* (Ap., 24:14, 35), which was consciously avoided by Melanchthon in the CA; rather it is the understanding of the Mass as a work *ex opere operato*. The Apology thereby refers expressly to Gabriel Biel (Ap., 4:210), for whom the Mass *ex opere operato*, in distinction to the sacrifice of the cross, has a finite value, both on the ground of the institution by Christ and also on the ground that it is offered up through the Church.[58] If one takes this background into account, a clarification of the essential question is possible and indeed has already been in large measure achieved in the Catholic-Lutheran dialogues.[59]

Penance, Confession

For Gabriel Biel[60] the effecting of the forgiveness of sins is ascribed to contrition (*contritio*), and absolution is given a purely declarative function. Over against this, the Apology opposes a "diminution of the power of the keys" and emphasizes, together with the CA and the Luther of 1530, the "power" of absolution, which, according to Ap., 12:41, "may properly be called a sacrament of penitence" (Cf. Ap., 13:4). Against the "pernicious error" "that the power of the keys guarantees the forgiveness of sins not before God but before the Church," "absolution is no less to be believed than if God's voice resounded from heaven," according to CA, 25:3–4 and the Luther of 1530. It is "not the voice or word of the man who speaks it, but it is the Word of God, who forgives sin, for it is spoken in God's stead and by God's command."[61]

"Those who despise private absolution understand neither the forgiveness of sins nor the power of the keys" (Ap., 12:101). To do away with it in the Church would be godless (Ap., 12:101); rather it "should be retained and not allowed to fall into disuse" (CA, 11).

The two parts of "true and right penance" are emphasized, namely, "to have contrition and sorrow, or terror, on account of sin" and "to believe in the gospel and absolution." This is to be seen against the background of the 1527 controversy between Melanchthon and Agricola over the value of preaching on penance and the law; it is directed against those "who preach faith without penance."[62]

"Amendment of life should then also follow" (CA, 12:5–6). At the religious discussions of 1530, the Lutheran side was prepared to accept "three parts of confession or penance," as was Melanchthon already in the Visitation Articles and in the report of the examiners (*Visitatoren*).[63]

OBJECTIONS AND FEARS RELATED TO A RECOGNITION OF THE CA[64]

A recognition of the CA does not involve a vote for Melanchthon against Luther but rather a vote for the official confessions which are accepted by the Lutheran churches; among these, Luther's *Small Catechism* and the CA have, according to the statement of the Lutheran World Federation, particular importance as confessional foundations.

For the interpretation of the CA, Melanchthon's *Apologia Confessionis Augustanae* is an "indispensable commentary." In it Melanchthon, unlike in the CA, slips into an extremely polemical tone in the evaluation of his Catholic partners in dialogue (cf. CA, 20:5 ff. with Ap., 18:2; Ap., 20:3). But in the essential questions themselves—and this is often overlooked—he confirms, in conjunction with the agreement reached in 1530 at Augsburg, the common Catholic-Lutheran basis (cf. the concept of sin and original sin, the evaluation of good works, the presence of Christ in the Lord's Supper, penance and ordination as sacraments, *gratia gratum faciens*, etc.). These positions taken by the CA and the Apology (and largely also by Luther in this period) are not identical with the positions of Luther and Melanchthon in 1520–21; this could be more thoroughly demonstrated on the questions of the freedom of the will, the concept of sin, the evaluation of the ancient ecumenical councils, and the concepts of Ministry and the Church.

The fears of T. Beer concerning (1) the unacceptable "forensic righteousness of Melanchthon" (!), and (2) a "passing over of merit" are based on false presuppositions and touch neither the CA nor the Apology.[65] The theological concern of Luther's distinction between *gratia* (grace) and *donum* (gift) is in fact fully taken up in the CA and the Apology. But Luther's christological stratagem is not utilized in this question in the CA (nor in the CA's teaching on the Lord's Supper: cf. Luther's teaching on ubiquity); neither is it considered in Luther's Catechisms or in the *Smalcald Articles*. On the other hand, salvation-historical thinking and passages cited from Scripture are more marked in the CA and the Apology, as is shown, for example, by the inclusion of the gift of the Holy Spirit in the teaching on justification. Still, here as well Melanchthon and the CA can reach back to a series of statements in Luther, as is clear on the question of sanctification through the Holy Spirit.[66] P. Hacker, pointing to Luther's letter to Jonas of 21 July 1520, sees "the common view of the CA as a cover-up to be literally justified by Luther's evaluation."[67] The fundamentally methodological question of the standard by which the judgment of a "cover-up" is "justified" cannot be answered by reference to Luther's statements. But even aside from this, a generally negative appraisal of the doctrinal statements of the CA cannot be found in the passages cited, even when these are read independently of the series of positive statements by Luther on the CA (cf. also Luther's letters to Melanchthon and Duke John of Saxony written on the same day). According to the context of the letter and the historical situation, Luther, with the slogan "conceal" (*verschweigen*), takes up the argumentation of "Satan," by which he means the Catholic opponents. What Luther has in mind in the points mentioned is the polemical settling of accounts with the opponents, as his contemporaneously written "Revocation of Purgatory" (*Widerruf vom Fegfeuer*) shows; over against the "Sophists" who now "conceal and cover up their abomination by much blubbering and crying" and who "out of their disgraceful hole try to give such an appearance that one should forget all their blasphemous teaching and substance"—against these he wants "again to draw out the old record."[68] The formulation "articles on the Antichrist pope" points in the same direction. In contrast to this, Melanchthon does not list an article (on the papacy) among the doctrinal articles which are necessary for preaching to the people but rather among the "odious" articles "which belong more in the school than in the preaching of the Church."[69] Against this background, the absence of this article in the CA is not a church-dividing teaching, but, on the contrary, it makes possible a nonpolemical and thorough discussion of this question of the papal ministry in contemporary Catholic-Lutheran dialogue, as in the U.S. dialogue, 1974–78.

Although a precise study of the relationship of the CA and the Council of Trent is still required, it must on the other hand be pointed out that the starting point for the council fathers' understanding of Luther was shaped by the collection of heretical Reformation statements which served Catholic controversial theology in 1530 by pointing out the difference between the CA and earlier Lutheran teachings.[70]

SUMMARY AND CONCLUSION

To recognize the CA as a witness to the faith of the Church is to understand the CA as it understands itself, namely, (1) as a witness in which *churches* bring their faith to expression[71] and (2) as a witness in which the faith with which the *whole Church* agrees is preserved.[72] Although the required brevity has permitted only a short sketch of the most important questions, nevertheless there are, in my opinion, no serious grounds on which to deny the CA this claim.

NOTES

1. Cf. on the individual groups: *Kirche und Amt. Neuere Literatur zur Ökumenischen Diskussion um die Amtsfrage,* collected by V. Pfnür, Beiheft 1 to *Catholica* (Münster: Aschendorff, 1975), pp. 24–32.

2. *One Baptism, One Eucharist, and a Mutually Recognized Ministry: Three Agreed Statements,* Faith and Order Paper No. 73 (Geneva: World Council of Churches, Publications Office, 1975).

3. *Accra 1974. Sitzung der Kommission für Glauben und Kirchenverfassung: Berichte, Reden, Dokumente,* ed. Geiko Müller-Fahrenholz, Beiheft zur *Ökumenischen Rundshau,* no. 27 (Korntal: Lembeck, 1975), p. 139.

4. For a full listing of the documents from the American Catholic-Lutheran dialogue, see Lindbeck/Vajta, p. 93, n. 1, below; cf. Harding Meyer, *Luthertum und Katholizismus im Gespräch*, Ökumenische Perspektiven 3 (Frankfurt: Lembeck, Knecht, 1973).

5. *Papal Primacy and the Universal Church* (Minneapolis: Augsburg Publishing House, 1974), par. 31–33.

6. *Lutheran World* 19 (1972): 259–73; *Worship* 46 (1972): 326–51.

7. Members on the Catholic side: Bishop H. L. Martensen (Catholic chairman), Cardinal H. Volk (from 1976: suffragan Bishop P. W. Scheele), J. F. Hotchkin, J. Hoffmann, S. Nagy (from 1976: S. Napiorkowski), Vinzenz Pfnür, C. Moeller, B. Kloppenburg (from 1976: Heinz Schütte, S. Schmidt S. J., P. Bläser). Members on the Lutheran side: George A. Lindbeck (Lutheran chairman), Bishop Hermann Dietzfelbinger, K. E. Skydsgaard (from 1976: L. Thunberg), K. Hafenscher, B. Weber, P. Nasution, A. Appel (from 1976: C. Mau), P. Højen (from 1976: D. M. Martensen), Vilmos Vajta, Harding Meyer.

8. Cf. *KNA-Ökumenische Information*, no. 6 (6 February 1974): 10–11; Vinzenz Pfnür, "Das Problem des Amtes in heutiger lutherisch/katholischer Begegnung," *Catholica* 28 (1974): 126.

9. Winfried Blasig and Wolfgang Bohusch, *Von Jesus bis Heute: 46 Kapitel aus der Geschichte des Christentums* (Munich: Kösel, 1973).

10. Cf. Vinzenz Pfnür, *Einig in der Rechtfertigungslehre? Die Rechtfertigungslehre der "Confessio Augustana" (1530) und die Stellungnahme der katholischen Kontroverstheologie zwischen 1530 und 1535* (Wiesbaden: Franz Steiner, 1970), pp. 285–92, 302.

11. Ibid., pp. 311, 118.

12. Cf. J. Lortz, *The Reformation in Germany*, trans. R. Walls (New York: Herder and Herder, 1968), 2: 61; cf. H. Tüchle, *Reformation und Gegenreformation*, in *Geschichte der Kirche* (Einsiedeln: Benzinger, 1965), 3: 80.

13. Pfnür, *Einig*, p. 136.

14. Ibid., p. 133.

15. Ibid., pp. 132–33.

16. Lortz, *Reformation in Germany*, 2:61.

17. *CR*, 2:433; cf. Pfnür, *Einig*, pp. 21–27.

18. Schmidt-Schornbaum, *Die Fränkischen Bekenntnisse* (Munich: Kaiser Verlag, 1930), p. 528.

19. F. W. Kantzenbach, *Die Reformation in Deutschland und Europa* (Gütersloh: Gerd Mohn, 1965), p. 19.

20. *WA Br*, 5:319, ll. 5–9; *LW*, 49:297–98.

21. Cf. the answering letter of the Duke of Saxony on 22 May, in *Archiv für Reformationsgeschichte* 53 (1962):193; cf. p. 194.

22. Cf. *WA*, 30^{II}:68, ll. 6–69, l.1; *WA TR*, 3:460, ll. 39–40; *LW*, 54:245:

"The reality and the words—Philipp. The words without the reality—Erasmus. The reality without the words—Luther."

23. Cf. Luther's letter of 6 July 1530 to Cordatus: "Impletur illud: 'Loquebar de testimoniis tuis in conspectu regum' " (*WA Br*, 5:442, ll. 14–16; *LW*, 49:354).

24. Cf. O. H. Pesch, *Theologie der Rechtfertigung* (Mainz: Matthias Grünewald, 1967), pp. 18–19.

25. Cf. *Assertio* (1520): "Everything happens with absolute necessity. This was also held by the poets" (WA, 7:146, ll. 7 ff.).

26. Ibid.; "Also God accomplishes the evil works in the godless" (WA, 7:144, ll. 33–34).

27. Cf. Pfnür's collection in *Einig*, pp. 226–27, n. 54.

28. DS, 1556 is formulated, for example, in conjunction with Art. 86 of Eck's "Four Hundred and Four Articles"; cf. Pfnür, *Einig*, pp. 115, 117.

29. Cf. Pfnür, *Einig*, pp. 328–29.

30. J. Ratzinger, "Was eint und was trennt die Konfessionen?" *Int. kath. Zeitschrift "Communio"* 1 (1972): 176; cf. his "Prognosen für die Zukunft des Ökumenismus," *Bausteine* 17, no. 65 (1977): 6–14.

31. Cf. Pfnür, *Einig*, pp. 101–2, 90.

32. St. A., 1:57, ll. 18 ff.; 1:281, ll. 28–29; CR, 15:1008.

33. Cf. Pfnür, *Einig*, pp. 14–20; S. Wiedenhofer, *Formalstrukturen humanistischer und reformatorischer Theologie bei Philipp Melanchthon* (Bern: Herbert Lang; Frankfurt and Munich: Peter Lang, 1976).

34. Karl Edward Förstemann, ed., *Urkundenbuch zu der Geschichte des Reichstages zu Augsburg* (Halle: Waisenhaus, 1835), 2: 488, 534–35; Ap., 18:10; Tappert, 226.

35. WA, 8:55, ll. 1–2; *LW*, 32:154; cf. Pfnür, *Einig*, pp. 66–84; E. Iserloh, *Luther und die Reformation* (Aschaffenburg: Pattloch, 1974), pp. 28–43, 88 ff. The question of whether Luther or Melanchthon was on the whole correct about Biel's theology can remain open here.

36. Cf. Pfnür, *Einig*, pp. 90, 187 ff., 228 ff., 254 ff., 392 ff.; Iserloh, *Luther*, pp. 90–91; H. Immenkötter, *Um die Einheit im Glauben* (Münster: Aschendorff, 1973), pp. 36–37; cf. also Ap., 2:35; Tappert, 104–5.

37. WA, 26:506; *LW*, 37:366; BS, 654; Tappert, 415:38—416:39. For Luther the concept of sanctification is not confined to "second justification," as these passages from Luther's *Large Catechism* and several others show (cf. T. Beer, *Int. kath. Zeitschrift "Communio"* 5 [1976]:190 ff.; WA, 30^I: 91, 94; *LW*, 51:166, 168; WA, 30^{II}:505; *LW*, 40:375; WA, 45:614; *LW*, 24:168). Also, in the *Large Catechism* (1:147) Luther renders *Sola fides vere iustificat* as "It is faith that properly makes us holy in God's sight"; cf. Ap., 3; cf. Pfnür, *Einig*, pp. 165–66; Tappert, 385:147.

38. CR, 15:459; cf. Ap., 7:15 (Tappert, 170): "The gospel brings . . . the Holy Spirit and the righteousness by which we are righteous before

God"; Ap., 7:13 (Tappert, 170): "The kingdom of Christ is the righteousness of the heart and the gift of the Holy Spirit"; Ap., 4:99 (Tappert, 121): "Faith is . . . a thing that receives the Holy Spirit and justifies us."

39. Cf. Pfnür, *Einig*, pp. 155–97. Cf. *WA*, 40^{I}:364, ll. 11–12; *LW*, 26: 229: "Christian righteousness consists in these two things: faith of the heart and imputation." Cf. Melanchthon (1535): "Those who commit (mortal sins) fall away from God's grace, that is, they cease to be looked upon (*gehalten*) as just" (*CR*, 21:448).

40. Cf. Pfnür, *Einig*, pp. 185 ff.

41. Ibid., pp. 198–208. Cf. Ap., 4:355; Tappert, 161: "Works . . . merit other bodily and spiritual rewards. . . . There will be distinctions in the glory of the saints"; Ap., 4:366; Tappert, 163: "Good works merit other rewards, both bodily and spiritual, in various degrees"; ibid.; cf. Ap., 4:367–68; *BS*, 229–230, German text: "Weiter sagen wir, dass die guten Werke wahrlich verdienstlich und meritoria sein. . . . Denn die Seligen werden Belohnung haben, einer höher denn der ander. Solch Unterschied macht der Verdienst." ("Furthermore, we say that good works are truly meritorious. . . . For the saints will be rewarded, one higher than the other. For merit produces such distinctions.") Cf. Ap., 1531 edition, 8: "Since then works are a certain fulfilling of the law, they are rightly called meritorious and it is rightly said that a reward gives rise to degrees of blessings" (*CR*, 27:423).

42. Cf. Immenkötter, *Um die Einheit*, pp. 37–39; Pfnür, *Einig*, pp. 152 ff., 256–64, 394–99.

43. Wiedenhofer, *Formalstrukturen*, p. 261.

44. CA, 8:1; Tappert, 33; Ap., 7:3 and 28; Tappert, 168–69, 173.

45. Ap., 7:20; Tappert, 171–72; cf. *WA*, 7:683, ll. 8 ff.; *LW*, 39:218. The passage which Luther cites in this connection, Luke 17:20–21, is replaced by Melanchthon with Ephesians 4:5–6 in the final edition of CA, 7.

46. CA, conclusion of part 1:1–2; Tappert, 47–48.

47. Cf. CA, 28:69; St. A., 7^{II}:277, n. 7.

48. Cf. Wiedenhofer, *Formalstrukturen*, p. 263; Vinzenz Pfnür, in K. Algermissen, *Konfessionskunde*, 8th ed. (Paderborn: Bonifacius, 1966), pp. 361–67; Pfnür, *Catholica* 28 (1974):118 ff.

49. Cf. Ap., 7:28, 47–48; Tappert, 173, 177; Ap., 12:40; Tappert, 187; Ap., 28:18–19; Tappert, 284. Cf. also H. Fagerberg, *Die Theologie der lutherischen Bekenntnisschriften von 1529–1537* (Göttingen: Vandenhoeck & Ruprecht, 1965), p. 247.

50. St. A., 6:21, 33–34. Cf. also P. Brunner, "Beiträge zur Lehre von der Ordination unter Bezug auf die geltenden Ordinationsformulare," in *Ordination und Kirchliches Amt*, ed. R. Mumm (Paderborn and Bielefeld: Bonifacius Verlag, 1976), p. 56.

51. Cf. the ordering which precedes CA, 13; Tappert, 35–36; Ap., 13:4;

Tappert, 211; "The genuine sacraments, therefore, are Baptism, the Lord's Supper, and absolution (which is the sacrament of penitence)."

52. Cf. Ap., 13:11; Tappert, 212; St. A., 2:501, ll. 16 ff.

53. Cf. Pfnür, Einig, pp. 45–64.

54. Cf. CA, 5, 8, 9, 13.

55. WA, 30^{II}:499; LW, 40:367; cf., on the other hand, WA, 5:125. Cf. Pfnür, Einig, pp. 213–21.

56. Cochläus, Septiceps Lutherus, c. 18; Fabri, Antilogiarum Babylonia, c. 3; CT, "De sacramento baptismi," canon 13 (DS, 1563). Cf. Luther: WA, 7:321, ll. 9–10; LW, 32:14.

57. Cf. Pfnür, in Algermissen, Konfessionskunde, pp. 373 ff.

58. Cf. Pfnür, Einig, pp. 51–62.

59. Eucharist as Sacrifice (New York: United States National Committee of the Lutheran World Federation; Washington: United States National Conference of Catholic Bishops' Commission for Ecumenical and Interreligious Affairs, 1967), pp. 187–97; "Catholic-Lutheran Agreed Statement on the Eucharist," Origins 8 (1979): 465–78.

60. Pfnür, Einig, pp. 77–82.

61. Ap., 12:7, 21; Tappert, 181, 185; WA, 30^{II}:485, ll. 6 ff.; LW, 40: 350; Ap., 12:39 ff.; Tappert, 187; WA, 30^{II}:454–55; cf., on the other hand, WA, 1:233, ll. 20–21; LW, 31:26.

62. CR, 26:9; Cf. E. Iserloh, Handbuch der Kirchengeschichte, vol. 4: Reform und Spaltung, ed. Hubert Jedin (Freiburg: Herder, 1967), pp. 357–58.

63. Immenkötter, Um die Einheit, p. 31; Pfnür, Einig, pp. 264 ff., 268–69.

64. P. Hacker, Int. kath. Zeitschrift "Communio" 5 (1976): 95 ff.; T. Beer and M. Habitzky, Int. kath. Zeitschrift "Communio" 5 (1976): 189–92; Catholica 30 (1976): 77–80.

65. Cf. T. Beer, Der fröhliche Wechsel: Grundzüge der Theologie Martin Luthers (Leipzig: St. Benno Verlag, 1974), 1:106: "In the Latin text of the Apology (4:73; BS, 198; Tappert, 117) Melanchthon mentions reward and merit, but he does not do so in the German text." Aside from the fact that in the "passing over of merit" the standard Latin text of the Apology is not taken into account, the reference to the German text, which was translated and somewhat arranged by Justus Jonas (!), is also faulty. For here—further on—it is explicitly said "that good works are truly meritorious" ("dass die guten Werke wahrlich verdienstlich sind") and that this merit constitutes the difference in the rewarding of the saints: "So haben sie denn eigen und sonderlichen Verdienst, wie ein Kind für dem andern" ("Thus they have their own special rewards, as one child before the other") (BS, 229, ll. 42, 60—230, l. 7; Tappert, 163:367–69). See above, n. 42. That "Melanchthon's forensic righteousness" "does not reflect Luther's

first righteousness" is not surprising since Melanchthon (Ap. 4:252; Tappert, 143) distinguishes this expression "nach richterlichem Gebrauch für gerecht erklären" (*usu forensi iustum pronuntiari,* "pronounced righteous in a forensic way") from the preceding first justification (*ex impio iustum effici,* "a wicked man is made righteous") in order to come to an understanding of James 2:24 (in distinction to the young Luther). In the second passage in the Apology in which one encounters this expression (Ap., 4:305; Tappert, 154), the forensic "declaring righteous" presupposes the alien righteousness of Christ communicated and freely given to us through faith (cf. the citations of 1 Cor. 1:30 and 2 Cor. 5:21!) (cf. Pfnür, *Einig,* pp. 155–81, especially 174–78; see above, n. 40).

66. See above, n. 38.

67. P. Hacker, *Int. kath. Zeitschrift "Communio"* 5 (1976): 95 ff.

68. *WA,* 30^{II}:367.

69. *CR,* 2:182–83.

70. Cf. Vinzenz Pfnür, "Zur Verurteilung der reformatorischen Rechtfertigungslehre auf dem Konzil von Trient," *Annuarium Historiae Conciliorum* 8 (1976): 407–28.

71. *Ecclesiae magno consensu apud nos docent* (CA, 1:1).

72. *Nihil esse receptum contra scripturam aut ecclesiam catholicam* (CA, conclusion of part 2:5; cf. conclusion of part 1:1).

The *Confessio Augustana* as a Catholic Confession and a Basis for the Unity of the Church

WOLFHART PANNENBERG

I.

Friedrich Heiler spoke of the "Catholicity of the *Confessio Augustana*" as early as 1930, at the time of its 400th anniversary,[1] but only in the last years has this theme become a topic of ecumenical discussion. It is now urged that the Catholic Church explore the possibility of recognizing the CA of 1530 as a witness of Catholic faith. This proposal was made in January 1974 at a session in Rome of the International Lutheran - Roman Catholic Working Group formed in 1973.[2] A half year later (19 June 1974), the diocesan Ecumenical Commission of Münster directed a similar suggestion to the German Catholic Bishops' Conference. The motion of the Ecumenical Commission on that occasion stated "that the CA advances no church-dividing doctrines and can be affirmed on the Catholic side as a witness to the faith of the Church universal."[3]

Thus a question which remained in a sense open at the time of the Reformation has been taken up anew by Catholics. To be sure, the CA was opposed at the Diet of Augsburg by a refutation, the *Confutatio*, which was presented for Protestant acceptance in the name of the Emperor on 3 August 1530. The intended publication of the *Confutation* did not take place, however, because the Emperor was concerned to keep the confessional question open until the meeting of the Council which the Protestants were demanding. Also, Clement VII received the CA and the Apology less unfavorably than did his Cardinal Legate, Compegi.[4] Nor did the Council of Trent explicitly pass judgment on the CA, and such a judgment later seemed of merely historical interest in view of the Council's doctrinal decisions. Yet there is a sense in which the Roman Catholic Church has never definitively answered the question raised by the CA. The latter claims that none of its teachings in the first twenty-one "chief articles" are "contrary or opposed" to Scripture or the catholic Church or the Church of Rome (as is expressly stated in the conclusion of part 1).[5] According to the CA, the dispute deals not at all with the "principal articles" of faith but "chiefly with various traditions and abuses" treated in the articles of the second part.

Protestant researchers in this area often view this self-understanding of the CA as a tendentious representation of reality. They see in it an expression of Melanchthon's efforts to minimize the genuine contradictions of faith which divided the two parties. They point to the "softening and concealment"[6] which occurred in the reworking of earlier drafts. This is particularly evident in Article 28, where the criticism of the papacy is reduced to a general critique of episcopal claims to secular authority. In Article 24 the rejection of masses for the dead was omitted and thus also the treatment of purgatory. The addition of Articles 20 and 21 led to including not only the necessity of good works but also the commemoration (though not the invocation) of the saints in the teachings retained by Protestants. Indulgences, pilgrimages, misuse of the ban, and jurisdictional disputes between priests and monks over the care of souls and pastoral duties were "discreetly passed over for the common good," as Melanchthon himself writes in the conclusion.[7]

Melanchthon's leanings towards peace and compromise led him substantially farther afield during the negotiations which followed the reading and delivery of the CA. Later critics of this tendency can appeal to Luther himself, who originated the description of Melanchthon as "treading lightly." This, however, was initially meant appreciatively rather than pejoratively, as is clear from Luther's letter of 15 May 1530 to the Elector: Melanchthon's Apology "pleases me greatly, and I know of nothing to improve or change in it. Anyway, it wouldn't work to try, because I can't tread so softly and lightly."[8] Yet on 21 July Luther wrote: "Satan is alive and thinks well of your treading lightly and dissimulating in the articles concerning purgatory, the cult of the saints, and, above all, the pope as antichrist."[9] To be sure, after its presentation on 25 June, Luther spoke of the CA as "plain and most beautiful,"[10] and thus identified himself with the final version.

Critics of Melanchthon's "pussyfooting" presuppose what happened later. They already know about the failure of his negotiating efforts during the Diet and especially about the Catholic rejection of the CA's own view that the religious conflict concerned abuses only and not fundamentals of the faith. The *Confutation* maintained in opposition to this that there were in fact contradictions on questions of faith. The CA's formulations of original sin, justification, the concept of the Church, and penance (in the article on confession) were unacceptable, and it failed to mention other truths of faith, such as the dogma of transubstantiation. This negative attitude hardened through the proclamation of the *Confutation* by the Emperor (or his secretary) on 3 August, and it hardened all the more because the following negotiations were unsuccessful.

From this Protestants also acquired the impression that the conflict was over faith, over doctrine. They thus adopted the judgment of the authors of the *Confutation* in opposition to the wording of the CA. Once they had adopted this viewpoint, it was naturally easy for them to see the readiness to compromise manifest in Melanchthon's peace efforts of 1530 as obscuring the special character of the Protestant position on faith in its opposition to the Catholic one. If, in contrast, one agrees with Melanchthon and the text of the CA that the whole dispute involved no ultimately contradictory doctrines, then his irenicism must be viewed as both prudent and consistent. The bloody wars of religion during the following centuries, and all the other unholy consequences of the confessional division, can only reinforce such an evaluation of Melanchthon's desire for reconciliation—assuming, that is, that there was no ultimate contradiction in faith.

For the CA, however, no such contradiction exists. There is unintended irony in the fact that precisely the adherents of the Lutheran Reformation have come to agree, under the pressure of historical development, with their opponents' judgment of the situation and disagree with their own basic confession (for the *Formula of Concord* understands itself as an interpretation of the CA and the Apology).[11] Given the inescapable historical conditioning of hermeneutical perspectives, this may be excused as a well-nigh unavoidable development,[12] but it can scarcely be regarded as an expression of strong faith. Faith would rather have been manifest in pointing, despite negative historical experiences, beyond the confessional divisions to an abiding unity in faith with the catholic tradition and Church. In any case, contemporary changes in the ecumenical situation should help us Protestants to overcome the limitations in our reception of the CA on this point and again to take more seriously its claim to formulate what is in accord with the faith of the catholic *and Roman* Church.[13] We are here confronted with a question which still remains open after four hundred years of church division, a question addressed not only to Catholics but also to the self-understanding of Lutheran churches and their theology.

It may well be asked whether this question of the catholicity of the CA does in fact still remain open in view of the subsequent dogmatic developments in the Roman Church through Trent, the two Vatican Councils, and the Marian dogmas of the last two centuries. That depends on how one interprets these developments. In any case, it is noteworthy that there are now Catholic theologians who affirmatively answer the question of the catholicity of the CA in the face of these developments. If the magisterium of the Catholic Church were to find itself in a position to confirm this judgment through the ordinary teaching of its bishops, or through a papal or conciliar pronouncement, this would be of much more than historical interest. It would be an event of immense contemporary ecumenical importance. The CA continues to be binding in Lutheran churches as a criterion for all later confessional developments. This makes it incumbent on Lutherans also authoritatively to clarify their own position. Is it or is it not true from their point of view that the new dogmas of Tridentine and post-Tridentine Catholicism have for the first time created difficulties for faith which the CA could in its day affirm as nonexistent? The answer to this question depends in large part on the contemporary self-understanding of Catholic theology and the Catholic Church. And this self-understanding in turn would be expressed for Protestants in a highly significant way by the recognition of the catholicity of the CA. Thus acceptance by both sides of the genuine catholicity of the CA might well serve as the basis for an understanding on subsequent dogmatic developments. In any case, the acceptance of its catholicity by the Roman Catholic magisterium would place the ecumenical dialogue on an entirely new footing, not only with Lutheran Protestantism but with Protestantism as a whole.

II.

Not only Catholics need to make up their minds about the catholicity of the CA, and their judgment naturally cannot here be anticipated; Protestant theology also has the task of clarifying the extent to which the claim of catholicity for the statements of the CA can be maintained in the light of contemporary theological knowledge. This requires consideration of the *Confutation's* arguments, of Melanchthon's answers in the Apology, and of Trent's treatment of the relevant questions. It would also be desirable to take into account the controversial literature of the sixteenth century and the Reformation reaction to Trent in, for instance, the exemplary shape which this took on the Lutheran side in the formulations of Martin Chemnitz in his *Examen Concilii Tridentini.* The latter must here be entirely omitted. All that can be done is briefly to survey the substantive issues which have already been raised.

The CA's claim to catholicity refers especially to the twenty-one articles of the first part. Only the succeeding seven articles, according to the conclusion, "were regarded as controversial."[14] They deal with points at which "some abuses have been corrected." In reference to these, the CA simply claims that "we have not acted in an unchristian or frivolous manner" but in accordance with God's command.[15] The CA grounds the use of both wine and bread for lay communion (Art. 22) in Christ's institution and asserts that the reforms which had been introduced in the liturgy of the Mass (Art. 24) harmonize with that institution. According to Article 25, the changes in the rite of confession are confined to a single point that "no one should be compelled to recount sins in detail, for that is impossible" and, furthermore, forgiveness is not dependent on such an enumeration. The abolition of mandatory fasts (Art. 26) is justified primarily in terms of Christian freedom from the law, but fasting itself is in no sense rejected. The CA rejects monastic vows (Art. 27) on the grounds that they are against human nature and weakness, opposed to the divine order, and all too easily combined with works-righteousness. Even if already taken, they can for these reasons be annulled. It defends the marriage of priests (Art. 23) in similar terms, and appeals, in addition, to 1 Timothy 3:2 and the order of the ancient Church in support of this step. Finally, the limitation of the power of bishops to spiritual matters (Art. 28) conforms to the distinction between the spiritual and secular realms.

It is doubtful that the controversy on these points can be regarded as entirely ended even today. To be sure, the fusion of the episcopal and papal offices with claims to secular authority has been eliminated by the course of history, and the rules on fasting have lost their binding force also in the Roman Church. Further, the liturgical reforms of Vatican II have in many respects justified the changes in the Mass introduced by the Lutheran Reformation. Vatican II encouraged the use of the vernacular[16] (which the *Confutation* declared unnecessary) and in contrast to the *Confutation* which emphatically opposed the Reformation's suppression of private masses, and also to Trent which continued to approve and commend them,[17] acknowledged in principle the communal character of the Eucharist.[18] The Second Vatican Council's ordering of the liturgy also largely conforms to the Reformation's insistence that the "real presence" is linked to the institution of the Lord's Supper for use by the congregation.[19] Further, the Council's emphasis on the connection between the eucharistic liturgy and preaching is yet another instance of the acceptance of an important Reformation concern.[20] In reference to communion in both kinds, the Council did not adopt the Reformation's view that this is necessary in order to have a eucharistic celebration which corresponds to Christ's institution, but it did provide room, although with limitations, for such celebrations.[21]

Thus many of the controversial questions discussed in the last seven articles of the CA are now pointless. Yet some persist. Monastic vows and clerical celibacy continue as part of the order of the Roman Catholic Church. Although these practices do not have the weight of doctrinal disagreements, yet it would be difficult for the Roman Church to concede catholic normativeness to the arguments of the CA against them. Perhaps, however, the Protestant attitude on these questions might be tolerable in our day within a catholic consensus of faith. The increased possibilities of dispensation and laicization have removed much of the plausibility from charges that monasticism and celibacy are wanton offenses against God's creation, order, and command. The most Protestants can expect from the Roman Church is that clerical celibacy not be made a condition for church fellowship (which is already the case in reference to the Eastern Church). Certainly a positive judgment on the catholicity of the CA as a whole would have been easier if Articles 23 and 27 had pleaded only for the *possibility* of different regulations on priestly celibacy and monastic vows than those which prevailed in the medieval Latin Church of the West. The universal validity claimed by the CA's argument on these points makes it doubtful that the Roman recognition of the catholicity of the CA, if possible at all, can cover more than the first twenty-one articles (to which, in any case, the claim primarily applies). While it is true that monastic vows and clerical celibacy are now also under discussion in the Roman Catholic Church, the arguments there employed do not exactly coincide with those of the CA. Protestants, however, can scarcely claim the same measure of catholic normativeness for the CA's arguments on these questions as for the articles of the first part of the CA.

Questions are also raised for Protestants by the Catholic acceptance of Reformation concerns through the liturgical reforms of Vatican II. They must ask to what extent they still take seriously what is said about the Mass at the beginning of Article 24: "We are unjustly accused of having abolished the Mass. Without boasting, it is manifest that the Mass is observed among us with greater devotion and more earnestness than among our opponents." Today this is not only not manifest, but it is not in fact the case. Among Lutherans, not to mention other Protestants, the Lord's Supper is for the most part no longer celebrated each week in the Sunday service, and when it is celebrated, it is often, at least in Europe, made into an addendum to the main service. Such practices directly contradict the CA. Furthermore, it can no longer be affirmed that "no conspicuous changes have been made in the public ceremonies of the Mass" other than the use of the vernacular and congregational singing. Lutherans cannot honestly appeal to the binding authority of the CA without confronting the problems raised by these considerations.

Yet these difficulties do not necessarily indicate doctrinal disagreements which would exclude the recognition of the catholicity of the CA. They concern the disputed questions of the second part, which, according to the CA, do not affect the consensus on the fundamental articles of faith. The one point at which this conviction is most questionable is in reference to the criticism in Article 24 of the sacrificial character of the Mass. Yet it seems that on this issue the sixteenth-century disputants unhappily missed each other's points. Article 24 directs its criticism not against any use whatsoever of the concept of sacrifice in reference to the Mass[22] but specifically against the thesis "that our Lord Christ had by his death made satisfaction only for original sin, and had instituted the Mass as a sacrifice for other sins" (CA, 24:21). Furthermore, it is in this sense, and only in this sense, that the *ex opere operato* effectiveness of the Mass was denied, namely, as if the ritual performance of the liturgical action propitiates God *ex opere operato*.[23] The *Confutation*, on its side, agrees, first, that there can be no talk of a sacrifice by a priest for actual sins which supplements Christ's sacrifice and, second, says that this has not been taught. (It does, however, ascribe to the Mass the power to remove the *punishment* for sin and thus to substitute for penitential satisfactions.)[24] In the Apology (Art. 24:62), Melanchthon replies to the second point by citing the teaching of a treatise (at that time attributed to Thomas Aquinas, but actually pseudonymous)[25] to the effect that sin itself is blotted out by the sacrifice of the Mass. Trent does not go into this question but describes the eucharistic sacrifice in terms which avoid the critique advanced by Article 24. The Mass simply *represents*, commemorates, and applies (*applicaretur*) to the forgiveness of daily sins the saving power of the sacrifice offered once for all (*semel*) on the cross.[26]

Trent, however, confirmed the character of the Mass as a propitiatory sacrifice and in so doing failed to reject the view attacked by the Protestants that this involves a propitiation for actual sins which supplements Christ's sacrifice. When it then went on and condemned the thesis that the Mass is a sacrifice only in the sense of being a praise and thank offering and a "mere" commemoration of the sacrifice on the cross, not a propitiation,[27] this inevitably awakened Protestant suspicions that it thereby affirmed a propitiatory function supplementary to Christ's sacrifice. It was in opposition to such an additional propitiatory function that the Apology had interpreted the Mass as a praise and thank offering.[28] The Protestant critique did not envision the possibility of speaking of a nonadditive propitiatory character of the Mass, founded in *anamnesis* (remembrance) and affirming simply that the liturgy in its sacramental performance participates in the sacrifice of Christ. It was precisely because of this that Trent's insistence on the propitiatory character of the sacrifice of the Mass could not help but be misunderstood by the Protestants, especially as the revelant anathema separates the propitiatory from the commemorative function of the eucharistic liturgy.

In our day, however, it seems that in fact no dogmatic conflicts remain on this question. Vatican II looks at the matter entirely from the viewpoint of *anamnesis*. It thinks of both the sacrificial role of the priest and the real presence of Christ in the elements in terms of Christ's presence in the eucharistic action as a whole.[29] As this approach is not contradicted by Article 24's rejection of the propitiatory function of the sacrifice of the Mass, there remains in this area also no insuperable barrier to the recognition of the catholicity of the CA.

We must now ask from a contemporary viewpoint about the doctrinal affirmations of the first part. Is their claim to agree with the teachings of the catholic and, indeed, Roman Church tenable? Vinzenz Pfnür thinks that it is, not only for the complex of themes centering on original sin and justification but also for the ecclesiological issues of Church, ministerial office, and sacraments.[30]

For Pfnür, the decisive consideration in reference to justification is that Article 4 does not teach a simply external and purely forensic justification but rather joins forgiveness of sins with the inner renewal effected by the Spirit.[31] It is a misunderstanding to suppose that justification by faith makes love useless. This was already recognized in the theological negotiations at the Diet of Augsburg. Eck found it possible to speak of a consensus "on the thing itself," and Melanchthon was able in the Apology to connect the concept of faith with the *gratia gratum faciens* (the grace which makes graced) on the grounds that love is the effect of faith.[32] The Apology also stresses that the article on justification does not universally exclude the biblical ideas of reward (and merit) but only the abuse of making them grounds for justification.[33] Pfnür is correct "that the position opposed by Luther and Melanchthon was advocated neither by the *Confutatio* nor by the Council of Trent while, on the other hand, the Reformation positions found in the catalogues of heretical statements and rejected from the Council of Trent to the present do not occur in the teaching of the CA and Apology."[34] It is true that a whole series of Tridentine canons on justification reject positions reminiscent of Reformation formulations,[35] but it is also clear that these formulations were understood and condemned in a sense different from that of the Reformers. Thus Article 4 of the CA is not directly affected.

In reference to original sin, Article 2 brackets and thereby leaves open the then debated question of whether the concupiscence which remains in the baptized after baptism is genuinely sin. Article 2 simply says that all the offspring of Adam are condemned by the sin in which they are born unless they are reborn through baptism and the Holy Spirit. The *Confutation,* however, suspected and rejected in this formulation the view of Luther's (already stigmatized by Leo X in 1520) that sin defined as concupiscence remains after baptism and is simply no longer imputed.[36] This view is the basis for Luther's *simul justus et peccator* (simultaneously justified and sinner) and was easily misused by anti-Lutheran polemicists to draw the (false) conclusion that for him baptism and justification change nothing in the human being. Melanchthon's Apology defends Luther's characterization of postbaptismal concupiscence as sin,[37] although Melanchthon himself was able in the theological discussions at Augsburg in 1530 and at Worms in 1541 to admit the Thomistic interpretation of concupiscence as consisting of a *materiale peccati* (substance of sin), which remains after baptism, and of a *formale peccati* (or guilt), which is removed.[38]

Significantly different forms of theological thought and of piety which have not yet entirely disappeared lie in the background.[39] Lutherans think of sin and the image of God in terms of the actual relation of human beings to God. They thus think of the image of God as identical to original righteousness, and of sin as involving the loss of both.[40] A similar actualism is evident in the way in which baptism and repentance are seen together in relation to the concupiscence which persists also in Christians. Thus, for example, repentance is described as the constantly renewed actualization of baptism. This view makes it difficult to do justice to the continuity of Christian existence founded in baptism, and it is therefore understandable that the *Confutation* distrusted the definition of original sin in Article 2.

Neither Luther nor Melanchthon, however, dissolved this continuity, and Article 2 itself expressly emphasizes the fundamental importance of baptism.[41] Yet it must be admitted that the abiding continuity of Christian being derived from baptism has not always been adequately expressed in Protestant piety, proclamation, and liturgy. The actualism of the confession of sins and the consolation of the gospel has too exclusively occupied the center of the stage. This unbalanced emphasis on a single aspect of the total Christian tradition involves dangers of which the churches of the Reformation need to become more keenly aware. This is especially true of the form these dangers have taken through the opposition which these denials evoked.

Thus, as far as the issues directly related to justification are concerned, the Lutheran-Catholic conflicts at the time of the Reformation are increasingly seen on both sides as related to differences in modes of thought which need not now involve substantive church-dividing disagreements. In our day, it is the ecclesiological differences which are considered the essential core of the confessional division. Yet Vinzenz Pfnür holds that in this area also the statements of the CA are genuinely catholic.[42] Even Protestants, however, need not maintain that they are complete. Article 7 acknowledges that the Church is one and will endure forever, and the "Church to which it testifies is not a Lutheran party church but the entire believing Christendom of all times."[43] The *Confutation* itself recognized that this is the meaning.[44] Yet it objected to the definition of the Church as "the congregation of saints" on the hypothesis that this excluded sinners and limited membership in the Church to the predestined (a view held by Huss and condemned at the Council of Constance in 1415).[45] In the Apology Melanchthon disposed of this misunderstanding by referring to the anti-Donatist statements of Article 8 (see Ap., 7:3) and defended the choice of the phrase "communion of saints" by reference primarily to the Apostles' Creed (7:8) but also by reference to the spiritual character of the Church as the people of God (7:14 ff.) and kingdom of Christ (7:16 ff.). Nor should an exclusively congregationalist sense be attributed to this formula. Rather it reflects terminology which goes back as far as Augustine.[46] It is also important to note that the Apology rejects the notion of a complete invisibility of the true Church in the sense of a "Platonic republic" (7:20).

The statement in Article 7 that it is enough for the unity of the Church that there be agreement in the teaching of the gospel and administration of the sacraments is in our day felt to be misleading even by Lutherans.[47] It ought not be construed restrictively but, as Pfnür rightly emphasizes, "is to be interpreted in terms of what it negates," namely, in opposition to compulsory uniformity in humanly instituted "ceremonies."[48] Even the *Confutation* agrees with this in reference to particular rites,[49] although uniformity is necessary in universal Christian rites which originated from the Apostles.

One must also agree with Pfnür that this depreciation of human traditions and ceremonies is not directed against the ministerial office. According to Article 5, the Ministry precedes the community of believers for it is instituted by God himself.[50] "The ministerial office is in no case to be included among the 'ceremonies instituted by men,' for, according to Article 5, the preaching office was instituted by God. In the CA, as everywhere in the Lutheran confessional writings, the office is not derived from the universal priesthood of all believers but from God's sending and commissioning."[51]

To this it must be added that in Article 14 the ministerial office is distinguished from the universal priesthood by the commission "publicly" to preach and administer the sacraments. Further, the form of ecclesiastical office which the CA had in mind was that of the bishop, although, in conformity to the tradition of the ancient Church, it saw this episcopal office as in principle identical to the pastoral office (*episcopi seu pastores*).[52] The question which is here raised regarding the relation of the presbyterate and the episcopate remains open to this day in the Roman Catholic tradition. Further, on the Lutheran side, the CA and the Apology, as well as Melanchthon's *Treatise on the Power and Primacy of the Pope* (1537), explicitly concede a secondary differentiation of the single ministerial office and cite the preservation of the unity of the Church as the criterion for such questions of church order.[53] The public character of the ecclesiastical office signifies that ministers do not act simply as private individuals, but, on the basis of their calling by the Church, they represent the person of Christ.[54] It is for this reason that there must be a public and orderly calling into this office within the Church (Art. 14).

One could wish that the scattered statements of the CA on Church and office contained a stronger emphasis on the relation of the unity of the Church to the ministerial task of preserving the unity of believers in their faith in Christ. From this perspective, the Ministry could well have been mentioned already in the treatment of the Church in Article 7 because church unity is impossible without a ministry of unity. To be sure, this point is implied by the statements of the CA. The agreement in the gospel and the sacraments which is necessary for the unity of the Church cannot be separated from the Ministry to which, according to Article 5, the preaching of the gospel and the administration of the sacraments is entrusted. Also what is said in Article 28:20 ff. about the "divine right" of "episcopal" jurisdiction (which includes the power to excommunicate and to reject false teaching) makes clear that the commission publicly to proclaim the Christian message embraces concern for the unity of believers in gospel teaching. However, the ecumenical and unitive implications of this understanding of the ministerial office are not clearly expressed in the CA, nor have they been fully effective in the ecclesial reality of the Lutheran churches. Yet they are unquestionably present and are important for judging the catholicity of the CA.

What, however, can be said of the sacraments? The CA spoke of only three (baptism, the Lord's Supper, and penance),[55] but it will be recalled that this was because the Reformation operated with a narrow concept of what constitutes "institution by Christ." As is indicated in the Apology (13:11), Melanchthon considered including ordination among the sacraments but acknowledged confirmation and extreme unction simply as rites originating with the Fathers, and marriage as instituted by God already in creation rather than first in the New Testament. He also noted that the Fathers (veteres) did not customarily speak of seven sacraments (Ap., 13:2) and concluded that the exact number is immaterial: "We do not think it makes much difference if, for purposes of teaching, the enumeration varies, pro-

39

vided what is handed down in Scripture is preserved" (Ap., 13:2). Trent, to be sure, threatened with anathema any departure from the number seven (DS, 601), but it also maintained that there are differences in rank (DS, 603). It was such differences which led Melanchthon not to count among the sacraments confirmation, extreme unction (Ap. 13:6), and, on other grounds, marriage (13:14–15). The CA itself says nothing explicitly on the question of number but simply singles out baptism, the Lord's Supper, and penance.

In reference to the articles on these three sacraments, the *Confutation* found no fault with that on baptism (Art. 9). It criticized the treatment of confession and penance (Arts. 11, 12) in part because of the failure to say anything about mandatory yearly confession, but primarily because of the reduction of the three parts of penance (contrition, confession and satisfaction) to two (contrition and faith). Contrary to what might at first be supposed, the main dispute at this point was not over the omission of "works of satisfaction." The CA speaks of good works as "fruits" which must necessarily follow penance, even though it does not number them among the constituents of the sacrament (13:6). A more important problem was the designation of faith rather than confession as the second part of penance. The *Confutation* objected to this substitution, and Trent rejected it (DS, 1704).

Perhaps this is the place in which there is the weightiest still unresolved difference in sacramental theology now that the questions of transubstantiation and of eucharistic sacrifice have lost their divisive sharpness because of the widespread agreement in ecumenical dialogues on the Lord's Supper. What the CA says in Article 10 on the Lord's Supper creates no difficulties, and its emphatic affirmation of the real presence (*vere adsint*) of Christ's body and blood can be read as adequately expressing the intention of the dogma of transubstantiation. The same cannot be said, however, of its statements on the sacrament of penance. Its reduction of penance to contrition and faith is anathematized by the Council of Trent more directly than is any other of its formulations, and it is hard to see, at least at first glance, how the contemporary Roman Catholic Church could recognize its catholicity. It is no accident that Melanchthon felt compelled in the Apology to deliver an especially detailed and passionate defense at this point. Yet a solution to this problem may be found in the fact that the CA deals with the theme of penance in two articles (11 and 12), and the second can be read as speaking of the theological content rather than the disciplinary ordering of the sacraments. It does not say that absolution can be pronounced without confession of sins but that contrition and faith suffice for forgiveness.[56]

Taken as a whole, the sacramental teachings of the CA challenge the church which professes to stand on this confession to ask what importance the sacraments actually have in its worship life. Melanchthon claimed in reference to confession (much as he had done in Article 24 in regard to participation in the Lord's Supper) "that most people in our churches use the sacraments, absolution and Lord's Supper, many times in a year" (Ap., 11:3). But has not the sacramental dimension of Lutheran church life drastically faded since then? Sacramental penance has changed into pietistic guilt feelings. It may well be that the disappearance of the sacrament of penance is of less concern than the neglect of the Lord's Supper, for "second repentance" was only for exceptional cases even in the ancient Church, while the Eucharist has always stood at the center of Christian worship life. Yet there are good reasons for deploring the pietistic sense of sin as a one-sided accentuation and narrowing of Protestant piety. The shift of emphasis from sacramental penance to a sense of guilt pervading the whole of life has historically contributed to an individualistic piety which is in general alienated from the sacramental life of the Church. At this point the CA is unquestionably more catholic than are the churches which in our day adhere to it. Any tendency to oppose a church of the word to a church of sacramental mediation is foreign to it.

Today the sacramental dimension is more likely to be regained in Protestant church life by starting with the Eucharist rather than with penance. The overemphasis on the theme of penance by both sides in the controversies of the sixteenth century was historically conditioned by developments which originated in the Middle Ages. Perhaps this excessive penitential emphasis—which influenced the conflict over the sacrifice of the Mass and distorted the understanding of the Lord's Supper—is in part responsible for that general estrangement from the communal sacramental life of the Church which began with the troubled conscience of the Reformation period. If so, it is all the more important to renew the Church's sacramental life—which the CA did not wish to damage—by stressing its center, namely, the liturgical celebration of the Supper of the Lord.

The CA's claim that its confessional affirmations are catholic need not prevent us from acknowledging the time-conditioned character of its formulations and emphases. Indeed, the appeal to such formulations can be heretical if one does not bear in mind their partial and historically limited nature. Thus only an interpretation which takes account of the one-sidedness and time-conditionedness of the CA can at the same time properly appreciate its catholicity.

NOTES

1. F. Heiler, "Die Katholizität der *Confessio Augustana*," *Die Hochkirche* 12 (1930): 6–7.

2. Vinzenz Pfnür, "Das Problem des Amtes in heutiger lutherisch/ katholische Begegnung," *Catholica* 28 (1974): 126.

3. The citation is from Pfnür, p. 4 above.

4. J. Ficker, *Die Konfutation des Augsburgischen Bekenntnisses: Ihre erste Gestalt und Geschichte* (Leipzig: Barth, 1891), pp. XCIX ff.

5. Tappert, 47:1.

6. J. von Walter, "Der Reichstag zu Augsburg 1530," *Lutherjahrbuch* 12 (1930): 49, in reference to the detailed evidence in Theodor Kolde, *Die älteste Redaktion der Augsburger Konfession* (Gütersloh: C. Bertelsmann, 1906), pp. 47 ff.

7. Tappert, 95:2–3.

8. WA Br, 5:319, ll. 5–9; LW, 49:297–98.

9. WA Br, 5:496, ll. 8–10. When Pfnür assesses Luther's remark about Melanchthon's "pussyfooting," he concludes that it refers more to the form of Melanchthon's text and is "in general positive," but Pfnür does not take up this second statement by Luther.

10. WA Br, 5:442, l. 14; LW, 49:354.

11. See the Preface to the Book of Concord of 1580. Tappert, 12.

12. In this sense one can agree with J. von Walter, who writes: "If the CA was presented on the presupposition that the teaching of the Protestants was not essentially different from that of the Catholics and that the disagreement chiefly concerned abuses in church life, then this presupposition must, of course, be recognized by the other side. *If that did not happen, then the Protestants are in possession of a confession which necessarily serves as a bulwark against every effort to conceal the religious as well as*

ecclesiastical opposition in which they stand to Catholicism" ("Reichstag," pp. 49–50; italics by Pannenberg). The problem with this statement is simply that von Walter regarded this question as having been negatively decided by history (p. 53)—as if history were already at an end. His concluding sentence makes this evident: "Thus the CA itself inevitably [*sic*] made illusory all the further attempts of its author to reach a political understanding" (p. 50).

13. Edmund Schlink, in his *Theology of the Lutheran Confessions,* trans. P. Koehneke and H. Bouman (Philadelphia: Fortress Press, 1961), p. xvii, correctly formulates this claim: "It is not the 'Lutheran' church (this designation is repudiated in the Confessions themselves) but the *una sancta catholica et apostolica ecclesia* which has spoken in the Confessions."

14. Tappert, 94:1.

15. Ibid., p. 49.

16. SL, 1, 36:2 and 2, 54.

17. DS, 1747 (*probat et commendat*). The *Confutation* argued that "by this abrogation of masses the worship of God is diminished, honor is withdrawn from the saints, the ultimate will of the founder is overthrown and defeated, the dead deprived of the rights due them, and the devotion of the living withdrawn and chilled. Therefore the abrogation of private masses cannot be conceded and tolerated." [Cited according to the translation of M. Reu, *The Augsburg Confession: A Collection of Sources with an Historical Introduction* (Chicago: Wartburg Publishing House, 1930), p. 370.]

18. SL, 1, 27. Cf. 2, 78 and esp. 55.

19. To be sure, the Tridentine condemnation of the limitation of Christ's presence to the *usus* (DS, 1654, cf. 1758) remains in force. Yet its meaning needs reinterpretation and further ecumenical discussion in the light of the liturgical renewal with its emphasis on the communal character of the eucharistic celebration. On the one hand, Catholics have accepted important elements of the Reformation emphasis on *usus* (use) while, on the other, the limitation of Christ's presence to the moment in which the elements are received need not be constitutive of the Reformation's position on this question.

20. SL, 52.

21. SL, 55. The necessity of communion in two kinds was denied by Trent (DS, 1731).

22. Tappert, 58–59.

23. "From this has come the common opinion that the Mass is a work which by its performance (*ex opere operato*) takes away the sins of the living and the dead" (Tappert, 58; cf. Ap., 24:27 ff.; Tappert, 254 ff.).

24. The *Confutation* denies "that Christ by his passion has made satisfaction for original sin and has instituted the Mass for actual sin, for this

has never been heard by Catholics, and very many who are now asked (most firmly) deny that they have so taught. For the Mass does not abolish sins, which are destroyed by repentance as their peculiar medicine, but abolishes the punishment due sin, (fulfills [*supplet*]) satisfactions, and confers increase of grace." Reu, *Augsburg Confession*, p. 370.

25. Opusculum 58, *De sacramento altaris*, c. 1 (cited in *BS*, 367, n. 1, with further references in *BS*, 93, n. 1).

26. DS, 1740.

27. DS, 1753 (canon 4).

28. Ap., 24:25 (Tappert, 253–54).

29. SL, 7.

30. See pp. 12–19 above.

31. See pp. 13–14 above with the references to CA, 5 and 18 (*iustitia spiritualis*).

32. See p. 14 above in reference to Ap., 4:116. The misunderstanding of justification *sola fide*, as if this could be by a faith which lacked love, was the basis for rejecting CA, 4 in the first draft of the *Confutation*. (See Ficker, *Konfutation*, p. 19. Cf. p. 30 in reference to CA, 6.) The final draft of the *Confutation*, however, bases its condemnation of CA, 4 on the latter's rejection of merit.

33. Ap., 4:362 ff. The *Confutation* criticized the rejection of the concept of merit as an offense against the biblical idea of reward: "Where there are wages, there is merit" (Reu, *Augsburg Confession*, p. 351). This objection, however, overlooks the fact that CA, 4 does not reject merit absolutely, but only as a ground for justification.

34. See Pfnür, p. 15 above.

35. See DS, 1551–83, esp. canons 9, 11–14, 19–20, 26–27.

36. In addition to objecting that the definition of original sin in CA, 2 obliterates the distinction between original sin and actual sin, for "to be without the fear of God and without trust in God is rather the actual guilt of an adult than the offense of a recently born infant," the *Confutation* rejects the declaration "whereby they call the fault of origin concupiscence, if they mean thereby that concupiscence is a sin that remains sin in a child even after baptism" (Reu, *Augsburg Confession*, p. 350). These statements refer back to Leo X's condemnation (DS, 1452–53) of the corresponding views of Luther (WA, 2:160, ll. 34–35; *LW*, 3:317; WA, 1:572, ll. 10 ff.; *LW*, 31:153–54). Cf. also Trent's canon 5 on justification (DS, 1515).

37. Ap., 2:35 ff.

38. The references are given by Pfnür, p. 23, n. 36 above. Cf. Ap., 2: 4, 35.

39. Matthias Kröger, *Rechtfertigung und Gesetz: Studien zur Entwicklung der Rechtfertigungslehre beim jungen Luther* (Göttingen: Vanden-

hoeck & Ruprecht, 1968), has rightly stressed the fundamental importance of Augustine's concept of sin for Luther's doctrine of justification.

40. Ap., 2, passim.

41. Cf. also CA, 9.

42. Pfnür, pp. 15–16 above.

43. A. Kimme, "Die ökumenische Bedeutung der Augsburgischen Konfession," *Die Aktualität des Bekenntnisses,* Fuldaer Hefte 21 (Berlin and Hamburg: Lutherisches Verlagshaus, 1971), pp. 9–74. The citation is from p. 30. Kimme adds that this article documents "most expressly the claim of the Lutheran Reformation to scriptural catholicity."

44. Reu, *Augsburg Confession,* p. 353. To be sure, the first draft of the *Confutation* complains that the Reformation preachers violated by their actions the unity affirmed by the CA (Ficker, *Konfutation,* p. 33).

45. Reu, *Augsburg Confession,* p. 353. Cf. Ficker, *Konfutation,* p. 33–34 and DS, 1201, 1206.

46. Documentation in S. Wiedenhofer, *Formalstrukturen humanistischer und reformatorischer Theologie bei Philipp Melanchthon,* vol. 2 (Bern: Herbert Lang; Frankfurt and Munich: Peter Lang, 1976), p. 222, n. 75.

47. See the comments by H. H. Harms, "Das Amt nach lutherischem Verständnis," *Luther* 44 (1973): 49–65, esp. 53.

48. Pfnür, p. 15 above.

49. "They are to be praised also in that they do not regard variety of rites as separating unity of faith, if they speak of special rites" (Reu, *Augsburg Confession,* p. 353).

50. Kimme, "Bedeutung," p. 31, interprets what Art. 7 says about the preaching of the gospel (*doctrina*) and the administration of the sacraments as specifications of Art. 5's statements about the ministerial office and sees Art. 14 as providing further clarification by its indication of the persons who should occupy the office.

51. Pfnür, p. 16 above.

52. CA, 28:30, 53. Cf. Kimme, "Bedeutung," p. 36 ff., and the following footnotes.

53. Tappert, 330 ff. Cf. CA, 28:55, 71, and Wolfhart Pannenberg, "Ökumenische Einigung über die gegenseitige Anerkennung der Ämter?" *Catholica* 28 (1974): 140–56, esp. 148, n. 14.

54. Ap., 7:28 bases the validity of the ministry of unworthy ministers in the fact that "they do not represent their own persons but the person of Christ, because of the church's call, as Christ testifies (Luke 10:16), 'He who hears you hears me.' When they offer the Word of Christ or the sacraments, they do so in Christ's place and stead."

55. This is the order in which the sacraments are treated from CA, 9 to 12 before Art. 13 on "The Use of the Sacraments." Cf. Ap., 13:4.

56. See the chapter by H. Jorissen, pp. 101–21 below.

On the Possibility of a Catholic Recognition of the *Confessio Augustana* as a Legitimate Expression of Christian Truth

HEINZ SCHÜTTE

I.

Removal of schisms and realization of the visible oneness of Christians is a gift we pray God for. We cannot bring it about by human powers. We can, however, serve this unity; the gift constitutes our task. We can do it by grace—in him who strengthens us.[1] It is a gift of God that separated Christians recognize this goal which they can affirm together and toward which they can strive by the grace of God: the unity of the churches, which remain churches and yet become one Church.[2] To express it more clearly, the Catholic, the Orthodox, the Anglican, the Lutheran Churches—to single out these—are to remain churches with their own patterns of piety and liturgy, with their own governments and ecclesiastical ordinances, and with their existing theological modes of expression. Yet they are no longer to be separated from one another but are to realize the one visible Church of Jesus Christ.

Christians can also say in common and affirm on what basis such a unity of churches in the one Church of Jesus Christ is to come about:[3]

—On the basis of the truth of the gospel, neither on a minimal nor on a maximal basis. "In essentials, unity"—in essentials, in what has been revealed by God, there must be unity. To express it another way, we seek oneness in confession, oneness in faith.

—In everything that does not belong to the essentials, to revealed truth, there can and must be the greatest possible freedom: "In whatever is doubtful, freedom." Therefore unity in diversity: not uniformity but pluriformity. Although true unity is utterly impossible where the truth is circumvented, it must nevertheless be said on the other side: "The claim of truth dare not be made where it is not compelling and unshakable. Nothing dare be imposed as truth which is in reality a form that has developed in the course of history and which stands in a rather close connection with the truth."[4]

—Love must rule everything. We are to be devoted to one another in serving, understanding love, ready to forgive one another even as our Father in heaven forgives us our guilt. We are to be ready in love to open paths for one another which can lead away from schism and to unity; we are to grasp every proposal which might be useful for a closer approach to the oneness willed by the Lord.

The CA has come under discussion as a basis for confessional unity between the Catholic Church and the Lutheran churches.[5] A reason for this is found in the CA itself, which expressly states its intention and conviction that it is in agreement with the teaching of the catholic Church.

The authors and signers of the CA did not—as, for example, the Lutheran theologian Werner Elert emphasizes—intend to found a new church; rather they wanted to confess their membership in the one, holy, catholic, and apostolic Church. It was not the purpose of the CA in 1530 to rupture the solidarity of the catholic Church "but rather to express it and restore it."[6]

The CA desires to adhere to the faith of the catholic Church. It appeals to the creeds of the ancient Church; it accepts the christological statements of the Councils of Ephesus and Chalcedon. The Protestant theologian Ernst Kinder writes: "By accepting the ancient creeds together with her own confessions as really authoritative, the Lutheran Reformation historically acknowledges the one true Church of Jesus Christ of all times and places."[7] The CA expressly declares its agreement with the catholic and Roman Church: "This is about the sum of our teaching. As can be seen, there is nothing here that departs from the Scriptures or the catholic Church or the Church of Rome, in so far as the ancient Church is known to us from its writers."[8]

That the CA desired to formulate the faith of the one, holy, catholic, and apostolic Church confessionally and did not desire to stand in antithesis to it is underlined by the statement: "The dispute and dissension are concerned chiefly with various traditions and abuses,"[9] which is to say that according to the understanding of the author and the signers of the CA the differences with the Roman Church concern only abuses, not essential doctrines of faith.

To gain a correct understanding of the text of the CA, one must also always start with the preface. In it the conviction is expressed that the framers and signers of the CA desire to live with the members of the Catholic Church "in unity and in one fellowship and Church, even as we are all enlisted under one Christ."[10]

The CA "was the basic ecclesiastical confession of early Lutheran Protestantism and has remained such,"[11] as the Lutheran theologian R. Hermann emphasizes.

In view of the intention of the CA and of its general authority as a confessional writing of the Lutheran churches—yes, and even beyond them also of other churches stemming from the Reformation—it is wholly understandable that the CA has (again!) come to be discussed as a possible basis for agreement. Cardinal Ratzinger has expressed himself as follows on this matter:

> The researches of the past few years converge in understanding that the CA as the basic Lutheran confessional document was drawn up as it was not only for diplomatic reasons, that it might be possible to interpret it under the laws of the empire as a catholic confession; it was also drafted with inner conviction as a searching for evangelical catholicity—as a painstaking effort to filter the bubbling cauldron of the early Reformation movement in such a way that it might give it the shape of a catholic reform. Accordingly, efforts are under way to achieve a Catholic recognition of the CA or, more correctly, a recognition of the CA as catholic, and thereby to establish the catholicity of the churches of the CA, which makes possible a corporate union while the differences remain.[12]

Such recognition of the CA by the Catholic Church would, according to J. Ratzinger, be

> far more than merely a theoretical-theological act which is negotiated by historians and church politicians. Rather it would be a concrete spiritual decision and to that extent a new historical step on both sides. It would mean that the Catholic Church would adopt its own way of realizing the mutual faith with that independence which is her right. Conversely, it would mean for those on the Reformation side to live and understand this text, which can be interpreted in a number of ways, in the direction of its original intention: in unity with the

dogma of the ancient Church and its original church structure. Taken as a whole it would mean that the open question about the center of the Reformation would be solved by a spiritual decision in the direction of a catholically lived CA and that the heritage of that time would be lived and accepted according to this hermeneutic.[13]

It is significant and important that the Executive Committee of the Lutheran World Federation has recommended that to begin with Lutherans take an open and positive attitude toward the discussions by the Catholic side. The chairman of the Commission on Ecumenism of the Lutheran World Federation, Bishop Dietzfelbinger, pointed to the 450th anniversary of the CA in 1980, and said that the Lutheran churches need to prepare carefully for the discussion of the CA as a common confession—also in view of the fact that many things have changed in the Catholic Church from what they were at the time of the Reformation.[14]

II.

In view of the proposal of a "Catholic reception" of the CA, a whole series of problems opens up. At the present moment the discussion is just beginning, and it would be helpful to make a brief survey of some of the questions which must be faced:

1. Critical remarks expressed by Protestant theologians concerning the CA.
2. The relationship of Luther and of Luther's theology to the CA.
3. The position of the CA among or in relation to the rest of the Lutheran confessional writings.
4. The correct interpretation of the CA in view of the divergent interpretations which have actually occurred.
5. The binding force and correctness of the *Confutatio*, which was the contemporary response to the CA.
6. The significance of the documents of the most recent Lutheran-Catholic dialogue for this project.
7. Difficulties in connection with a reception of the CA for Catholic theology and the Catholic Church.
8. Problems which arise for Lutheran theology and the Lutheran Church in view of a possible Catholic reception of the CA.
9. Common tasks for Lutherans and Catholics in view of a possi-

ble acceptance of the CA as a basis for corporate Lutheran-Catholic unity.

Although in the following we will comment on these problems, it goes without saying that this is not intended to make a more careful and thorough discussion unnecessary.

1. Critical remarks made by Protestant theologians concerning the CA:

—According to the view of a number of Protestant theologians, the CA contradicts Luther's theology on decisive points. It is said that already Luther himself stated that the CA was "stepping softly." But especially it is said that this confession does not consistently carry through Luther's understanding of the universal priesthood of all believers, that is, that in those writings by Luther which truly reflect the Reformation, nothing is said of the *rite vocatus,* that is, of valid ordination as the prerequisite for the public ministry of word and sacrament.[15]

—The judgment by the CA that the real difference is not about doctrines of faith but about a few abuses is said to be untrue, for in the CA certain essential controversies had regrettably been passed over in silence, in particular the papacy, purgatory, and the sacrifice of the Mass. Heinrich Bornkamm writes:

> Hoping to reach agreement at the Diet and fearing a religious war, Melanchthon endeavored to express agreement with the doctrine of the Roman Church as much as possible; he ignored a number of particularly thorny questions (especially the papacy and purgatory) and even permitted himself to be carried away enough to write the untrue sentence: 'The dispute and dissensions are concerned chiefly with various traditions and abuses' (conclusion of part 1), which he was then compelled at Wittenberg in the *editio princeps* (1531) to alter while the work was being printed. Thus the CA alone cannot be regarded as a sufficient presentation of Reformation teaching. At the very least one must take in addition Melanchthon's Apology, which is in many instances more forceful, his *Treatise on the Power and Primacy of the Pope,* and Luther's *Smalcald Articles.*[16]

—In a certain respect the director of the Commission on Faith and Order of the World Council of Churches, the Reformed theologian Lukes Vischer, criticizes the CA when he remarks with respect to Article 7: "The formula *'satis est'* non satis est."[17]

51

It would not be well to ignore criticism of this kind by Protestant theologians. Someone would certainly bring such objections into the discussion anyway. We turn to these criticisms and attempt to answer them with a few remarks.

2. With respect to the relationship of Luther and of Luther's theology to the CA.

Luther expressed his opinion of the CA a number of times. While at the Coburg, he asked for Melanchthon's draft in order that he might express his opinion concerning it. Luther's opinion is contained in a letter to his Elector dated 15 May 1530. It reads: "I have read through Magister Philip's *Apologia*; it pleases me very well, and I know nothing which should be improved or changed, neither would it be proper, for I cannot step so gently and softly. May Christ our Lord grant that it may bring much good and rich fruit, as we hope and pray. Amen."[18] The Protestant theologian K. Stürmer writes with respect to this remark by Luther: "Thus it fell, the word about stepping softly. Anyone who listens carefully, however, will not be able to hear any kind of reproach in Luther's judgment, rather the contrary."[19] This was not the only time the Reformer expressed a positive view of the CA; R. Hermann remarks that after the presentation of the CA, Luther spoke of it as *confessio plane pulcherrima*, a "quite wonderfully beautiful confession,"[20] and that at the end of the Diet of Augsburg he expressed his acknowledgement to Melanchthon.[21] On the other hand, a remark about "stepping softly" in a letter to Justus Jonas, 21 July 1530, has a negative connotation, namely, when Luther wrote that the failure to designate the pope as antichrist was now coming home to roost.[22]

More significant is a confrontation of the CA with a basic theological viewpoint which Luther held from about 1519 to 1521 and perhaps as late as 1523. In several of his writings from this period there is found an understanding of Church and Ministry which cannot be harmonized with certain ecclesiological statements of the CA, but to which some Protestant theologians appeal in a one-sided manner as characteristic of Luther and on the basis of which they raise critical objections against the CA, or on the basis of which, by modifying certain articles, they seek to interpret the CA.

In an attempt to convey Luther's fundamental understanding, K. G. Steck takes as his basis Luther's writing *Ad librum eximii Magistri Nostri Mag. Abrosii Catharini, defensoris Silvestri Prieriatis acerrimi, responsio* from the year 1521.[23] In it Luther writes that the Church— like its foundation, Jesus Christ, on whom it is based—is invisible and spiritual, perceptible only by faith. As far as Matthew 16:13–19 is concerned, Luther says: *"Igitur sicut Petra ista sine peccato, invisibilis et sola fide perceptibilis, ita necesse est et Ecclesiam sine peccato, invisibilem et spiritualem sola fide perceptibilem esse: opportet enim fundamentum esse cum aedificio eiusdem conditionis"* (As the Rock is without sin, invisible and spiritual, perceptible only in faith, so it is necessary that also the Church should be without sin, invisible and spiritual, perceptible only in faith: for foundation and building must be of the same quality).[24] For Luther—as H. J. Iwand explains in his comments on this passage—the *Petra* (the Rock) is not Simon Bar-Jona but the hearer of the revelation of the Father. Therefore, according to Luther, Christ founds his Church upon faith in which he himself is present,[25] not on Simon Peter. (That no exegete today any longer considers such an interpretation appropriate is well known.) However, if the Church—as Luther at that time clearly thought—is invisible, then by what sign can I know that the Church exists? Steck asks with Luther and answers with him: By baptism, bread, and gospel. "For where you see baptism, bread, and gospel present and efficacious . . . no matter where, no matter by what person (administered), . . . no matter who distributes the Lord's Supper and proclaims the gospel, there you need not doubt that the Church exists."[26] And Steck adds—pointing directly at CA, 14— "Nothing is said here about *rite vocatus* (rightly called), nothing!"[27] It is a fact that also Article 7 of the CA is sometimes interpreted from this perspective: someone appeals to a saying by Luther that everyone who has been baptized may boast that he is already pope, bishop, and minister and considers the question of the Ministry solved from such a one-sided emphasis on the universal priesthood of all believers, but must then suffer himself to be told that the practice of ordination, widely practiced since the Reformation, would really have been unnecessary.[28]

As the Lutheran theologian W. Elert has shown,

Luther was soon converted, and that very thoroughly and permanently, from the above-mentioned notions. His better insight prevailed at three points. First of all, the notion of the universal rule of the emperor is shattered for him. In the second place, Luther breaks with the view that the emperor is the defender and advocate of the Church. . . . In the third place, however, there follows also during the 1520s the . . . change in his conception of church government. . . . Here his practical experience and his continuing growth in theological understanding are at work together. . . . Where it is left to individuals how they want to organize, there without exception mobs and sects come into being. Already the activity of Karlstadt in Wittenberg in 1521 convinced Luther in a practical way that it is impossible to carry out the congregational principle. These practical experiences mark the start of the church visitations beginning in 1526 which led to the origin of the territorial churches. Hand in hand with this, as already said, went his growth in theological understanding. Again he moves in a twofold direction. For one thing, now his individualistic thinking, which took its starting point from the universal priesthood, is supplemented with corporate thinking. In the concept of "body of believers" the emphasis is shifted from the believers to the body. . . . Whatever is said from that time on by Luther about church organization must be understood as referring to the Church, not to the individual congregation. . . . This totality, that is, the Church, has indeed the right to create organs for itself, to transfer her functions to individuals. However, and this is the other point in his theological progress, she is by no means to decide according to whim whether she will do it. The ecclesiastical Ministry which she transfers to individual officeholders through calling and ordination does not have its origin in practical considerations and necessity. Rather it was instituted by Christ himself. . . . Even as Luther had, in his struggles with the fanatics and sectarians, recognized the impossibility of turning over the Church, like the civil government, to "Mr. Everyman," so he now recognized also the deeper reason as far as the Church is concerned. The Church does not exist as a result of the goodwill of the believers but solely because of the real presence in word and sacrament of the exalted Christ, who has authoritatively set the ministry of proclaiming the word in opposition to the authority of "Mr. Everyman."[29]

According to Elert, it is a fateful error to stop with Luther's writings completed by 1523 when searching for his opinions, because he overcame many one-sided views as his theology progressed. A comparison of the CA with Luther's understanding around 1530 no longer leads to things which cannot be harmonized, as is the case with statements between 1519 and 1523.

3. The CA in the context of other Lutheran confessional writings.

As H. Bornkamm appropriately remarks, points in controversy which are missing in the CA are discussed in other confessional writings. Therefore the CA needs to be supplemented by other confessional writings. The question then is, Will not then agreement and union on the basis of the CA become impossible? For example, Bornkamm mentions the *Smalcald Articles*. In this document, drawn up in 1537, it becomes plain "what they sought at that time to formulate at the risk of their very existence as the message of the gospel and . . . defended stubbornly," as the Lutheran theologian Ernst Wolf writes.[30] By the message of the gospel they meant the article of the justification of the sinner through Jesus Christ: through the crucifixion and resurrection of Jesus Christ the redemption and justification of the sinner was accomplished; it is imparted to men "without the works of the law, on the ground of faith," as St. Paul argues in the Epistle to the Romans. According to the *Smalcald Articles,* the entire protest against the pope is based on this chief article; nothing in this article can be given up; on it rests all that must be practiced and taught against the pope.[31] In other words, the opinion prevailed that the pope and the Church at that time stood for a totally different doctrine of justification, a doctrine opposed to the gospel. Careful study—no longer ruled by polemical thinking—has, however, shown that the doctrine of justification no longer divides Lutherans and Catholics if one disregards the one-sided emphasis in Luther's writings (monergism of God, the bondage of the human will) and all kinds of aberrations in the popular piety of that time. At the General Assembly of the Lutheran World Federation in Helsinki in 1963, the conclusion was reached that the Catholic doctrine of justification could, from the Lutheran standpoint, no longer be dismissed as false, unbiblical, and unevangelical.[32] The Lutheran theologian Wenzel Lohff has stated that this has consequences also for the rejection in the *Smalcald Articles* of the pope on the basis of the doctrine of justification:

> Luther and the theologians who followed him demanded of the Roman Church freedom to understand the gospel in terms of justification. It can be said that as a result of more recent efforts by Roman Catholic theologians, the basis of the conflict can almost be regarded as

removed, all the more so because also in the Reformation tradition the interpretation of justification has developed further. If these circumstances are taken into consideration, the conflict on the basis of which Luther's criticism of the papacy arose appears to have been removed.[33]

As a further point of controversy not treated in the CA, H. Bornkamm mentions what was popularly called *Fegfeuer*. The dogma does not speak of *Fegfeuer* but of *purgatorium,* that is, of cleansing, which really means an event. H. U. von Balthasar has proposed the following attempt at resolving the controversy. With the reduction of *Fegfeuer* from a "place" to a "condition," according to Balthasar,

> little would be accomplished unless one decided to locate the cleansing power of this condition in the encounter of the still uncleansed sinner with the Kyrios, who appears in order to judge him. On the other hand, one will have to agree with Joachim Gnilka ("Ist 1. Kor. 3:10–15 ein Schriftzeugnis für das Fegfeuer?" [diss., Würzburg, 1955]) when, after a review of the whole tangled exegesis of this passage, he follows most recent exegetes by interpreting the "testing fire" of the "Day of the Lord" as the Lord coming at the last judgment, and also in his conclusion that this fire (using Isaiah 66:15–16 as a parallel) represents merely "a picture of the majesty of God revealing himself, of the unapproachability of the Holy One." On the other hand, we cannot deny that Scripture does not teach two judgments or days of judgment, but only one, and that we must therefore envision the particular judgment after death (no matter how abstractly we imagine it) in a dynamic connection with the final judgment. If this proposal succeeds in making *Fegfeuer* understandable as a dimension of the judgment, of the confrontation of the sinner with the "flaming eyes" and the "fiery feet" of Christ (Rev. 1:14; Dan. 10:6), much would appear to have been gained for the ecumenical dialogue.[34]

Together with the papacy, the *Smalcald Articles* reject the Mass: "If the Mass falls, the papacy will fall with it."[35] It is well known that the *Smalcald Articles* say that "the Mass in the papacy must be regarded as the greatest and most horrible abomination because it runs into direct and violent conflict with the article of justification."[36] On the Lutheran side there was the conviction that the Mass was understood as a sacrifice in addition to the sacrifice of Christ on the cross, and therefore the Mass was tantamount to a denial of the all-sufficient sacrifice offered once for all. The results of newer discussions and labors show that it is not necessary that we "remain eternally divided and opposed the one to the other,"[37] which is the conclusion drawn by the *Smalcald Articles*. A document has been worked out by the international Lutheran-Catholic dialogue on questions concerning the Eucharist. It deals with all disputed questions, including the question of the relationship between the sacrifice on the cross and the sacrifices of the Mass; differences remain, but where there is a correct interpretation of the Eucharist, there are no antitheses between Lutherans and Catholics which must separate the churches. The Institute for Ecumenical Research of the Lutheran World Federation has concluded that as a result of the ecumenical dialogue,[38] agreement has been achieved or can be achieved with respect to questions of the Eucharist, such as sacrifice, atoning sacrifice, and sacrifice by the Church.

These hints appear to indicate that a Catholic reception of the CA may not, in spite of its connection with the other Lutheran confessions, be impossible in principle.

4. With reference to the divergent interpretations of the CA.

We shall focus on two examples. How is *ministerium* in Article 5 to be understood? What is the meaning of *satis est* in Article 7 of the CA?

"Does 'ministry of teaching the gospel and administering the sacraments' refer to a specifically defined service or to the general activity of the ministry of word and sacrament?" H. Fagerberg, a Lutheran theologian, asks.[39] In other words, does *ministerium* refer to a special Ministry bestowed on special persons or only to a function which can be performed by any and every Christian? Fagerberg lists the opposing views:

> Höfling and Persson opt for the second possibility, Höfling by placing the Ministry very close to the universal priesthood, Persson through his repeated assertion that the activity in question could as a matter of principle be performed by "whoever wants to." These interpretations, however, practically considered, find no support in the confessional writings; rather the confessional writings understand *ministerium* in a technical sense as a special, limited activity which is entrusted to those persons called to it.[40]

It is true that all Christians are commanded to bear witness to the gospel by word and deed; however, the special office of the Ministry (the office of pastor, teacher, and priest) for the guidance of the congregation, the public proclamation of the gospel in word and sacrament, and for presiding over the celebration of the Lord's Supper is committed to specific persons through ordination, as must be concluded from Article 14 (*rite vocatus*) and must be said against K. G. Steck's understanding. As far as Fagerberg's analysis of P. E. Persson's opinion is concerned, the following criticism must be made: Persson was a participant in the official Lutheran-Catholic dialogue and concurred with a document in which it is emphasized that this office is not merely functional but is bound to specific bearers of the office. Persson expressly acknowledged that he holds this understanding and remarked that he is erroneously alleged to think of the office as something merely functional.[41]

Appeal is sometimes made to Article 7 of the CA for the view that any and every Christian could proclaim the gospel publicly and administer the sacraments. There it is said that it is sufficient (*satis est*) for the true unity of the Church to agree concerning the teaching of the gospel and the administration of the sacraments. This sentence can be understood correctly if, on the one hand, Article 14 is taken seriously (that only a validly ordained person is called to public proclamation and the administration of the sacraments) and, on the other hand, attention is given to the sentence immediately after the statement about *satis est*: "It is not necessary that human traditions or rites and ceremonies, instituted by men, should be alike everywhere."[42] There need be no objection if by *satis est* the greatest possible freedom is demanded concerning human regulations as long as there is agreement about revealed truth. If, however, by the *satis est* the pure proclamation of the word and the right administration of the sacraments are set down as absolutes, detached from the ordained bearer of the office, in other words, if one sees in Article 7 of the CA a structural instead of a regulative understanding of the Church, if one believes that one can "define" Church without a special, ordained Ministry, then Lutherans stand in opposition to the doctrine of the Ministry held by the Catholic and Orthodox churches. (On the basis of a thorough investigation we are convinced that this, although it is the opinion of some individuals, is not the understanding of the Lutheran churches.)

The Reformed theologian L. Vischer has emphasized the positive side of *satis est* but has also warned against using the formula uncritically. "It becomes a hindrance when it is made into a principle and transferred uncritically into present-day circumstances."[43] According to Vischer, the CA offers only an incomplete answer to the question of what is necessary for true unity. "It is, for instance, not quite clear to what extent the office of the Ministry—instituted by God, according to Article 5—is a prerequisite for the establishment of unity."[44] True unity cannot be guaranteed merely by preaching and administering the sacraments, without a special office; according to Vischer, the formula *satis est* is even dangerous because it does not deal fully with the problem of unity. *Satis est* has, as he points out, "often been misused to diminish the importance of questions of organization. . . . But wherever community is discovered, it demands realization. Therefore it also demands a strategy calculated to achieve the aim of unity and common witness. The weakness of the CA lies in the fact that it weakens rather than furthers the will to do this; . . . the formula *'satis est' non satis est.*"[45] We wish to remark that Vischer calls attention to a danger one should take note of; however, if the CA is correctly understood, this danger can certainly be avoided, and it is not the intention of the CA and of its author and signers to reduce the Church to the proclamation of the gospel and the administration of the sacraments without ordained bearers of the office. The confessors at Augsburg had no intention of founding a new church; rather they wanted to reform the existing church and apply the touchstone of the correct proclamation of the gospel and administering the sacraments to the real Church of the time.

5. To the question of the obligatory nature and correctness of the *Confutatio*[46] as a contemporary of the CA.

One asks oneself today why the CA was not, in accord with its own intention, accepted by the Roman Catholic side in 1530 as a confession of the faith of the one, holy, catholic, and apostolic Church. In seeking an answer one must not forget the status of polemics at that time. One needs to keep in mind furthermore that serious points of controversy are not discussed in the CA, as Lutheran theologians concede; to that extent one could hardly have stopped with the CA.

To be sure, already in 1530 the *Confutatio* was not the answer of the Catholic Church; rather it was drawn up at the request of the

Emperor and in his name; it was a theological opinion; many of its answers and especially their proofs are more than doubtful (for instance, the defence of celibacy, which is based on Old Testament regulations, is surely a negative evaluation of conjugal love and surrender).[47] After the Apology of the CA, the *Confutatio* has been rendered out-of-date, as a Catholic theologian, E. Iserloh, admits.[48]

That the *Confutatio* is not to be regarded by Catholics as the answer of the Catholic Church and that careful reflection is required and is today taking place is clear from the fact that after the Second Vatican Council official discussions began between Lutherans and Catholics. In view of the convergences and agreements which have been achieved on important controversial points, the question now is:

6. What is the significance of the documents of the official Lutheran-Catholic dialogue for a possible Catholic recognition of the CA as a basis for Lutheran-Catholic unity and fellowship?

The report of the international Lutheran-Catholic dialogue, "The Gospel and the Church,"[49] was submitted to a number of faculties and church leaders; they were asked to respond to it. The resulting opinions can be summed up briefly in two sentences:

—The report "The Gospel and the Church" is welcomed as the conclusion of the first phase of the official Lutheran-Catholic dialogue.

—There is general desire for a continuation of the studies and discussions because there can be real unity only if the antitheses are thoroughly overcome.

As a necessary complement to the MR, the Lutheran-Catholic dialogue instructed two subcommittees to draw up two documents, one on the Eucharist and one on the Ministry, giving special attention to the episcopate and to the relation of this office to the Church. The document on the Lord's Supper, or Eucharist, has meanwhile been worked out and has already been accepted in principle by the plenary commission without a dissenting vote. It consists of two parts. In the first part everything is said which Lutherans and Catholics are able to confess jointly. In the second part past and present controversies are discussed; the question is asked in all honesty whether there are some antitheses that still must separate the churches, or whether, in spite of every possible difference in language and emphasis, unity in the truth is possible. The latter appears to be the case. It is quite possible that major difficulties may show up with respect to the Ministry (episcopate, teaching office, Petrine office) in the Church, although answers given by the official Lutheran-Catholic dialogue in the United States are promising.[50] As has been done in the documents mentioned, the attempt to overcome past and present controversies should be made against the background of the CA. In this way the CA would gain credence, and any criticism and skepticism on either the Lutheran or the Catholic side which might doubt that the differences had been truly eliminated would either be obviated or else met.

In addition, the newer documents of the dialogue have found a frame of reference in the CA. Finally, by drawing the CA into the discussion, the legitimate concern that the CA does not mention all controversies completely, and in this respect is in real need of being supplemented, could at least in part be taken up.

7. What difficulties and problems arise from the idea of a Catholic reception of the CA for Catholic theology and the Catholic Church?

As Bishop Dietzfelbinger, the chairman of the Committee on Ecumenism of the Lutheran World Federation, emphasized at Uppsala in 1976, the dogmas proclaimed after the schism of the Western Church have raised problems which were not yet present in 1530, and they ought to be solved before a reception of the CA by the Catholic Church.

Therefore earnest efforts are necessary by the Catholic side to demonstrate in a convincing manner that the dogmas in question are in conformity with the gospel. This is the case for the Mariological dogmas of 1854 and 1950 and no less for the primacy and infallibility of the pope. As the Lutherans in a document of the official bilateral dialogue in the United States have stated, it is necessary "that papal primacy should be so structured and interpreted that it unequivocally serve the gospel and the unity of the Church and that its exercise of authority not subvert Christian freedom."[51] In addition, the synodical, collegial structure of the spiritual office (a synod of bishops with and under the Minister in the Petrine office; a college of presbyters together with and under their bishop) would have to be clearly recognized, even as Jesus originally made the Twelve the prototype of the

61

spiritual office.[52] All stages of the historical development of the Church remain subject to the canon and standard which Christ originally established.[53]

Apart from this problem, the CA poses a few serious questions for Catholic theologians themselves, above all concerning the subject of repentance, as a comparison of Article 12 with the text of the Council of Trent which refers to it shows; a careful examination must be made to determine what was the intention of both statements and whether as a result the possibility of agreement exists.[54]

It is true that the second part of the CA is concerned with abuses, with matters which, in the opinion of the confessors at Augsburg as well as according to the judgment of Catholic theologians, do not fall within the area of *regula fidei,* of the truth of the faith, but under the *regula disciplinae,* that is, that are not part of unchangeable divine revelation but under changeable ecclesiastical law in which change is quite possible;[55] nevertheless dogmatic statements are touched upon in part 2 of the CA; therefore it is necessary to make clear what the demands for reform have reference to, in other words, that matters of faith are not being attacked. We consider such a clarification possible.

8. What problems arise for Lutheran theology and for the Lutheran Church from the possibility of the Catholic Church recognizing the CA as a basis for corporate unity between the Lutheran churches and the Catholic Church?

A Catholic theologian needs to exercise great restraint if he wishes to point out problems in Lutheran theology and the Lutheran Church. We mention briefly: the question of the actual recognition of the CA or of the faith confessed in it together with the ancient creeds of the Church; the fact of the diverse estimates of the binding force of the CA as well as of the other confessional writings—are they "binding exposition of Scripture by the Church"[56] or can they, because of their "historical conditioning," claim only indirect relevance at present, which is how Paul Jacobs characterizes their evaluation by a certain group of Lutheran theologians?[57] "Failure by the churches to be bound to the confessions"[58] would have to be met resolutely. We have already referred to the problem of diverse interpretations of the CA; there would need to be a way of limiting interpretations which cannot be harmonized with the faith of the one, holy, catholic, and apostolic Church, for the confessors at Augsburg wanted to maintain this faith.

9. What support could be developed jointly by Lutherans and Roman Catholics for declaring the CA to be a basis for corporate unity between the Lutheran churches and the Roman Catholic Church?

In what has been said until now, it has become plain that there are many concerns and problems for Lutherans as well as for Catholics which they should face together. This does not prevent the preparation of additional special studies by one side or the other.

A commentary could be prepared jointly, giving as briefly as possible explanations that are in part complementary, in part corrective; there could be a jointly prepared description of what constitutes unity and liberty. The process of reception would have to be worked out together; there would have to be much more prayer for unity in truth and love in joint services of prayer and repentance, for without ecumenical spirituality, without unity in the Holy Spirit, the unity of the churches in the one Church of Jesus Christ is not possible. Spiritual ecumenism must be viewed as "the soul of the whole ecumenical movement," as the Catholic Conference of German bishops in 1976 emphasized, citing Vatican II.[59] J. Ratzinger has stated what he thinks the prospects are for realizing corporate unity between the Lutheran churches and the Catholic Church:

> That is a question which is better answered by action than by specu-
> lation, . . . by thinking and acting with respect for the other person in
> his search for what is essentially Christian and by considering unity as
> an urgent good which demands sacrifices, whereas separation must in
> each and every case be justified. It means that the Catholic does not
> work for the rejection of the confessions and for the destruction of
> what is churchly in the Lutheran sphere but that, to the contrary, he
> hopes for the strengthening of their confessions and of their churchly
> reality.[60]

We need to look for what unites when we read the Lutheran Confessions; we need to understand the other *in bonam partem*. The question of the prospects for realizing corporate unity between the Lutheran churches and the Catholic Church is, according to Ratzinger, in the last analysis a question of the forces which are presently at work in Christendom. . . . A Christianity of faith and faithfulness seeks unity; it lives its faith as a definite decision about its content and is precisely for this reason in search of unity. . . . This is a faith which makes the highest demands on a person, renders him utterly powerless, and requires his unlimited patience and readiness for ever-renewed cleansing and deepening. But then, it so happens that Christianity rests entirely on the victory of the improbable, on the adventure of the Holy Spirit, who leads man beyond himself and precisely in this way leads him to his true self. Because we trust this power of the Holy Spirit, we therefore hope for the unity of the Church and put ourselves at the disposal of the ecumenism of faith.[61]

God willing, we shall observe the 450th anniversary of the CA. It would be a significant event if Lutheran and Catholic Christians could more nearly achieve what the confessors at Augsburg intended: removal of the schism, and visible unity of the churches in the one Church of Jesus Christ—in the truth, in freedom, and in love. We would then be able to proclaim the glad tidings about Jesus Christ, the Redeemer of all men, in a more credible fashion.

NOTES

1. Phil. 4:13.

2. Cf. J. Ratzinger, "Die Kirche und die Kirchen," *Reformatio* 13 (1964): 105; H. Schütte, *Protestantismus*, 2d ed. (Essen: Fredebül and Könen, 1966), pp. 541–42.

3. Cf. H. Schütte, *Um die Wiedervereinigung im Glauben* (Essen: Fredebül and Könen, 1960).

4. J. Ratzinger, "Prognosen für die Zukunft des Ökumenismus," *Bausteine* 17, no. 65 (1977): 10.

5. This happened first at the international Lutheran-Catholic dialogue, then in the essay by Vinzenz Pfnür, pp. 1–26 above, and finally in the above mentioned essay by Ratzinger, "Prognosen," p. 12.

6. W. Elert, "Die Bedeutung der Augsburgischen Konfession im theologischen Denken und in der geistesgeschichtlichen Entwicklung," in *Ein Lehrer der Kirche*, ed. M. Keller-Hüschenmenger (Berlin: Lutherisches Verlagshaus, 1967), p. 103.

7. E. Kinder, *Der evangelische Glaube und die Kirche* (Berlin: Lutherisches Verlagshaus, 1958), p. 131.

8. CA, conclusion of part 1; BS, 83c; Tappert, 47:1; cf. Kinder, *Glaube*, p. 134.

9. *BS*, 84d; Tappert, 48:2.

10. *BS*, 44–45; Tappert, 25:4.

11. R. Hermann, "Zur theologischen Würdigung der Augustana," *Luther-jahrbuch* 12(1930): 162; cf. also Vilmos Vajta and H. Weissgerber, eds., *Das Bekenntnis im Leben der Kirche* (Berlin: Lutherisches Verlagshaus, 1963).

12. Ratzinger, "Prognosen," p. 12. If here and in the following we speak of "corporate union while the differences remain," this means—as is clear from the goal sketched in the beginning—that churches which had been separated but in the future would be united would, without prejudice to full fellowship in witnessing, Christian service, sacraments, public ministry, and basic structure, retain their special confessional profile. We repeat: the goal is the unity of the churches, which remain churches (!) and yet become one Church. Cf. the essay by H. Meyer, pp. 69–80 below, who agrees fully with this statement of the goal.

13. Ratzinger, "Prognosen," p. 12.

14. Cf. Hermann Dietzfelbinger, pp. 95–100 below.

15. Karl G. Steck, "Ecclesia—creatura verbi," in *Von Einheit und Wesen der Kirche*, ed. J. Beckmann et al. (Göttingen: Vandenhoeck & Ruprecht, 1960), p. 50.

16. H. Bornkamm, "Augsburger Bekenntnis," *RGG*[3] 1:735.

17. L. Vischer, ". . . satis est?* Gemeinschaft in Christus und Einheit der Kirche," in *Christliche Freiheit—im Dienst am Menschen*, ed. Karl Herbert (Frankfurt: Lembeck, 1972), pp. 243–54.

18. *WA* Br, 5:319, ll. 5–9; *LW*, 49: 297–98; "fast wol" at that time meant "very well"; cf. Wilhelm Maurer, *Historischer Kommentar zur Confessio Augustana*, vol. 1 (Gütersloh: Gütersloher Verlagshaus, 1976), p. 24.

19. K. Stürmer, "Bekennen oder Leisetreten," *Jahrbuch des Evangelischen Bundes* 17 (1974):54.

20. R. Hermann, "Zur theologischen Würdigung," p. 163.

21. Ibid.

22. Ibid.

23. Cf. Steck, "Ecclesia," pp. 41, 48 ff.

24. *WA*, 7:710, l. 1.

25. *WA*, 2:190, l. 8; H. J. Iwand, "Zur Entstehung von Luthers Kirchenbegriff," in *Festschrift für Günther Dehn*, ed. W. Schneemelcher (Neukirchen: Verlag der Buchhandlung des Erziehungsvereins, 1957), p. 154, n. 21.

26. Steck, "Ecclesia," pp. 49–50, following Luther, *WA*, 7:720, l. 34.

27. Steck, "Ecclesia," p. 50.

28. Cf. H. Schütte, "Bemühungen zur Überwindung von Lehrdifferenzen zwischen den Reformationskirchen," *KNA—Ökumenische Information*, no. 27 (1976): 6.

29. Elert, "Lutherische Grundsätze für die Kirchenverfassung," in *Ein Lehrer der Kirche*, pp. 116–17.

30. E. Wolf, *Peregrinatio*, vol. 1, *Studien zur reformatorischen Theologie und zum Kirchenproblem* (Munich: Chr. Kaiser, 1962), p. 117.

31. *BS*, 416–17; Tappert, 292:5.

32. W. Andersen, "Das theologische Gespräch über die Rechtfertigung in Helsinki," in *Helsinki 1963: Beiträge zum theologischen Gespräch des Lutherischen Weltbunds*, ed. E. Wilkens (Berlin: Lutherisches Verlagshaus, 1964), p. 35.

33. W. Lohff, "The Papacy and the Reformation: 2. Would the Pope still have been the Antichrist for Luther today?" *Concilium: Religion in the Seventies*, vol. 64 (New York: Herder & Herder, 1971), pp. 261–62.

34. H. U. von Balthasar, "Eschatologie," in *Fragen der Theologie heute*, ed. Joh. Feiner, Jos. Trütsch, and Fr. Böckle (Einsiedeln: Benziger, 1957), p. 411.

35. *BS*, 419; Tappert, 294:10.

36. *BS*, 416; Tappert, 293:1.

37. *BS*, 419; Tappert, 294:10.

38. "Stellungnahme des Strassburger Instituts zum lutherisch-katholischen Abendmahlsgemeinschaft," in *Um das Amt und Herrenmahl: Dokumente zum evangelisch-katholischen Gespräch*, ed. G. Gassmann et al. (Frankfurt: Lembeck, 1974), p. 137.

39. H. Fagerberg, *Die Theologie der Lutherischen Bekenntnisschriften von 1529 bis 1537* (Göttingen: Vandenhoeck & Ruprecht, 1965), p. 243.

40. Ibid., p. 243.

41. H. Schütte, *Amt, Ordination und Sukzession* (Düsseldorf: Patmos, 1974) p. 164; in a letter Persson corroborates this description as correct.

42. *BS*, 61; Tappert, 32:3.

43. L. Vischer, ". . . *satis est?*" p. 250.

44. Ibid., p. 251.

45. Ibid., p. 253.

46. See *CR*, 27:1–243.

47. *Confutatio, CR*, 27:208–11.

48. E. Iserloh, "Confutatio," *LThK*² 3:37–38.

49. The so-called *Malta Report;* see the list of abbreviations for full bibliographical details.

50. Cf. *Lutherans and Catholics in Dialogue*, vol. 4: *Eucharist and Ministry* (New York: United States National Committee of the Lutheran World Federation; Washington: United States National Conference of Catholic Bishops' Commission for Ecumenical and Interreligious Affairs, 1970), pp. 7–23; *Lutherans and Catholics in Dialogue*, vol. 5: *Papal Primacy and the Universal Church* (Minneapolis: Augsburg Publishing House,

1974), pp. 9–38; for a full bibliographical listing see Lindbeck/Vajta, p. 93, n. 1, below.

51. *Papal Primacy*, p. 22, sec. 30.

52. J. Ratzinger, "Die bischöfliche Kollegialität," in *De Ecclesia*, vol. 2, ed. J. Barauna (Freiburg: Herder, 1966), pp. 44–45.

53. J. Ratzinger, "Primat," *LThK*² 8:761.

54. Cf. CA, 12 with DS, 1704. In this connection see the contribution of Hans Jorissen in this volume, pp. 101–21 below.

55. K. Adam, *Una Sancta in katholischer Sicht* (Düsseldorf: Patmos, 1948), pp. 65–66.

56. Edmund Schlink, *Theology of the Lutheran Confessions*, trans. P. Koehnecke and H. Bouman (Philadelphia: Fortress Press, 1961), pp. xvi–xviii.

57. P. Jacobs, *Theologie reformierter Bekenntnisschriften* (Neukirchen: Verlag der Buchhandlung des Erziehungsvereins, 1959), p. 14.

58. Schlink, *Theology*, p. xv.

59. *Ökumenisches Direktorium*, Part III, following *Unitatis Redintegratio* 8 at Vatican II.

60. Ratzinger, "Prognosen," p. 12.

61. Ibid., p. 13.

The *Augustana* Accepted by Rome?
What Lutheran and Catholic Theologians
Can Contribute to This Goal

HARDING MEYER

Recognition of the CA by the Roman Catholic Church! It is an ecumenically fascinating thought and in agreement with the CA's own original intention. One would like to grasp it with both hands, undergird it with additional arguments, and with solemn entreaties lay it on the hearts of the Lutheran churches. Yet a number of pressing questions stand in the way. They are questions which point to tasks which must be performed, not questions which will necessarily cause the project to fail.

There are, first of all, questions concerning the proper form and presentation of the project itself. Here it is necessary to achieve somewhat greater clarity in order that one may know precisely what is wanted and what is not wanted. For instance, the question of terminology arises, but very soon it turns out to be more than a matter of mere terminology. Does the action referred to mean "recognition," "reception," or "acceptance" of the CA? All three terms have been used in the discussion up to this time, generally interchangeably, but is it not possible that they stand for very different things? Is the projected recognition, reception, or acceptance to be "by the Catholic Church," "as catholic," "as a Roman confession," "as a legitimate expression of Christian truth," "as an independent expression of catholic belief," or "as a testimony to the faith which the churches have in common?" One meets with all these formulations. Furthermore, divergent interpretations of these formulations[1] are not only possible but presumably even exist. At once the additional question arises: What is the real *purpose* of such a recognition, and therefore what would be accomplished by it? Here also it would be necessary to achieve greater clarity and unanimity before too much publicity is given to the thought of a Catholic recognition of the CA and thus give rise to opinions which can sometimes be revised only with great difficulty. If one considers the viewpoints expressed up to this time (Vinzenz Pfnür, the Ecumenical Commission of the Diocese of Münster, Joseph Ratzinger, Heinz Schütte) and attempts to arrange them in a sequence, a graduated definition of the goal seems to appear. To begin with, (1) the intention could be carefully to correct the Roman Catholic judgment of the Reformation by taking the CA of 1530 as a criterion and hermeneutical key for understanding what the Reformation was about. The intention would therefore be to make a historical-theological evaluation. On the basis of this primarily historical-theological statement, recognition of the CA could then (2) express the fact that the central confession of the Lutheran churches today represents a legitimate confession of the Christian faith and that a church in which this confession occupies a central place and possesses binding authority is the Church of Jesus Christ. This would then be a theological-ecclesiological judgment. Finally, (3) there could follow from that judgment an ecumenical-ecclesial decision: the realization of full church fellowship on the basis of a CA which has binding force in the Lutheran churches, is not understood by the Catholic Church as a Roman Catholic confession, but would be recognized as a legitimate confession of the Christian faith.

Such a graduated definition of the goal could prove helpful. The efforts to achieve Catholic recognition of the CA would by no means have to embrace all three steps at once. Already the first step would be worth every effort. One ought, however, to be conscious of that internal dynamic which leads toward the following steps once the first step has been taken.

If, however, the CA is actually to be a meetingplace between the Catholic and the Lutheran churches and if its recognition by Catholics is to make church fellowship possible, then everything depends on efforts that really and truly have that CA in mind with which the Lutheran churches live, and not another. This is not simply decided by the form of the text but by the context which has developed through history or by the *Sitz im Leben* of this confession. In other words, it is necessary in connection with all further efforts for a

Catholic recognition of the CA to reflect constantly on the historical differences which developed in various ways between the CA of 1530 and the CA which has become a confession of the Church and with which the Lutheran churches have since that time lived and still live. Unless this historical distance is earnestly taken into consideration, there is an acute danger that the CA will not become a meetingplace, but that only a sham encounter occurs, whereas in reality a new and tragic misstep has been taken.

I would like to sketch briefly two points on which attention to the historical differences seems to me to be particularly important and describe a third point somewhat more in detail.

1. The accumulated burden of the history of separation.

Herbert Immenkötter prefaces his examination of the deliberations at Augsburg with what Luther said a few years after the Diet of Augsburg: "I fear that we shall never again get as close together as we did at Augsburg."[2] In fact, after Augsburg the Protestant line and the Catholic line again increasingly diverge. With the breaking off of the Regensburg Colloquy in 1546, the period of religious dialogue has also come to an end. After 1555 the confessional borders are essentially fixed. From that time on they are separated churches, separated in fact and in law, each with its own historical development. With the exception of a few episodes, there is an increasing movement in divergent directions in worship, in spirituality, in theology, and in church doctrine.

Of course, the text of the CA was not changed through the subsequent history of separation. But is the CA not changed by the way it has been received, understood, used, and lived in later years in the Lutheran churches? One is compelled to say that the CA, since it is a confession of the church, is influenced in its content by the changing historical context. Therefore the accumulated burden of the history of separation rests upon it also. This cannot and must not be ignored if one wishes to deal with that particular CA which is today the confession of the Lutheran churches.

Let us take as an example the Scriptural principle of the Reformation. It is a well-known fact that the CA does not speak of this. One can go even further and say that the CA in its whole way of arguing

71

does not represent a strict understanding of *sola scriptura* as it had crystallized during the early years of the Reformation struggle, but sees "the relationship between Scripture and tradition in a more differentiated way."[3] But does not the renewed sharpening of this controversial question, on the one hand, through the decree of Trent (DS, 1501) and, on the other, through the statements of the *Formula of Concord*[4] affect the understanding and interpretation of the CA in the Lutheran churches? Two references will make this clear. The confession of the Protestant-Christian Batak Church, which belongs to the Lutheran World Federation, is a confession which in a sense takes the place of the CA there and which has been formulated in evident dependence on it. It contains an article on "The Word of God" (Art. 4) in which *sola scriptura* is emphasized very sharply. This Batak Confession has been recognized by the LWF as "in substantial agreement" with the Lutheran Confessions and, therefore, in particular with the CA. This is an indication of how, in the judgment of the Lutheran churches, the Reformation understanding of Scripture belongs as a matter of course to the substance of the Lutheran Confessions and thus also to the CA. The controversy concerning the *sola scriptura* was sharpened anew during the history of separation which came after the CA. How difficult it is to keep this controversy out of the content of the CA itself is shown also by Peter Brunner's position, in which he by no means stands alone. The understanding of justification as it is presented in the CA implies (so he thinks, and so also others think) the *sola scriptura*, the basic meaning of which is "that no superior court, even if it were the council of bishops together with the bishop of Rome, dare intrude between the believer and this Word." That this is so, that therefore the understanding of justification in the CA implies this *sola scriptura*, Brunner believes, becomes apparent in its full sharpness only in light of the history of separation, namely, "in light of the dogmatic development of the doctrine about the papacy" as it came to its conclusion in Vatican I.[5] On the issue of Mariology, a similar projection has to be made from the subsequent history of separation back to the CA. As is well known, the CA does not mention the mariological problem, not even where it could have found a place at that time, that is, in Article 21 (The Cult of Saints). It is already different in the Apology, which interprets Article 21 of the CA in such a way that with it, even though in a very restrained manner, certain forms of Marian piety are rejected.[6] It was bound to happen that, in the course of the history of the separation, the understanding of the CA should be influenced by the sharpening of this controversy through the intensification of a certain kind of Catholic piety toward Mary which eventually led to the official Marian dogmas. Therefore, although the CA does not contain an explicit rejection of Catholic Mariology, one could say there is an implicit rejection of this kind in the CA, and it becomes explicit in the course of the history of separation.

If efforts on behalf of a Catholic recognition of the CA are really to become ecumenically fruitful, they have to take note of the fact that the CA is encumbered with the accumulated burden of the history of separation. Therefore one will have also to consider questions which in the CA as such were not treated at all. Thus our approach makes the effort for a Catholic recognition of the CA more comprehensive and more difficult than if it were concerned only with the wording of the CA. But this makes it at the same time more genuine and more promising. By no means are these efforts bound to fail for this reason. For also belonging to the "historical difference" which lies between the CA of 1530 and, if I may express it thus, the CA of 1977 is the fact that in the meantime there has taken place not only a deepening of the divergences but, in more recent times, also a contrary movement toward convergence, as is apparent in the ecumenical research and the interconfessional dialogues of our time.[7] This is true also with respect to the controversial questions mentioned above; therefore efforts for a Catholic recognition of the CA need not sidestep them.

2. The form of the unity we seek.

An additional point at which it will presumably be necessary to reckon very emphatically with the historical distance between the CA of 1530 and our present situation is the question about the form of the ecclesiastical fellowship or unity which a Catholic recognition of the CA would serve and even for which it would, as Schütte says, be the "basis."

The situation in 1530 was undoubtedly that the unity of the Church still essentially existed. It is true that the unity was seriously threatened, but it was not yet broken; it was seriously disturbed but not yet suspended. That is how it was without doubt perceived by many at that time, as, for example, Hubert Jedin shows and admits, although he himself judges this to have been "a fateful illusion."[8] The Diet of Augsburg itself was admittedly an expression of this view, as were also the later religious colloquies, which were always politically supported or even politically induced. Those who parleyed there were still not separated churches but "religious parties." The CA is, in its intention and in its statements, to be understood only against this background: it wants by all means to preserve the still-existing unity—the "peace" of the Church, as it says again and again—in the acute crisis of theological disagreements. What those of the Lutheran persuasion wanted to accomplish by their Confession and even gain by entreaty is *toleration* of a specifically formulated proclamation and practice, which the CA expresses and seeks to justify, *within* the still-existing ecclesiastical fellowship and the existing ecclesiastical structures.

For more than four hundred years, the situation has been totally different: now there are separated churches. Therefore the task is totally different now than it was at that time. It is no longer a matter of *maintaining* and *guarding* the existing unity in a crisis situation, but a matter of *regaining* the unity of the Church which has in fact been shattered and splintered into independent, institutionalized, particularized churches separated by clear lines of demarcation.

Thus the question arises to what extent the model of unity which the CA intends—that is, the concept of toleration or integration of a group characterized by a specific form of proclamation and practice within the Roman Catholic Church and its structures—is still applicable in view of the changed situation, or whether we must search for another, perhaps analogous, model or concept of ecclesiastical communion.

What has been said about this question in the present discussion of a Catholic recognition of the CA?

There are a few explicit statements about this in Ratzinger and in Schütte. They speak of "corporate union amid differences." Schütte illustrates this, quoting Ratzinger, by speaking of a "unity of the

churches, which remain churches and yet become one Church." The
different churches "are to remain churches with their own forms of
piety and ceremonies, with their own governments and constitutions,
with their own ways of speaking theologically. But they are no longer
to be separated from one another but are to realize the one visible
Church of Jesus Christ."[9]

Here indeed his terminology is difficult to follow, although the idea
itself is clear. Without doubt, what he emphasizes is that without
prejudice to full fellowship in witness, Christian service, sacraments,
and ministry, the hitherto separated but now united churches are
permitted to retain their special spiritual, theological, and institutional heritage, in short, retain a confessional identity. With this one
can only agree most emphatically. It is only within the limits of such
a concept of unity that a Protestant-Catholic ecclesial fellowship is
conceivable. One must ask himself all the more, however, whether
the concept "corporate union" is not then an unfortunate one and
highly subject to misunderstanding. It is certainly true that the concept here is meant, first of all, in opposition to the idea of a "unity
through the conversion of individuals." But in ecumenical usage this
concept had been formulated with precision and given a fixed meaning by the time of Edinburgh (1937).[10] It is identical with the concept
of "organic union" and thus indicates a concept of unity which is not
characterized by the preservation of but by the abandonment of
confessional independence and identity in favor of a new transcon-
fessional identity. Moreover, the concept of "corporate union" in the
context of the Edinburgh Declarations is intentionally contrasted with
and definitely wants to be more than "mutual recognition." Unity
through "corporate union" was the fundamental idea at Edinburgh
and, as is well known, is also today still the standard for broad currents within the ecumenical movement. Is not the present discussion
of a recognition of the CA, by contrast, wholly centered on the idea
of a "recognition" of the other in his otherness and individuality?
Does not Ratzinger himself say: "A Catholic recognition of the CA
. . . would mean that by this step the Catholic Church would take on
its own form of the realization of the common faith as well as the
independence that is its due"?[11] Whether this is the case or not, also
in these questions which do not in the final analysis arise because of

historical developments since the CA of 1530, there are still clarifications needed in both form and content in order that it may be apparent in a less ambiguous manner that the unity concept which most nearly corresponds with the thought of a Catholic recognition of the CA is the concept of mutual recognition.

3. The CA is joined together with the other confessional writings.

Naturally, in the first stages of the investigation of the question whether a Catholic recognition of the CA is conceivable, attention must essentially be focused on the CA as such. This is what Pfnür and Pannenberg have done. It becomes apparent, however, in the case of both that in the efforts for a Catholic recognition of the CA, one cannot simply stop with the text of the CA. At the very least this text is in need of interpretation, of commentary, of explanatory supplement. Pfnür consults in particular the results of the discussions at Augsburg and Melanchthon's Apology. Pannenberg resorts in addition to more recent theological and liturgical developments in the Catholic Church or to insights gained in more recent ecumenical dialogues and ecumenical research. Therefore Schütte rightly calls for the mutual preparation of a "commentary with . . . explanatory statements which are in part supplementary, in part corrective"[12] as a prerequisite for a Catholic recognition of the CA.

That efforts in behalf of a Catholic recognition of the CA cannot stop with the mere wording of the CA had become apparent already at Augsburg, where the alternative of recognizing or rejecting the CA was very soon given up in favor of theological negotiations. These were intended to lead to formulas of agreement or unity on questions which were still in dispute (for example, in the doctrine of original sin, the article on justification, or the concept of repentance) and for a short time appeared to accomplish this result.[13] The same phenomenon is apparent in the religious colloquies of succeeding years (Leipzig 1534, 1539, Hagenau/Worms/Regensburg 1540–41). For the most part, they start with the text of the CA but then go beyond it on the decisive points to new joint statements, formulations, and documents.

The text of the CA, however, was and continues to be in need of being interpreted and supplemented not only insofar as its recognition by the Catholic Church is concerned. It is and was in need of being interpreted and supplemented also insofar as it is a binding confession of the Lutheran churches. A most important fact for understanding the CA is that although the CA is indeed the *central* Lutheran confession, in reality it has never been and is not now the *only* binding Lutheran confession. There is in fact not a single Lutheran church—I say this in spite of a few particular historical exceptions and ecclesial peculiarities—which has constituted itself and identified itself as Lutheran in view of its confessional basis *sola Augustana*. Besides the CA there always were and are, in addition to the symbols of the ancient Church, also other confessional writings held by the Reformation. This was true even at the Smalcald Convention (1537), when the CA was raised from what had hitherto been in fact a confession—in some ways one could even say a private writing by Melanchthon—to the status of a universally binding confessional writing and then received as such by the Protestant princes and estates and incorporated into the constitutions of the territorial churches. Already on that occasion Melanchthon's Apology and the *Treatise on the Power and Primacy of the Pope* were placed side by side with it. To these were added later the other Lutheran confessions compiled in *The Book of Concord*. Heinrich Bornkamm's carefully nuanced evaluation of the CA reflects Luther's very mixed opinions about the CA and appears to be confirmed by the conduct of the Lutheran churches themselves. "The basic ideas of Protestant doctrine . . . stand out with great clarity" in the CA, nevertheless the CA "alone . . . cannot be considered a sufficient presentation of Reformation teaching."[14]

This means that the CA is what it is only in relation to the other Lutheran confessional writings. It cannot be lifted out or subordinated to this collection of confessional writings which help determine its meaning and content. Therefore to the extent that present efforts for a Catholic recognition of the CA aim at more than subsequent reverence for an especially congenial Reformation document but regard the CA as a confession of the Lutheran Church, to that extent these efforts must take this fact and its significance into consideration.

In his well-known essay for the anniversary of the CA in 1930, Friedrich Heiler very pointedly recognized and highlighted this problem: through its incorporation into the corpus of the other Lutheran confessions, he points out, the confession of 1530 in reality became a *Variata Confessio,* that is, a "confession which has a different meaning and task than that document 'which . . . was delivered to the Emperor Charles V at the Diet in 1530.' " Heiler does not merely describe this development. He judges it at the same time as disastrous, as an "inner contradiction . . . which has to be resolved."[15] His solution, to be sure, seems questionable. He proposes, on the one hand, separating the CA from the body of the other confessional writings, on the other, examining, supplementing, and correcting the CA itself according to the criterion of what he calls "the authority of the catholic Church," that is, of the tradition of the whole Church which is expressed through the ecumenical councils.[16] At the very least, separating the CA from its connection with the other confessional writings would not only be anachronistic but would, above all things, fail to understand the CA as a confession of the Lutheran churches.

Naturally, the fact that the CA is joined together with the other Lutheran confessional writings makes Catholic recognition of the CA more difficult and laborious. One dare not, however, sidestep these difficulties as if only after they have been met would Catholic recognition of the CA achieve ecumenical importance. Catholic recognition of the CA will by no means become impossible because the CA is joined together with the other Lutheran confessional writings. For the question is not Catholic recognition of the whole *Book of Concord;* this would be absurd for the simple reason that in that case it would be demanded of the Catholic partner that he be "more Lutheran" than the majority of Lutheran churches.

The problem which results from the fact that the CA is joined together with the other Lutheran confessions can be solved only by theological interpretation. One will therefore have to take as his point of departure that in many respects the ecumenical openness which characterizes the statements of the CA is noticeably narrowed the moment one views and understands these statements in the context of the other confessional writings. To mention just a few examples:

Article 10 of the CA on the Lord's Supper is narrowed in an anti-Catholic sense when in the *Smalcald Articles*,[17] and then especially in the *Formula of Concord*,[18] the doctrine of transubstantiation is criticized and even formally condemned; the controversial question of original sin remaining after baptism, which was not touched in CA, 2, is taken up in the Apology,[19] and later on in the *Formula of Concord*,[20] and described in terminology which clearly seems to conflict with the doctrinal decisions of the Council of Trent (DS, 1515); the statements of the CA about the Ministry, Church, and the office of bishop do not touch on the problem of the office of the papacy but are then interpreted by the often very critical expressions in other confessional writings about papal primacy.[21]

All this does not at all mean that there would be no way to overcome these and similar reinterpretations of the CA, for it was originally open.

There is within the corpus of the Lutheran confessional writings sufficient latitude for an interpretation which preserves the ecumenical openness of the CA more strongly than might at first glance seem possible. Furthermore, the CA, as is generally acknowledged, occupies a central position among the other confessional writings so that it is wholly legitimate and acceptable to address critical questions to and make interpretations of the other confessional writings from the perspective of the CA. Finally, none of the Lutheran confessional writings possesses the character of an irreformable dogma. They continue to be—as they themselves express it[22]—historically conditioned confessions, subject to the critical norm of Holy Scripture and open to new insights which arise in new historical situations and in confrontation with new challenges.

In short, it is always necessary in the efforts for a Catholic recognition of the CA to take into account the fact that the CA is joined together with the other Lutheran confessional documents if this recognition really has in mind that CA with which the Lutheran churches live. Where the content of the CA appears to be ecumenically limited by this fact, these limitations must be broken through by theological efforts. The task would therefore be to interpret the other confessional writings in the light of the CA by making use of newer theological insights, churchly developments, and the results of ecumenical research and discussion. This task could, as Schütte suggests, be begun by a Catholic-Lutheran commentary on the CA.

NOTES

1. Cf. the chapter by Walter Kasper in this volume, pp. 123–29 below.
2. *WA TR*, 4: 495, ll. 7–9; cf. Herbert Immenkötter, *Um die Einheit im Glauben: Die Unionsverhandlungen des Augsburger Reichstages im August und September 1530*, 2d ed. (Münster: Aschendorff: 1973), p. 10.
3. Vinzenz Pfnür, p. 12 above; cf. also *Einig*, pp. 14–19.
4. *BS*, 767 ff.; Tappert, 464:1–2 and 503–4:3.
5. "Reform—Reformation, Einst—heute," *Kerygma und Dogma* 13 (1967): 181–83.
6. *BS*, 321–22, 324; Tappert, 232:25–28 and 234:34.
7. Cf. Lindbeck/Vajta, pp. 81–94 below.
8. Hubert Jedin, *A History of the Council of Trent*, vol. 1, trans. E. Graf (London: Thomas Nelson and Sons, Ltd., 1957), p. 357.
9. Cf. Schütte, p. 47 above.
10. The corresponding texts are found, for example, in Lukas Vischer, ed., *A Documentary History of the Faith and Order Movement 1927–1963* (St. Louis: Bethany Press, 1963), pp. 61–64, esp. nos. 121–26.
11. J. Ratzinger, "Prognosen für die Zukunft des Ökumenismus," *Bausteine* 17, no. 65 (1977): 12.
12. See above, p. 63.
13. Cf. Immenkötter, *Einheit*.
14. H. Bornkamm, "Augsburger Bekenntnis," *RGG*[3] 1:735–36.
15. "Die Katholizität der *Confessio Augustana*," *Die Hochkirche* 12 (1930): 185, cf. 201.
16. Ibid., p. 186, cf. pp. 190, 204.
17. *BS*, 452; Tappert, 311:5. Tappert's translation "better" for the Latin *optime* and the German *aufs beste* is unfortunate. The correct translation would be "perfectly."
18. *BS*, 801, 1010; Tappert, 571:14; 575:35; 588:108.
19. *BS*, 153 ff.; Tappert, 105:36; 106:45.
20. *BS*, 849–50; Tappert, 510–11.
21. *Smalcald Articles*, *BS*, 427 ff.; Tappert, 298 ff.; *De potestate et primatu papae tractatus*, *BS*, 471 ff.; Tappert, 320 ff.; *Formula of Concord*, *BS*, 1060–61; Tappert, 614–15.
22. *BS*, 767 ff.; Tappert, 464 ff.

The Augsburg Confession
in Light of Contemporary
Catholic-Lutheran Dialogue

GEORGE LINDBECK and VILMOS VAJTA

The fact that since Vatican II church-sponsored bilateral dialogues have existed between Lutherans and Catholics is one of the factors which have made it possible once again to take seriously the CA's claims to catholicity. These dialogues have not been carried on in a vacuum. They are part of a broader movement in scriptural studies and in historical and systematic theology. They have influenced and been influenced by ecumenical discussions, especially those carried on within the Faith and Order movement which is now part of the World Council of Churches. Their task in part is to evaluate the work previously done by scholars and thus serve as a stage in a process by which, as at Vatican II, the labors of theologians help shape the official positions of churches.

The trend of the dialogues has in many respects brought both sides closer to the CA. Lutherans and Catholics have drawn nearer to each other and thus also to the stand taken by the Reformers at Augsburg in 1530. This convergence has not been the result of a deliberate effort to be ecumenical but rather is the consequence of seriously attempting to carry out the assignment given by the churches. Their mandate has been to explore the historic controversies in order to determine what can and cannot now be said in common. Because of the great changes in the theological and practical situations, the sharp antitheses of the past have in many cases been weakened or disappeared. What is shared by the two traditions once again bulks large, just as it did for the CA.

It is the purpose of this essay to examine some of these interconnections between the CA and the dialogues. We shall confine our

81

attention to the most important. The first major dialogue (1965 to the present) is the one sponsored in the United States by the Commission on Ecumenical and Interreligious Affairs of the Catholic Bishops' Conference and by the United States Committee of the Lutheran Federation (now called Lutheran World Ministries) in cooperation with the Lutheran Church—Missouri Synod. It has produced six reports published in books together with supporting essays.[1] The other dialogue venture which will concern us is international and is sponsored by the Vatican Secretariat for Christian Unity and the Lutheran World Federation. It has had two rounds. The first (1967–71) issued the *Malta Report*,[2] while the second (1974–) has so far published only one document, *Das Herrenmahl* (*The Eucharist*),[3] but is also concerned with other themes.

1. Starting Points

The first of these dialogues, that in the United States, chose the Nicene Creed as its initial topic. It thus recognized the centrality of the christological and trinitarian affirmations of the early Church for what Lutherans and Roman Catholics hold in common. While there was no conscious intention of imitating the CA at this point, the correspondence is complete. That confession also starts with the classic trinitarian and christological doctrines as the basis for the common catholic faith which it claims to profess in its first part, in the first twenty-one articles. The primacy of the ancient creeds is also underscored by the fact that three of them (the Apostles', Nicene, and Athanasian Creeds) are placed first, before the CA, in *The Book of Concord,* the official collection of Lutheran confessional writings. It is only when the two sides start with this shared heritage, and thus deal with the divisive issues in a christological and trinitarian context, that they can hope to reach agreement.

The theme chosen for the first international dialogue, "Gospel and Church," was not intended to indicate any particular priority among topics but simply to name the characteristic contrasting emphases of the two traditions: "gospel" for Lutherans, and "Church" for Catholics. Yet the parallelism with the CA is once again striking. The CA is concerned with the Church, not simply with the gospel. Its focus is not on a free-floating gospel but rather, as Article 7 makes clear, on the Church as the place in which the gospel should have the normative role. Thus the second part, devoted to the ecclesiological and liturgical consequences of reforming the Church in the light of the proclamation of the gospel, is much more extensive. Similarly, the bulk of the MR, as of the dialogues as a whole, deals with questions of church order and of worship. It is quite wrong to suggest, as is sometimes done, that this is a betrayal of the centrality of justification by faith. As the CA testifies, the importance and meaning of this doctrine becomes apparent only by dealing with its implications for the concrete life of the Church. To be faithful to the catholic intentions of the CA and thus open the way to unity, one must give an ecclesiological interpretation both of it and of the Reformation (as the dialogues in effect have done) rather than focus on the specifically Reformation emphases in isolation.

2. Scripture and Tradition

The critical thrust of the Reformation attack on church tradition came neither from Scripture alone nor from justification alone but from an interpretation of Scripture as centered on justification. The question of whether the Reformation critique still applies depends, therefore, on whether the views of tradition and of "human ordinances" (*traditiones humanae*) against which it was directed have remained the same. Clearly they have not. Roman Catholics share the contemporary exegetical consensus on the relation of Scripture and (oral) tradition, which is quite different from that prevailing in the sixteenth century. Vatican II emphasizes the priority of the gospel tradition transmitted in holy writ and omits reference to extrabiblical tradition as an independent source of knowledge of revelation. There is therefore now convergence on a question which, although not expressly treated by the CA, was clearly one of the most divisive issues of its time. This convergence is reflected by the new way in which the MR speaks of the gospel as supremely normative for evaluating all developments in the church: "Neither the *sola scriptura* nor formal references to the authoritativeness of the magisterial office are sufficient. The primary criterion is the Holy Spirit making the Christ event into a saving action" (18). The same conviction is implicit in the work of the U.S. dialogue and has been explicitly articulated in its most recent common statement, "Teaching Authority and Infallibility in the Church" (1978).[4]

3. Justification

We have already suggested that Article 4 on justification in the CA ought to be read in conjunction with earlier articles, especially CA, 3, "The Son of God." Salvation is *propter Christum*, on account of Christ, and only because of this *per fidem*, through faith. Later articles such as CA, 6, "The New Obedience," and CA, 20, "Faith and Good Works," are also indispensible for an understanding of justification. The doctrine is seen in a variety of dimensions, the most important of which is christological.

A similar comprehensive approach to justification combined with historical-critical methods make it possible to speak in our day, as does the MR, of a "far-reaching consensus . . . in its interpretation" (26). Both sides agree "that the event of salvation to which the gospel testifies can also be expressed comprehensively in other representations derived from the New Testament, such as reconciliation, freedom, redemption, new life, and new creation"(27). This possibility of expressing the same reality in a variety of ways was also affirmed, it may be noted, in the discussion of contemporary reformulations of justification at the Helsinki Assembly of the Lutheran World Federation in 1963. In any case, a christologically oriented and pluriform interpretation of justification has been assumed by the dialogues and, indeed, has made them possible.

Such an approach is challenged, however, not only by intellectualizations of the doctrine which were common in the age of orthodoxy and which tend to equate justifying faith with the acceptance of theological formulations, but also by the currently popular exegetical concentration on Saint Paul's main letters to the neglect or exclusion of other parts of the New Testament witness. When these letters are read in terms of certain philosophies of existence or experience, they sometimes lead to the abandonment of the christological affirmation of the ancient creeds and to the reduction of justification to an "existential" within human life. They also are at times accompanied by a rejection of what is called "early Catholicism" in the New Testament and by the attempt to distinguish "a canon within the canon."

Thus justification as "the center of Scripture" becomes not a hermeneutical center, as it was for the Reformers, but a principle of selection among the New Testament writings. The contemporary Roman Catholic - Lutheran convergence is closer to the Reformation doctrine as expressed at Augsburg than to this type of modern interpretation of justification *sola fide.*

4. Church and Ministry

In turning to the implications of justification for the order and practise of the Church, we must note that this doctrine not only limits and corrects ecclesiological affirmations, but that it also positively requires them. There is nothing accidental about the connection between CA, 4 and 5. "In order that we may obtain this faith, the ministry of teaching the Gospel and administering the sacraments was instituted. For through the word and the sacraments, as through instruments, the Holy Spirit is given, and the Holy Spirit produces faith, where and when it pleases God, in those who hear the Gospel" (CA, 5:1–2).

It could not be more clearly said that justification is neither received nor given without the Church's Ministry. Exactly the same position is adopted in both the U.S. and international dialogues. The MR, for example, states that "the ministry of reconciliation belongs to the work of reconciliation. In other words, the witness of the gospel requires that there be witnesses to the gospel"(48). The Ministry, one might say, belongs within the pneumatic event of justification. The doctrine of justification has corrective consequences for the understanding of the Church and Ministry, but it does not diminish their importance.

This point is often forgotten when it is supposed, as Lutherans have often done, that the Church is first referred to in CA, 7, where it is designated as the *congregatio sanctorum,* the assembly of saints. The purpose here, however, is not to define the Church (as if it could exist without the Ministry) but to indicate the locus within which the ministerial office is exercised: "the assembly of saints *in which* the gospel is taught purely and the sacraments are administered rightly" (CA, 7:1). Conversely, a ministerial hierarchy without the people of God is irreconcilable with the gospel. This Reformation emphasis is also present in the MR: "The church as a whole bears witness to Christ; the church as a whole is the priestly people of God. As *creatura et ministra verbi* (creature and servant of the word), however, it stands under the gospel and has the gospel as its superordinate criterion"(48).

Whether Roman Catholics could have said this before Vatican II is a question which we cannot here pursue. What is important is that Lutherans and Catholics now agree "that the office of Ministry stands over against the community as well as in it and that the ministerial office represents Christ and his over-againstness to the community only in so far as it gives expression to the gospel" (MR, 50). If this point is taken seriously, it opens the way for the acceptance of the CA on a crucial ecclesiological point: the mutual recognition of Ministries. In the U.S. dialogue, Catholics recommended consideration of such a recognition just as clearly as did the Lutherans (*Eucharist and Ministry*, pars. 35, 54), but in the MR they were rather more cautious (63–64).

5. Structures of Ministry

To the degree that contemporary Lutherans view the gospel Ministry as constitutive of the Church, they move nearer to the CA, but Catholics also are drawing closer, namely, in their understanding of church structures. Historical work has made it necessary to recognize that "the understanding and shaping of the ministerial office has undergone considerable change and development" (MR, 55). It therefore becomes possible to restructure the Ministry in order to fit new situations. The medieval episcopacy, for example, with its worldly entanglements (criticized in CA, 28) has largely disappeared.

Nevertheless, despite this new flexibility, Catholics continue to think of distinctions between pastor, bishop, and pope as essential, while Lutherans view them as accidental. The bishop's powers as enumerated in CA, 28:5, for example, are the same as those of any ordained minister. The distinctions in the ranks of the hierarchy are said in the later Lutheran Confessions to be of human rather than divine origin (for example, Ap., 14:1), *ius humanum* not *ius divinum*. The CA implicitly agrees. Only if episcopal (and, by implication, papal) authority were acknowledged as human rather than divine could the Reformers think of accepting it, for if it were divine, resistance to it when it opposes the gospel would be illegitimate.

These problems have been discussed in the contemporary dialogues with results which at least partly break the impasse of the sixteenth century. After noting that priests sometimes ordained in pre-Reformation times and that different ministerial structures can exist in different periods and places, the U.S. dialogue says "that the episcopal structure and constitution of the Roman Catholic Church does not in itself represent a problem for Lutherans" (*Eucharist and Ministry,* pars. 19–22, 28). The MR, while not speaking directly of episcopacy, also emphasizes historical variability and concludes that "the office of the papacy as a visible sign of the unity of the churches is therefore not excluded in so far as it is subordinated to the primacy of the gospel by theological reinterpretation and practical restructuring"(66). This point was subsequently developed at much greater length in the U.S. *Papal Primacy and the Universal Church.* Further, both dialogues have recognized the inadequacy of the sixteenth-century distinction between *ius divinum* and *ius humanum* (for example, MR, 31) and have drawn from this the conclusion that, in the light of the historicity of all structures, it is not possible to say that the distinctions and the powers of the different ranks of Ministry belong exclusively in one category or another. What is essential is that Christian freedom not be violated by any minister, whether pastor, bishop, or pope (for example, *Papal Primacy and the Universal Church,* p. 31). They thus agree with the CA's desire to preserve the historic structures for the sake of peace and unity, and yet also recognize the right and duty of disobedience when officeholders in the church oppose the gospel (although Catholics would not agree that this duty of disobedience extends as far as the establishment of separate church orders). This double demand of loyalty and possible resistance to church authorities is part of the pathos of an ecclesiology founded on justification by faith.

6. The Sacraments: Baptism and the Eucharist

The major sacramental problems at Augsburg were not the same as in the contemporary discussions. The Roman *Confutation* criticized the CA's treatment of penance and its failure to enumerate the seven sacraments. Melanchthon's reply to the second of these objections was that the number of sacraments is a terminological question which can be answered differently depending on how one defines the word (Ap., 13). With this the dialogues appear to agree (see the discussion of whether ordination is a sacrament in MR, 59, 61) but have not dealt with the question at length. Penance also has been mentioned only in connection with other topics, especially baptism. Instead, attention has been focused on what, by universal agreement, are the two main sacraments, baptism and the Lord's Supper.

Baptism. Baptism was chosen as the second topic to be considered in the U.S. dialogue not because it has traditionally been an area of disagreement, but of agreement. The purpose here, as in the discussion of the Nicene Creed, was to test the genuineness of the apparent consensus. Both sides could agree that baptism is "for the forgiveness of sins" and that it can be administered to infants, but behind these affirmations the historic differences over the understanding of sin and of the relation of baptism to penance quickly reemerged. The discussions of penance in particular "brought out a sharp difference in theological ways of thinking and speaking" (*One Baptism for the Remission of Sins,* p. 74).

Nevertheless the group decided that as far as baptism is concerned, these differences are chiefly of historic rather than contemporary importance. One reason for this view was the consensus among the biblical scholars that the New Testament view of baptism was very different from traditional views held by Catholics and Lutherans. The overwhelming emphasis in the early Church was on baptism as a rite of initiation into the community rather than as an individualistic means of receiving forgiveness and the infusion of grace or faith. Thus the great challenge is not to resolve controversies which involved inadequate understandings of baptism on both sides but to rethink baptismal theology and practise in the light of a better understanding of Scripture and tradition and the changed situation of the Church. Further, the differences in this area are not church-dividing because the major Christian traditions recognize the validity of each other's baptisms. For these reasons, the dialogue group, to the disappointment of some, did not attempt a thorough discussion but turned to other themes.

The Eucharist. In contrast to baptism, the Lord's Supper is the point in which the division of the churches in worship is most painfully apparent. It has been dealt with at length in both the CA and in contemporary dialogues.

The presence of Christ in the Eucharist was not seen as a controversial question by either the CA or the Roman *Confutation,* but in view of the often divisive emphasis on transubstantiation in succeeding centuries, the real presence was naturally first considered. It was rather quickly agreed in the U.S. dialogue that both traditions fully affirm the reality of Christ's eucharistic presence and that the difference in expressing or conceptualizing this reality need not be church-dividing (*The Eucharist as Sacrifice,* pp. 191–97).

The Mass as sacrifice was a much more serious issue for the sixteenth-century Reformers, but here again the U.S. dialogue found that the clarifications in the understanding of the eucharistic sacrifice introduced both at Trent and more especially in recent times removed what the Reformers objected to (*The Eucharist as Sacrifice,* pp. 188–91). These results have been confirmed and amplified in the international dialogue's recent common statement, *The Eucharist* (*Das Herrenmahl*).[5]

This latter document also deals at length with the abuses treated in CA, 22 and 24. The controversy over communion in two kinds (CA, 22) has lost its virulence now that Roman Catholic practise since Vatical II grants possibilities for lay reception of the cup. The greater symbolic adequacy of communion under both species has been affirmed, and thus the justice of the CA's protests has been in part conceded. Further, Lutherans acknowledge that Christ is fully present under both species and at times have been known to administer communion in one kind in instances of urgent pastoral need.

Similarly, Catholics have in effect granted that at least some of the objections to private masses in CA, 24 were justified. The international dialogue's common statement *The Eucharist* says that "since the Second Vatican Council, a significant change has taken place in the liturgical practice of the Catholic Church which underlines the superiority of 'the communal celebration with attendance and active participation of believers—whereby it still holds good that in each case the Mass has its public and social character'" (par. 63; the quotation is from Vatican II, SL, 27; cf. DS, 747). Indeed, even the name *missa privata* is no longer official, and the rubrics speak instead of *missa sine populo* (masses without a congregation) with the understanding that at least a server shall assist the celebrant. Thus private masses in the form criticized by the CA are no longer officially sanctioned.

What, however, of the theology which, according to the CA, led to the "infinite proliferation of masses" (24:23)? The papists were accused of holding that "Christ had by his passion made satisfaction for original sin and had instituted the Mass in which an oblation should be made for daily sins, mortal and venial. From this has come the common opinion that the Mass is a work which by its performance (*ex opere operato*) takes away the sins of the living and the dead" (CA, 24:21–22). The view mentioned here was never official doctrine. It arose from a late medieval amalgamation of teaching about the efficacy of mass suffrages and Scotist eucharistic theory and is now scarcely held by anyone. Nevertheless, as Vinzenz Pfnür concludes in his discussion of the matter, "it is not surprising that the *opus operatum* thus understood became, in the Reformation polemic, the absolute contradiction of justification by faith."[6] Now, however, as *The Eucharist* volume makes clear, the *opus operatum*, like the sacrificial understanding of the Eucharist to which it is closely linked, is not a point of contention.[7] Here again Roman Catholics need to acknowledge the catholic intention of the CA, and the Lutherans must ask whether they can continue to say of contemporary Roman Catholic practices that they "diminish the glory of Christ's passion" (24:24).

In some ways, indeed, eucharistic practice in Roman Catholicism is now closer than in Lutheranism to that recommended by the CA. According to the CA, "one common Mass is observed among us on every holy day, and on other days" (24:34), and it also claims that these masses are "celebrated with the greatest reverence" (24:1). The reverence may remain, but frequency was not maintained except in restricted circles (such as among Grundtvigians in Denmark or at Neuendettelsau under the influence of Löhe in the nineteenth century). Frequent communion may again be spreading under the influence of the liturgical movement, but this development has proceeded far faster and further in the Roman Catholic Church. There also, to be sure, it is a recent development. For a long time there were many masses but few communicants. In the twentieth century, however, especially since Vatican II, communal masses and congregational communion have become standard.

Finally, the CA urges that the sacrament is to be used in faith (24: 30). This agrees with the stress on the active participation of the faithful in the *Constitution on the Liturgy* of Vatican II. It thus appears that none of the abuses of the Mass attacked by the CA have gone unreformed by the Roman Church, and that there are therefore no obstacles in this area to recognizing its catholicity.

7. Intercommunion

Admission to communion, however, remains a major problem. It is discussed in the CA in terms of the "power of the keys," that is, the power to admit and exclude from the Lord's table. There is no doubt about the existence of the power for the CA: "None is admitted unless they are first heard and examined" (24:6). "Confession has not been abolished in our churches, for it is not customary to administer the body and blood of Christ except to those who have been previously examined and absolved. The people are very diligently taught concerning faith in connection with absolution" (25:1-2). Bishops are empowered "according to the Gospel . . . to exclude from the church ungodly persons whose wickedness is known . . . without human power, simply by the word"—*sine vi humano, sed verbo* (28:21). Catholics would agree to these preconditions for communion, yet the interpretation of them in the two traditions is markedly different.

On the Lutheran side, it is difficult or impossible on Reformation grounds to refuse communion to any baptized Christian who professes repentance and wishes to receive. Roman Catholics, in contrast, continue to exclude all non-Catholics (except for special regulations for the Eastern Orthodox and for emergencies). *Communicatio in sacris* is thus hindered not only, as is often supposed, because of the non-recognition of Lutheran ministerial orders by the Roman Catholic Church but also because of a difference in the understanding of church discipline, of the power of the keys. How major an obstacle this is has yet to be discussed in the dialogues.

The disciplinary gap has, to be sure, greatly narrowed since the sixteenth century because the churches can no longer make use of "human power," that is, civil penalties, to enforce their spiritual sanctions. It has become necessary to rely on the word, that is, on instruction and proclamation (including proclamation in the spiritual counseling of individuals) and on the widespread use of general, rather than private, confession and absolution. The way in which communicants are "diligently taught" and "previously examined and absolved" is by being addressed by the message of judgment and grace in the eucharistic celebration. Once this is done, Lutherans are inclined to hold that they cannot properly be denied access to the sacrament. This is not equivalent to what is often meant by "open communion," for there is here no invitation to those who do not agree with what is proclaimed and celebrated. At the same time, it is the one addressed who must respond to Christ's invitation, and here not denominational affiliation but repentance and faith are decisive. It is on these grounds that the Lutherans in the MR conclude that "a celebration of the Lord's Supper in which baptized believers may not participate suffers from an inner contradiction and from the start, therefore, does not fulfill the purpose for which the Lord instituted it. For the Lord's Supper is the reconciling acceptance of men through the redemptive work of Jesus Christ" (72).

The Catholic participants in the formulation of the MR were divided on this question of intercommunion. Three unreservedly agreed with the recommendation "that church authorities, on the basis of what is already shared in faith and sacrament and as a sign and anticipation of the promised and hoped for unity, make possible occasional acts of intercommunion as, for example, during ecumenical events or in the pastoral care of those involved in mixed marriages" (73). Two, however, thought that such acts should be unilateral rather than reciprocal, while another two believed that there should first be full recognition of ministerial orders. Roman Catholic Church discipline, in any case, remains opposed to intercommunion, and the difference at this point between the two traditions arises, as it did already at Augsburg, from a disagreement over church governance and the lack of Catholic recognition of Lutheran Ministries.

Conclusion

Roman Catholics and Lutherans are returning after 450 years to a position comparable, though by no means identical, to that which existed at Augsburg. The bilateral dialogues have helped produce a limited fellowship between the two traditions on the basis of one baptism, a shared acceptance of the ancient creeds, and a new understanding of the catholic concerns expressed by the CA. It is only because of this rapprochement that the proposed recognition of the CA becomes thinkable.

Recognition, however, is not an end in itself. Its significance lies in the encouragement which it could give to further developments. One such development would be the reconciliation of ministries, whose significance as a manifestation of the visible unity of the Church within the plurality of gifts and varieties of Christian witness cannot be overestimated. Some would hold that beyond this there is a further stage of integration or "corporative union" (Ratzinger) of the churches, but whether this or some other form of unity is in fact the goal of ecumenical efforts is a question on which there is as yet by no means complete agreement.

One thing is clear, however. If Lutherans and Catholics are to progress on the road to unity, some kind of shared recognition of the essential catholicity of the positions taken by the CA will have to develop. Those who are concerned for the united witness of all Christians to the Lord Jesus Christ will hope and pray that this development will take place sooner rather than later.

NOTES

1. These have been published in a series under the general title *Lutherans and Catholics in Dialogue*: vol. 1: *The Status of the Nicene Creed as Dogma of the Church* (1965); 2: *One Baptism for the Remission of Sins* (1966); 3: *The Eucharist as Sacrifice* (1967); 4: *Eucharist and Ministry* (1970); 5: *Papal Primacy and the Universal Church* (1974); 6: *Teaching Authority and Infallibility in the Church* (1979). The first four volumes were published jointly by the United States National Conference of Catholic Bishops' Commission for Ecumenical and Interreligious Affairs, Washington, and the United States National Committee of the Lutheran World

Federation, New York. Volumes 5 and 6 were published by Augsburg Publishing House, Minneapolis. References to these volumes will be made by citing the individual volume and paragraph.

2. The German and English texts together with supporting essays are in *Evangelium-Welt-Kirche: Schlussbericht und Referate der römish-katholisch/ evangelisch-lutherischen Studienkommission, "Das Evangelium und die Kirche," 1967–1971,* ed. Harding Meyer (Frankfurt am Main: Lembeck/ Knecht, 1975); see MR in the Abbreviations.

3. *Das Herrenmahl* (Paderborn: Bonifacius and Frankfurt: Lembeck, 1978); "Catholic-Lutheran Agreed Statement on the Eucharist," *Origins* 8 (1979): 465–78.

4. *Theological Studies* 40(1979): 113–66.

5. See n. 3 above.

6. Vinzenz Pfnür, *Einig in der Rechtfertigungslehre? Die Rechtfertigungslehre der "Confessio Augustana" (1530) und die Stellungnahme der katholischen Kontroverstheologie zwischen 1530 und 1535* (Wiesbaden: Franz Steiner, 1970), p. 64.

7. *Das Herrenmahl,* pp. 93–100.

Lutheran Difficulties
Which Stand in the Way of a
Catholic Recognition of the
Augsburg Confession

HERMANN DIETZFELBINGER

When the Executive Committee of the Lutheran World Federation was assembled for its annual meeting in Uppsala in August 1976, the following recommendation was accepted during the discussion of the dialogue with the Roman Catholic Church: "The Lutheran churches ought to make known their openness toward and their interest in Roman Catholic discussions which revolve about the possibility of a reception of the CA as a legitimate expression of Christian truth."

The observer from the Vatican Secretariat for Christian Unity, Prof. Dr. Schütte, was present and responded:

> In 1980 we will observe, God willing, the 450th anniversary of the CA. It would be a significant event if we could approach more closely to the real intent of the CA, that is, unity of the churches, which remain churches and yet become one Church, oneness in the truth of the gospel while preserving the greatest measure of pluriformity and of that freedom for which Christ has made us free, oneness in love by which all the world is to recognize that we are Christians. . . . We do not close our eyes to the fact that the efforts for a Catholic reception of the CA as a basis of confessional unity will not be easy. But I can say here that Cardinal Jan Willebrands, the President of the Secretariat for Christian Unity, takes a positive attitude toward this endeavor.

A number of features are worth noting at this point. For one thing, it seems to me that it becomes evident how seriously the question of a positive stance toward the CA is being considered in the Roman Catholic Church. For another, it may be of significance for the Roman Catholic Church that the Lutheran churches not only in Germany and Europe but everywhere in the world are being challenged to take part in what is being done. Therefore this matter will also come up for discussion at the general assembly of the Lutheran World Federation at Dar-es-Salaam in June 1977. Furthermore, Schütte, while correctly characterizing the intention of the CA, has also honestly called attention to the difficulties which are connected with this undertaking. If I am now called upon to describe from a Lutheran perspective the theological and ecclesiastical difficulties which could arise from an eventual recognition of the CA by the Roman Catholic Church, I am assuming the basic work done on this subject by Wolfhart Pannenberg. He has already given an inventory of the problems and also called attention to the most important theological questions which arise, for instance, in the doctrine of sin, of the sacraments, and of the Church.* I shall try to take up the larger issues in the hope that airing the difficulties will not serve to intimidate but rather to foster courage.

One needs to hold his breath for a moment: for ecumenical discussion (whose uncertainty and even stagnation is at present often bemoaned) a positive stance by the Roman Catholic Church toward the CA would, even leaving all other possible results out of consideration, be a call to action which could hardly come in a stronger way. As a matter of fact, the CA has been waiting for a positive response (would that this might come in 1980!) ever since it was publicly read on 25 June 1530. In the meantime almost 450 years have passed. Again and again it becomes apparent how difficult it is to bridge the chasm created by the years during which we have grown farther and farther apart theologically, historically, and linguistically. We can measure this chasm from three points of view. Has not the Roman Catholic Church changed since 1530? We ourselves, the Lutheran Church, have changed. The position of the CA has also changed.

1. The CA affirms expressly in its doctrinal part, that is, in the first 21 of its 28 articles, that its teaching "is not contrary or opposed to that of the universal Christian Church, or even of the Roman Church" (CA, conclusion of part 1:1). This claim is underlined by an appeal to all of church history, in particular to the Nicene Creed. Moreover, all that is raised by way of criticism in the last seven articles concerning both

*See above, pp. 35–41.

forms of the sacrament, the marriage of priests, the Mass, confession, monastics vows, and so on, is not described as a fight against false doctrine but as a concern for eliminating abuses. Thus the CA is not a renunciation of the catholic Church but an acknowledgement of it and an expression of the conviction that "we are all under one Christ and should confess and contend for Christ" (preface to the CA, 11).

To be sure, we must ask what that Catholic Church is which it acknowledged. Here serious difficulties surface for us. The Roman Catholic Church has changed in many respects since 1530. Especially during the past few decades, we have followed with profound sympathy the outer and inner changes which have taken place in it during the course of the Second Vatican Council. Reforms which the CA expressly awaited have also been set in motion. We ourselves have received many impulses to renewal which have led us to discover once again how many things separated Christians have in common. On the other hand, we dare not in the midst of this process of rapprochement ignore the developments which have taken place in the opposite direction during the past centuries and which have been made permanent by a number of important doctrinal documents. To show how individual decisions by the Council of Trent are to be harmonized with a modern recognition of the CA is, of course, a task for Catholic theologians themselves. We are especially troubled by the dogmas which have come into being during the past 150 years, namely, concerning Mary and the papacy. The peace-loving Melanchthon did not write of the office of the pope in the CA. Would he be able to proceed in the same manner today after the promulgation of the dogma of papal infallibility? As far as Mariology is concerned, the Lutheran Church surely also needs to discuss the role of Mary in order that biblical insights which have been lost or shortchanged among us may be uncovered and taken seriously. On the other hand, I consider the problems to be more difficult than they are at times represented to be by the Protestant side. Thus the question arises for us as we face a changed Roman Catholic Church whether we today can hold the same opinion as the CA does, that is, that the controversies which arose at the time of the Reformation had only to do with different positions about abuses and not with the foundations of the faith.

2. However, the Lutherans of 1530 have also changed. At that time they were a group within the Roman Catholic Church and desired to remain catholic. How is the word *catholic* understood today in the Lutheran Church? In the course of centuries, particularly under the influence of religious conflicts, it has assumed a different sound and content for many Lutherans, so that it is by no means easy for them to find their way back to the original meaning. The struggle during the past few years to arrive at a common text for the Apostles' Creed is an example of this. It was impossible to reach agreement concerning the "catholic" Church. Lutherans did not become a group in the Catholic Church but an independent church; in accord with Luther's will, they did not call themselves Lutheran, yet that is how it turned out. And the CA, which continues to want to be a catholic confession and which was made in the presence of and for all Christendom, nevertheless is no longer only a confessional and reasoned document for the fellowship in the one catholic Church. Instead, it has become (after Holy Scripture and the creeds of the ancient Church) an important part of the doctrinal foundation of the Lutheran Church in all the world and in many cases a document with legal significance.

Therefore we must ask: What changes in direction would recognition of the CA by the Roman Catholic Church bring about in the churches of the Reformation? Who would we be if the Roman Catholic Church were to recognize the CA? We speak today of the crises of identity in which many confessional churches find themselves because of currents of intellectual and spiritual changes. Perhaps also the Lutheran Church would, in some of its parts, have to count on such an identity crisis. Such a step on the part of the Roman Catholic Church could become a test for the Lutheran Church to show its true colors, since in the CA as well as in the other Lutheran confessions it is not a particular denomination but the *una sancta* which has spoken, and to show to what extent it will also in the future regard itself not merely as Protestant but as catholic in the original sense. I am of the opinion that it ought to face this question of identity resolutely and not seek to evade it.

3. Through what has been stated above, it has already become apparent that also the position of the CA itself has changed since it was

publicly read in 1530. Its importance and rank have not decreased. In 1648 the Reformed churches stemming from Calvin were included in the religious peace of Westphalia as "relatives of the CA." The CA plays an important role as a confessional document also in many united churches in Germany. Because the year 1980 marks not only the 450th anniversary of the CA but also the 400th anniversary of *The Book of Concord,* which is very important for the unity of the Lutheran churches, it must be remembered that also *The Book of Concord* simply desires to express "the correct understanding of the CA." From this it follows, however, that as one defines his stance toward the CA one cannot ignore the other confessional writings, such as the Apology of the CA or the *Large* and *Small Catechisms* of Martin Luther. If the CA avoided a statement concerning the papacy because peace was still hoped for in 1530, Luther himself vigorously made up for this in the *Smalcald Articles* of 1537, which must also be counted among the Lutheran confessions. Therefore a discussion of "recognition" by the Roman Catholic Church will certainly have to be conducted primarily with reference to the CA. But at the same time the totality of the Lutheran confessions will also have to be considered.

With this we are face to face with the chief problem. The case of the Lutheran Confessions is unique. Although they (principally the CA together with the *Small Catechism*) determine the teaching, piety, and shape of the Lutheran Church, they do not in the last analysis intend to derive their authority from themselves. They intend to be nothing else than an interpretation of Holy Scripture—to be sure, not by an individual theologian but, even if by an individual, an interpretation by the Church of Jesus Christ itself. The Lutheran Confessions are not a code of canon law of the Lutheran Church and do not want to be understood as ecclesiastical law. Rather they are open to Holy Scripture and submit to its judgment. The condemnations expressed in them also need to be examined carefully from the viewpoint of the way Holy Scripture defines our relationship to each other today. Their validity and binding force is therefore a derived one, derived from Holy Scripture and subject to it. Dialogue concerning the CA would certainly have to be conducted by us on the basis of such presuppositions. That our confessional writings, including the CA, would thereby become a mighty call to repentance to the Lutheran Church, a summons to return to Holy Scripture, must here be said plainly. We cannot in all honesty avoid the fact that today the CA in some of its sections poses questions to the church which takes its name from this confession rather than being a polemic against the Roman Catholic Church of that time. We cannot, for instance, affirm "without boasting" today that the Mass, that is, the eucharistic service, "is observed among us with greater devotion and more earnestness than among our opponents," as Article 24 of the CA has it. In any case, the question of the recognition of the CA by the Roman Catholic Church requires all of us to face up to the question of the interpretation of Holy Scripture, that is, whether we are able to stand together on the basis of Scripture. This question, it seems to me, is more important and pressing than all sorts of premature questions about organizational possibilities or structural consequences in case the Roman Catholic Church takes the step being discussed. This question presents the final difficulty but also the great promise of the whole undertaking, for surely it is to such searching in particular that God has promised the assistance of his Holy Spirit.

Does the Teaching of the *Confessio Augustana* about Repentance Stand in the Way of Its Recognition by the Catholic Church?

HANS JORISSEN

THE CONNECTION BETWEEN THE DOCTRINE OF JUSTIFICATION AND THE DOCTRINE OF REPENTANCE

The possibility of the recognition of the CA as a legitimate expression of the universal and in this sense catholic faith by the Catholic Church must be shown most of all in connection with those questions in which a different understanding of faith and revelation, judged by the center of Christian revelation, appears to be deeply divisive of church fellowship. As far as the absolutely central question of justification is concerned, the careful and detailed investigation of Vinzenz Pfnür concerning the doctrine of justification in the CA and the Apology, on the one hand, and of the polemic Catholic theology of Reformation times, on the other, appears to have demonstrated the essential agreement in principle (in spite of the maze of polemics) in a convincing manner.[1] Therefore Wolfhart Pannenberg sees as "the weightiest still unresolved difference" which appears to stand in the way of recognition of the CA as catholic by the present-day Catholic Church or which lets such a recognition "appear, at least at first glance, difficult to imagine," not the doctrine of justification but the statements of the CA, especially CA, 12, about the sacrament of penance, "which were also directly placed under anathema by the Council of Trent in a way not true of any other formulation of the CA."[2] Melanchthon himself, to be sure, had emphatically, even vehemently, worked out in the Apology the inner connection between the doctrine of justification and the doctrine of repentance: for this article (that a man receives the forgiveness of sins through faith) "is the chief issue on which we clash with our opponents and which we believe all Christians must understand. . . . For the doctrine of penitence and the doctrine of justification are very closely related" (Ap., 12: 59). "The issue at hand is a great one, the chief doctrine of the gospel, the forgiveness of sins" (Ap., 21: 10). Recognition of agreement on the essential content of the doctrine of justification will therefore at least presuppose that there will also be no insurmountable antithesis in the doctrine of repentance, even as on the other side the doctrine of repentance will have to pass the test of really agreeing with the doctrine of justification.

PRIOR HERMENEUTICAL REFLECTIONS

The Lutheran doctrine of repentance is centered on faith in the free, forgiving grace of God in Christ, which is therefore without merit on man's part and, parallel with this, on faith in the efficacious promise of forgiveness in absolution by virtue of the power of the keys bestowed by Christ. It is directed not only against the insufficient penitential theology of late nominalism (this theology was the mother of many misconceptions, especially as it was expressed by Gabriel Biel)[3] but even more strongly against wrong attitudes and abuses in the practice of repentance when it is perverted into legalism and externalism. It is especially on account of these things that the discussions became heated. Honesty demands that wrong developments in the ecclesiastical discipline of penance, and indeed also such as were harmful to people, be openly admitted not only in the penitential discipline of the ancient Church (for example, unrepeatability or lifelong defaming consequences; finally these brought about the collapse of the Church's institutionalized practice of repentance) but also in the development of so-called private confession. Wrong developments must be especially admitted in the rise of the so-called *Tarifbusse*, which included the demand for substantial completeness in confession, the extreme and excessive interpretation of which became a central focus of passionate protest by the Reformers, as did the disastrous practice of redemptions and commutations which finally led to the traffic in indulgences.[4]

The debates about *opera satisfactoria* or *satisfactionis* ("satisfactory works" or "works of satisfaction") are also to be viewed against this background. One will therefore have to keep this historical setting carefully in mind in order not to miss the precise point in question and the intention and thrust of the claims and charges in each individual case. It is therefore not permissible to play down and treat as harmless wrong developments in theology and practice on the one—let us say the Catholic—hand, and on the other hand to evaluate the protests and attacks by the Reformation side as abstract or didactic statements, detached from their concrete settings. If the questions with which we are faced are to be discussed in an objective fashion, it will be necessary not only that one disregard antiquated viewpoints but also that there be on the Catholic side an explicit and positive recognition of the rightness and importance of the Reformation protest for the sake of the truth of the gospel.[5] The Reformation concept of the doctrine of repentance was presented to the council fathers at Trent only in the form of theses, or lists of errors, and in this sense in *abstracto*,[6] and this must also be taken into consideration in an evaluation.

THE INSTITUTIONALIZED REGULATION
OF PENANCE

It is from the positive statements of the CA and of the Apology about the doctrine of repentance that every discussion of this doctrine must begin. These statements will show that, at least de facto, the structure of the sacrament of penance as a complex event between the activity of the sinner and the forgiving activity of God through human and ecclesiastical mediation receives its full due, so that there is actual agreement with catholic teaching. Luther also expresses this structure quite clearly, for example, in the *Large* and *Small Catechisms*. Let me say to begin with that it does not seem to me unimportant to point out that in conformity with Luther and the other Lutheran Confessions the statement that "private absolution should be retained" (and therefore also private confession), found in the beginning of CA, 11, could, in view of the crisis which has developed about the sacrament of penance in the present Catholic Church, become for this church itself, very differently from the time of the Reformation, a matter of real importance. In this fashion, the basic assertion just cited from CA, 11 (cf. CA, 25) could become the common starting point, based on trust in the gospel of reconciliation, for pastoral endeavor in order to revitalize and reappropriate the sacrament of penance. This positive concern, as Luther, for example, expresses it in the *Large Catechism*,[7] could (if freed from historical and subjective limitations) become the common guide, on the one hand, for a relevant, gospel-oriented hermeneutic and, on the other, for a pastoral revitalization of the sacrament of penance, for it would be understood as the glad tidings of forgiveness in Christ offered to and bestowed by the Church.

Let us address ourselves to specific questions:

1. Apology, 13 numbers absolution (which it calls the sacrament of penance) among the sacraments which are properly so called. The sacramental character of repentance is expressed with sufficient clarity by its position in CA, 11 and 12, for it is placed after the articles on baptism (CA, 9) and the Lord's Supper (CA, 10), as well as just before CA, 13 (The Use of the Sacraments). The essence of the sacrament of penance is seen in absolution: "absolution (which is the sacrament of penitence)" (Ap., 13:4). "Absolution may properly be called a sacrament of penitence" (Ap., 12: 41). This definition of the essence of the sacrament of penance is in accord with the tradition of Scotist scholasticism. In it, in contrast to the Thomistic understanding, the actions of the penitent, although indeed indispensable prerequisites for a fruitful reception of absolution, do not become constitutive parts of the essence of the sacrament itself. The Council of Trent did not, according to the testimony of the documents of the Council, want to decide this dispute between the scholastics. Consequently the understanding championed in the CA and in the Apology can be held without contradicting the teaching of the Council of Trent. According to CA, 12, the sacrament of penance has special importance for those who have lapsed after baptism and are returning to repentance. Through absolution they receive forgiveness of sins (cf. Ap., 12:1). In absolution the power of the keys, which was given to the Church by God through Christ, is efficacious. "The power of the keys administers and offers the Gospel through absolution, which is the true voice of the Gospel" (Ap., 12:39; cf. 11:59). "It is not the voice or word of the man who speaks it, but it is the Word of God, who forgives sin, for it is spoken in God's stead and by God's command" (CA, 25:3–4). "Therefore we must believe the voice of the one absolving

no less than we would believe a voice coming from heaven" (Ap., 12:40–41)—"according to the statement, 'He who hears you, hears me'" (Ap., 12:40); "absolution . . . is the Word of God that the power of the keys proclaims to individuals by divine authority. It would therefore be wicked to remove private absolution from the church," for "those who despise private absolution understand neither the forgiveness of sins nor the power of the keys" (Ap., 12:99–101). Although the true voice of the gospel sounds forth in absolution, the confessional writings nevertheless do not for this reason identify absolution with preaching. Absolution and preaching are different actions.[8] We need to point out in this connection that the CA and its Apology (as well as Luther in *Von den Schlüsseln,* written in 1530)[9] teach the efficacy of absolution as canceling guilt before God more decidedly than their opponents (in particular G. Biel): "The keys truly forgive sins before God" (Ap., 12:40). Decidedly and even passionately they reject the "vicious error" that the power of the keys extends only to the remission of guilt before the church but not before God, or that it refers to the conversion of eternal into temporal punishments or to a partial remission of temporal punishments (Ap., 12:6–8, 21–22, 118, 139). We cannot enter into the historical background of the penitential theory which is here being opposed. It developed out of early scholastic contritionism, which spread through Peter Lombard and continued to find some champions even in scholasticism, although they were without doubt inadequate. This theory does not go beyond a purely declarative function of absolution in the forgiveness of sins, and therefore the chief function of absolution is the imposition of satisfactions or penalties.

It seems important to me that in this connection the resolute and theologically justified protest against the undermining or obscuring of the "blessing," of the "power of absolution," and of the "power of the keys" (Ap., 11:9; 12:10) is directly connected with stressing the forgiveness of sins freely bestowed on account of Christ through faith, that is, the righteousness of faith, as also with the equally resolute rejection of every kind of works righteousness: "Previously the whole power of absolution had been smothered by teachings about works, since the scholastics and monks teach nothing about faith and free forgiveness" (Ap., 11:2; cf. also 12:65, 116, 118; CA, 12:10). This shows, on the one hand, that receiving forgiveness through faith does not compete with the forgiveness, valid before God, that is effected by the power of absolution (cf. esp. Ap., 12:39-43) and, on the other, that the protest is aimed at even the slightest semblance of the forgiveness of sins "because of our merits and works" (cf. esp. Ap., 12:116-17). It seems to me that if the question of the abuses is set aside, the rejection of the imposition of penalties, which the opponents considered the chief function of the power of the keys, was more than a little determined by the theological understanding of absolution just outlined, and this rejection must therefore be understood as a pointed rejection of the opponents' theology of absolution, for their theology obscures the power of absolution. The two functions of absolution are not impugned by this, but the "binding" does not refer to the imposition of penalties but to the act of denouncing and excommunicating such as are unwilling to repent (Ap., 12:176). Therefore the power of the keys and its efficacy are not rejected; on the contrary, what is rejected is a specific (theologically inadequate) theory about the power of the keys and its negative effect in the practical administration of the keys. In this connection it must be stated that the statements by the Council of Trent about the imposition of penalties and satisfactions[10] are not dogmatic definitions in the strict sense and, as will become clear below, do not exactly deal with the position of the CA and the Apology.

2. The absolutely indispensable and necessary prerequisites for receiving forgiveness of sins by the penitent are, according to CA, 12 and the Apology, contrition and faith. This faith, which must of necessity be added to contrition and which first makes contrition a salutary thing, is not (as Ap., 12:60 emphatically declares against the way faith is misunderstood in the *Confutatio*)[11] the faith which precedes the virtue of penance but special faith in the promise of forgiveness by Christ (cf. also Ap., 12:35, 44, 54), justifying, quickening, comforting, and supporting faith (Ap., 12:36, 52). This faith distinguishes the contrition of Peter from that of Judas (Ap., 12:8, 36). Therefore contrition and faith are, as the Confessions show from Scripture, the "chief parts" of the (virtue) of penitence (Ap., 12:44-45, 52). The sacrament of penance is not therefore excluded from

but is expressly included in justification by faith. Thus acts done by penitents are brought into relation to the sacrament of penance, to absolution. "In speaking of faith, therefore, we also include absolution" (Ap., 12:39). Indeed, faith is received and strengthened through the word of absolution, "which is the true voice of the Gospel" (Ap., 12:42–43). This clear doctrine of repentance "adds to the honor of the power of the keys and the sacraments, it illumines the blessing of Christ, and it teaches us to make use of Christ as our mediator and propitiator" (Ap., 12:32).

The need for faith in all of our Christian life and for directing the "acts of the penitent" toward the sacrament of penance is again clearly set forth in the debate with the opponents (here, the *Confutatio*). The opponents are asked whether reception of absolution is a part of penitence. In case they wanted to separate the confession of sins from absolution by means of subtle distinctions, it would be necessary to ask what value confession without absolution would have. If it would have no value, they would surely have to grant that faith is a part of penitence since it is impossible to obtain absolution without faith (Ap., 12:61).

From the passages quoted—which must, of course, be evaluated in their total context—three things can be concluded: first of all, to Christian penitence in its entirety belongs also the sacrament of penance, namely, absolution. Second, for the sinner to receive the forgiveness of sins through absolution, contrition and faith are non-negotiable prerequisites. To this must be added, in the third place: contrition and faith are not meritorious works but "works of God in men" (cf. Ap., 12:53). Therefore also the forgiveness of sins does not come "*ex opere operato* because of contrition but by that personal faith by which each individual believes that his sins are forgiven" (Ap., 12:59).[12] It is precisely to exclude the meritoriousness of contrition as the "cause" of the forgiveness of sins that Melanchthon so emphatically stresses the need for faith: "We insist that this faith is really necessary for the forgiveness of sins" (Ap., 12:60; cf. esp. also 12:91–93).

That in this sense faith as "the second part of penitence" (CA, 12; Ap., 12:35) belongs of necessity to contrition must be held fast also on the part of Catholics without qualification. This was expressly affirmed in the discussions of the virtue of penitence at the Council of Trent by a number of the council fathers.[13]

3. Apology, 12:98 introduces the section on "Confession and Satisfaction" with a reference to "the great importance of preserving the true teaching about contrition and faith, the two parts of penitence," and declares: "We have therefore concentrated on the explanation of these doctrines and thus far have written nothing about confession and satisfaction." The words *superiores partes* can be understood both in the sense of sequence (the above named parts) and also in the sense of importance. It is precisely the latter interpretation, certainly the primary one, which makes the whole an important theological passage and interprets also the second part of the quotation (for in fact there was heated debate about confession and satisfaction). Two things follow from this: First, there is (and this must be and is admitted by Catholics) a "ranking" among the "acts of penitents." While confession and satisfaction can at times be omitted, for example, on account of physical impossibility, contrition and faith are absolutely requisite and indispensable. Second, confession and satisfaction are not thereby excluded from the totality of penitence. Contrition and faith are indeed the *praecipua partes*, the principal and chief parts (for which reason penitence, according to CA, 12, in its proper sense consists of these two parts), but they are not therefore (in an exclusive sense) the only parts.

The Confessions say expressly that the confession of sins is retained on account of absolution: "The preachers on our side diligently teach that confession is to be retained for the sake of absolution (which is its chief and most important part), for the consolation of terrified consciences, and also for other reasons" (CA, 25:13). "We also keep confession, especially because of absolution, which is the Word of God that the power of the keys proclaims to individuals by divine authority" (Ap., 12:99; cf. 11:59). In agreement with Luther, the esteem for and benefits of confession are stressed everywhere in the CA and Apology, and believers are admonished to receive the sacrament frequently (CA, 25; Ap., 11:3). It would, as the passages already quoted show, be restricting the doctrine advocated in the CA and the Apology if one wanted to understand the retention of confession exclusively from the standpoint of consoling consciences or as having only a pastoral-pedagogical basis (although even this is not a minor concern). It is certainly important in the case of any confession leading to absolution that there be an explicit and sincere inner confession in which a person recognizes and confesses before God that he is a concrete sinner. Let the reader compare here, for example, Ap., 12:107: "Such confession, made to God, is itself contrition. For when confession is made to God, it must come from the heart and not just from the voice, as in a play"; compare also Ap., 12:170, a quotation ascribed to Chrysostom: "In the heart contrition, in the mouth confession, in the deed complete humility." A mere outward confession, understood as an outward work without inner contrition before God and without faith, is rejected (cf. also Ap., 12:95). A bit later we shall have to give closer attention to confession and to questions—in part still open—connected with confession.

4. There are no weighty disagreements with regard to "satisfaction" as such. We need to take our starting point from the basic declaration that the death of Christ is the real satisfaction for sin and for the punishment of sin (Ap., 12:140; 146–47). The satisfaction of Christ is appropriated by us through faith and sacrament "for the remission of sins," not by our own meritorious works. Yet repentance is and remains a constant task for the Christian life. Repentance must, however, bring forth good works as fruits of repentance (CA, 12:5; Ap., 12:174). There can be no true conversion or contrition without outward works of repentance and good fruits. Inner repentance demands embodied, concrete expression (Ap., 12:131; 148). An act of repentance is demanded which shows itself in reformation of life (Ap., 12:164), in newness of life (Ap., 12:45). It is not to be understood in a Platonic sense, as though it meant merely a hypocritical change of mind: "Mortifying, quickening, putting off the body of sins, being raised—we are not to understand these terms in a Platonic sense as counterfeit changes; but mortification means genuine terrors, like those of the dying, which nature could not bear without the support of faith" (Ap., 12:46); "penitence ought not to be a fraud but an improvement of the total life" (Ap., 12:170). According to a quotation ascribed to Augustine, "true satisfaction means

cutting off the causes of sin, that is, mortifying and restraining the flesh" (Ap., 12:168). The condemnation of sin, the "judging of ourselves" (according to 1 Cor. 11:31), must show itself in active contrition, that is, in the amendment of life and in the good works demanded by the gospel (Ap., 12:163–64).

In this sense Melanchthon is also willing to consider "fruits worthy of repentance, that is, improvement of the whole life and character" as a third part of (the virtue of) repentance (as being added to the two chief parts, namely, contrition and faith—Ap., 12:163–64), although he would, for his own part, rather adhere to the division into two parts, not in order by some means to play down good works but in order by this means to show clearly those parts of repentance which, on the part of the sinner, are absolutely necessary. These parts are in this sense essential parts of repentance (they properly belong to it in conversion or regeneration and in the forgiveness of sins). By this means Melanchthon also intends to emphasize the faith demanded in repentance, whereas good works are the consequences of regeneration and of the forgiveness of sins (Ap., 12:58; cf. 12:131). This faith comes into being and shows itself in repentance, and it grows and is strengthened through the good works born of repentance: "For this purpose we are reborn and receive the Holy Spirit, that this new life might have new works and new impulses, the fear and love of God, hatred of lust, etc. The faith we speak of has its existence in penitence. It ought to grow and become firmer amid good works as well as temptations and dangers. . . . From these statements the fair-minded reader can judge that we very definitely require good works, since we teach that this faith arises in penitence and ought to grow continually in penitence" (Ap., 4:349–50, 353).

Punishment also is not excluded from repentance: "We grant that revenge or punishment is necessary for penitence, but not as a merit or price. . . . In a formal sense revenge is part of penitence because regeneration itself takes place by constantly mortifying the old life," which is then elucidated "etymologically"; "Penitence is so called because it holds punishment" (Ap., 12:148—*poenitentia quasi poenae tenentia*). Mitigation of the punishments of sin through repentance (Ap., 12:164) is as little excluded as is the honoring of God through good works and the divine reward for these works (Ap., 12:174; 12:139).

As one surveys the whole discussion, it becomes clear that this doctrine of repentance does not offer forgiveness of sins "at a cheap price" and that none of the penitential acts required by the Catholic theology of penitence (contrition, confession, satisfaction) is omitted. In penitence as it has been sketched here, the essential thing in satisfaction is repentance itself, fully rendered.

In the following sections the questions on which there seem at first glance to be weighty theological differences will be considered individually.

FULL CONFESSION AND THE
DIVINE INSTITUTION OF CONFESSION

1. Although the Church as a matter of principle has retained confession, CA, 9 and CA, 25:7–12 reject the necessity of enumerating all trespasses and sins: "In confession it is not necessary to enumerate all trespasses and sins." The Apology devotes long and vehement discussions to this question. Therefore a precise understanding of the point in question is of the utmost importance. What precisely is being rejected? In seeking an answer to this question, both elements in the above statement must be given equal weight: "enumeration" of "all sins." The basis for rejection is (as it is for Luther): "For this is impossible" (CA, 9; Ap., 9:8). People, and in particular compliant people, would be driven "to hopeless despair" by it (cf. CA, 25:9; Ap., 9:10), their consciences bound with inescapable snares (cf. Ap., 9:6–7) and weighed down with endless torture (cf. Ap., 9:7; 10; 12: 11). For "our wretched human nature is so deeply submerged in sins that it is unable to perceive or know them all, and if we were to be absolved only from those which we can enumerate, we would be helped but little" (CA, 25:9; cf. Ap., 9:8).

This rejection is directed squarely against the decree of the Fourth Lateran Council (1215) concerning penance (DS, 812), according to which every believer is obligated, as soon as he has reached the years of discretion, to confess "all his sins" at least once each year. Already the theology of the thirteenth century (Thomas Aquinas) had understood this regulation in a more precise and restricted sense: "all sins which one remembers."[14] With this and an additional elucidation (instead of "each believer" it is now "the sinner"), and also without the obligation "at least once each year," the regulation is taken over by the Council of Florence (1439); however, along with this limitation, the duty of a complete confession is particularly emphasized: "It is necessary in oral confession that the sinner confesses all sins which he remembers . . . fully" (DS, 1323). The authors of the *Confutatio* can find support in this statement when in opposition to CA, 11 they insist on complete confession of all transgressions which come to mind after careful scrutiny of the conscience (*CR*, 27:103). With this the debated point could, theoretically, have been considered settled.

As the response in the Apology shows, however, Melanchthon was here not concerned with a theoretical question but with a very practical pastoral concern which stands at the very center of the gospel as the joyful tidings of divine forgiveness (cf. Ap., 12:1–2). The objection is not even directed against the regulation of the Fourth Lateran Council per se as much as against the casuistry which the "Summists," the composers of canonistic confessional manuals, had developed in connection with it (Ap., 11:7, 9; cf. 7:32). "The whole church throughout Europe knows how consciences have been ensnared by it!" However, "these terrors made no impression on wild and profane men" (Ap., 11:7–8). All this would have been "more tolerable if they had added one word on faith, which consoles and encourages consciences," but about this "there is not a syllable in this heap of constitutions, glosses, summae, and penitential letters. They say nothing about Christ. They only recite lists of sins" (Ap., 11:9; cf. 12:12).

In the minds of Luther and Melanchthon, all this is connected with the slogan "enumeration of sins." To say it once again in the words of the first draft of the Apology: "Whereas men should have been instructed about absolution and faith, it was the sole concern of the writers and teachers to accustom men to enumerate their sins while faith was passed over with the deepest silence."[15] Here the cardinal point of the discussion stands out clearly, and it is from here that the constantly recurring reproach about mere works-righteousness becomes understandable.

It would be a mistake and not in accord with the historical facts if one would, by pointing to the "theoretical" solution of the *Confutatio,* impute immoderate exaggeration to Melanchthon as he stubbornly tried to maintain his position. The attack is directed against crass abuses in the practical administration of the sacrament of penance. Evidence of this is also the fact that in the negotiations in the interest of unity at the Diet of Augsburg, Article 11 was moved from the first part, which contains the doctrinal articles, and assigned to the discussions in the second part concerning abuses (cf. CA, 25).[16] To sum up, what is rejected is the obligation to "enumerate all sins," for this is self-torturing, scrupulous, mathematically exact, exceeding the ability of people. It never releases a person from doubt and the terrors of conscience and finally drives him to despair. It is an obligation which (and this is the decisive reproach) is not even counterbalanced by the comforting, cheering, and liberating message of God's gracious forgiveness for Christ's sake, through faith, and not on the basis of our merit and works. In opposition to this, the glad tidings of confession and absolution are emphatically set forth (cf. Ap., 11:1–2; 12:3–4, 35–36, 39–43, 98–101).

It would be a serious misunderstanding to interpret the rejection of this kind of "enumeration of sins" as a disparagement of the value of confession[17] or as habitual laxness. This is contradicted, on the one hand, by the fact that Luther criticizes the decree of the Fourth Lateran Council on confession by saying that it could be fulfilled only if interpreted loosely;[18] on the other hand, Luther expresses his highest regard for confession as a "unique remedy for troubled consciences."[19] He also presupposes sincerity in confession and care in examining one's conscience.[20] The *Small Catechism* offers instruction based on the Ten Commandments on "How Plain People Are to be Taught to Confess." Those sins are to be confessed "which we know and feel in our hearts,"[21] the "sins which bite into the heart and trouble us."[22] "If, however, anyone does not feel that his conscience is burdened by such or by greater sins, he should not worry, nor should he search for and invent other sins, for this would turn confession into torture."[23] As far as the secret sins of the heart are concerned, the following statement by Luther could be a guide: "If such sins of the heart belong at all to confession, it is those about the sinfulness of which the person who confesses is perfectly clear."[24] It follows from all this that the statement in CA, 25:7 about confession—that enumeration of sins is not necessary and that "no one should be compelled to recount sins in detail, for this is impossible"—must not be misinterpreted as if it counseled laxness.

In this connection a twofold observation with respect to the Council of Trent is significant. During the closing discussions about the completeness of confession, in order to avoid misunderstanding, the council fathers in their doctrinal decisions intentionally did not use the phrase "enumeration of sins," which occurs in the list of errors (instead of *enumerate* they used the term *confess*—DS, 1707). Besides, they made the restrictions of the Council of Florence even more precise by limiting the duty to confess to "all mortal sins which the person confessing remembers after necessary, careful consideration," and this was not done "in order to warn against laxness in the interpretation of the decree of Florence but surely rather in order to say that when searching the memory, an earnest and reasonable preparation is expected, and not an attitude of scrupulosity."[25]

2. Against this background, one can approach what is undoubtedly the weightiest question raised by the Council of Trent, namely, the question whether complete confession is a matter of "divine right" or necessary for salvation. Against the CA, the *Confutatio* had emphasized the necessity of complete confession for salvation: "Complete confession . . . is necessary for salvation" (*CR*, 27:159). On the other hand, Melanchthon, in a number of passages in the Apology, clearly denies that the "enumeration of sins" is a matter of "divine right" and necessary for salvation (Ap., 11:6–8, 10; 12:11–12, 23, 102, 110–11). Becker is of the opinion that Melanchthon's view was condemned almost word for word by the Council of Trent (DS, 1707).[26] I consider this only partially correct. It is correct if one tears the statements of the Apology out of their contexts and then takes them as abstract didactic statements. But one must consider the overtones for Melanchthon of the key word *enumeration*—one may call it a word of provocation (as we have said above, it was not used in the condemnation because the council fathers at Trent clearly recognized the misunderstanding connected with it). If one lets the

statements stand in their concrete historical contexts, then Becker's opinion will need to be considerably modified. We shall show this in connection with two important statements.

In opposition to the "endless enumeration of sins," to which, as he says, so much effort is devoted in the treatises on confession, although most of this is based on human traditions yet is demanded of people "under the pretext that it is by divine right"—to all this Melanchthon sets in opposition absolution, of which he says that it is in truth "by divine right" but of which the opponents speak only incidentally and "coldly" (Ap., 12:11–12). The antithesis: the exaggerated and "fictitious divine right" ("they demand this enumeration under the pretext that it is by divine right") and the disregard of what is "really by divine right" is then sharpened still further by the accusation that the opponents "pretend that the sacrament grants grace *ex opere operato,* without a right attitude in the recipient," whereas they do not even mention faith, which lays hold of absolution and comforts consciences.

In the text which follows (Ap., 12:110–11), Melanchthon comes to grips with the *Confutatio.* After expressly admitting the value and benefit of confession, he continues: "Examination . . . must be controlled, lest consciences be ensnared; for they will never be at rest if they suppose that they cannot obtain forgiveness of sins without enumerating all their sins. In the *Confutatio* our opponents have maintained that complete confession is necessary for salvation; this is completely false, as well as being impossible. What snares this requirement of complete confession has cast upon consciences! When will the conscience be sure that its confession is complete?" It is quite plain how Melanchthon understands the "complete confession" demanded by the *Confutatio,* namely, as a self-tormenting search for and endless recording and enumerating of sins.

Melanchthon is correct when he says that an enumeration of sins so understood cannot appeal to divine right (cf. also CA, 25:9–10). It is necessary to listen carefully for the beat and the secondary overtones, which really shape the music here.

As far as Melanchthon's view of the penitential discipline of the ancient Church is concerned, we may quote the competent judgment of H. Jedin: "It is hardly debatable that certain historical assertions

115

of the Reformers were closer to the truth than were the assertions of the Catholics."[27]

The *Confutatio* had declared that "complete confession" was not only necessary for salvation but that it was also "the nerve center of Christian discipline and of all obedience." Therefore the princes and cities are admonished that "they should act in conformity with the orthodox Church" (*CR*, 27:159–60). One is compelled to ask whether this is not dangerously close to making confession an instrument of domination and whether the passionate attacks of the Reformers against tyranny over consciences[28]—attacks made precisely because of their high regard for the sacrament of penance—are not justified.

If we now compare the statements of the Apology with the statements of the Council of Trent, we are forced to conclude: that which Melanchthon opposes is not exactly what is condemned by the Council of Trent, and what the Council of Trent places under the anathema is not really what Melanchthon meant.

But the question of the divine right of confession calls for an even more basic analysis, which we shall at least begin here. As far as the sacraments are concerned, Luther considers only that as being by divine right which can be traced back directly to an institution by Christ in Scripture. Therefore absolution, since it is efficacious in the power of the keys, is a sacrament; therefore also public confession is for him something sacramental and by divine right. This is not, however, true of secret confession since, he holds, it cannot be proved from Scripture, although he in no way denies its value.[29] Today, however, a new theological situation has developed, for theology on both sides is no longer able to trace back Church, baptism, the power of the keys, and even the Lord's Supper to the earthly Jesus with the same apodictic certainty as was the case in earlier times.[30] Therefore both sides must join together in a new way in order to find criteria for discerning what is by divine right and what is institution by Christ. Here it seems that the "consensus of the Church" might serve as the hermeneutical key for it basically rests on the origin of the Church, the kerygma, and the mission to ministry through the self-revelation of the resurrected and exalted Christ, which then, with the assistance of the Holy Spirit, unfolds in history through the Church's interpretation and appropriation of the revelation in Christ. This process of proper interpretation is not mechanical but the abiding task of the Spirit-led Church(es). Also for Luther and Melanchthon the "consensus of the Church" had gained increasing importance.[31] On the central point addressed by Melanchthon, "that we obtain the forgiveness of sins by faith for Christ's sake and not for the sake of our works" (Ap., 12:66–67), the churches have now achieved "consensus."

The Council of Trent also finds the basis for the divine right of confession in the consensus of the Church, as the thorough investigation by Becker shows.[32] In the strict sense the dogmatic decision is aimed only at sacramental confession in general and as such, that is, without taking into consideration the two variations: secret or public. About secret confession it is said only that it does not run counter to institution through Jesus Christ (DS, 1706). This last-named point is in full agreement with Luther, the CA, the Apology, and the other confessional writings, as is proved by the fact that the Reformers retained the practice of confession. As far as the duty of confessing secret sins (sins of the heart) is concerned, the pertinent statement by the Council of Trent (DS, 1707) is at least not a bare definition,[33] standing alone, but is an integral part of the dogmatic statement about the duty of confessing mortal sins (each and every mortal sin). If one compares with this the corresponding statement by Luther: "If, however, they are to be confessed, I say that it is only those of which he clearly knows that he has purposed them in his heart contrary to the divine commandments, that is, not mere thoughts,"[34] one could hardly consider this to be a weighty difference. Finally, as far as "mortal sins" are concerned, agreement also in this ought not to be difficult.[35] Certainly also the CA considers it a real possibility that a justified person may fall after baptism and lose the Holy Spirit, and it is for those who have fallen after baptism that the sacrament of penance has its particular importance (CA, 12:1–2, 7–9). Also with respect to attaching the power to absolve to the ecclesiastical Ministry, there is no difference in principle between Luther and the CA.[36]

If one subjects the statements on the sacrament of penance to calm, objective scrutiny, one can with good reason give a negative answer to the question whether on this question there are really profound and irreconcilable differences.

SOME REMARKS WITH RESPECT TO
ARTICLE 12 OF THE CA

Wolfhart Pannenberg proposes as a possible solution for "the weightiest still unresolved difference" in the doctrine of repentance— namely, that CA, 12 speaks of only "two parts" of repentance (contrition and faith) instead of the traditional "three parts" demanded also by the Council of Trent (contrition, confession, satisfaction)—to read Article 12 with the understanding "that it is not speaking of the institutional form of the sacrament but of the theological content of repentance."[37] With this we must fully agree. For, as a matter of fact, confession is not here replaced by faith, as our explanations have already shown, but the discussion here is about subjective repentance, an inner act of repentance (contrition) to which faith of necessity belongs as an indispensable component. Thus the two parts of repentance (contrition and faith) of which Article 12 speaks are not placed in opposition to the three parts or the three acts of the penitent (contrition, confession, satisfaction). Rather, if we abide by the above division, the two parts belong intrinsically to the "first act" of the penitent person. Two more reasons can be cited for this in addition to what has been said. First, the Apology itself, in defending CA, 12, refers the two parts, especially the necessity of faith, to the first act of the penitent person. It closes the respective statements with the remark: "All this happens in the first step" (Ap., 12:1–11) and proceeds from there to a discussion of confession and satisfaction. Second, during the negotiations for unity at the Diet of Augsburg— in which Melanchthon himself participated—full unity was achieved concerning the fact that contrition must of necessity include faith and also concerning "the three parts of repentance" (contrition together with faith, confession, satisfaction.)[38]

Both the *Confutatio* and the Council of Trent suffer from terminological misunderstandings. They came about chiefly through the "snares of language," for the language of the CA about the two parts of repentance was almost bound to be associated with the traditional way of speaking of three parts in the minds of the opponents since this terminology was customary in the ecclesiastical theology of penitence (so also the Council of Florence—DS, 1323). In addition,

Pfnür has shown with sufficient clarity that the *Confutatio* was not primarily interested in clarifying the point at issue. Nevertheless it was already cleared up at the negotiations for unity with the express agreement of Johannes Eck. That the Council of Trent failed to see the meaning of the statements in CA, 12 was due to the fact that the council fathers had before them only a list of errors with citations consisting of individual sentences torn out of context (cf. *CT*, 7¹:233–34). A number of the fathers, however, expressly stressed the correctness of their statements as far as the virtue of penitence is concerned.

This much is therefore certain: the anathema of the Council of Trent (DS, 1704) does not fall upon that which CA, 12 and the Apology intend. Therefore also the respective source material in Denzinger needs to be cleared up. The corresponding doctrinal decisions of the Council of Trent no longer need to be considered as the "weightiest still unresolved difference in the doctrine of the sacrament" and to stand as a hindrance in the way of a possible recognition of the CA.

No agreement could be reached on satisfaction at the unity negotiations in 1530, on "whether satisfaction is necessary for blotting out the punishment of sin."[39] This controversial question must also be understood in terms of its historical background. The distinction between the guilt (*culpa*) of sin and the punishment (*poena*) of sin first rose in the School of Saint Victor during the twelfth century in order, on the basis of the contritionism of the early Middle Ages (according to which the forgiveness of sins occurs already in contrition), to deny that a genuine function can still be ascribed to the power of granting absolution. In view of the full recognition of the true nature of satisfaction in the sense of "fruits of repentance," as is held by Luther, the CA, and the Apology, this controversial question possesses no dogmatic relevance today.

The ecclesiastical command to use confession has not been able to prevent the present crisis in the sacrament of penance in the Catholic Church any more than there has been a fulfillment of Luther's optimism. He believed that if only confession "would be rightly taught ... such a desire and love for it would be aroused that people would

119

come running after us to get it, more than we would like."[40] To take up together the pastoral task indicated by this problem could help lead to agreement about repentance.

NOTES

1. Vinzenz Pfnür, *Einig in der Rechtfertigungslehre?* (Wiesbaden: Franz Steiner, 1970).

2. W. Pannenberg, p. 40 above.

3. For the theological background compare esp. Pfnür, *Einig*, pp. 29–88.

4. Cf. H. Jorissen, "Beichte oder Busse?" in *Bestellt zum Zeugnis,* Festgabe für Bischof Pohlschneider, ed. K. Delahaye, E. Gatz, and H. Jorissen (Aachen: Einhard, 1974), pp. 217–32, esp. pp. 220–22.

5. Cf. Pfnür, *Einig*, p. 386.

6. *CT*, 7¹: 233–39.

7. *BS*, 730–33; Tappert, 459–61.

8. H. Fagerberg, *Die Theologie der lutherischen Bekenntnisschriften* (Göttingen: Vandenhoeck & Ruprecht, 1965), p. 101, n. 35; cf. Pfnür, *Einig*, pp. 82, 217–18.

9. Cf. Pfnür, *Einig*, pp. 82, 217–18.

10. Sess. XIV, esp. canon 15, with the corresponding chapter (DS, 1715; cf. 1962).

11. *CR*, 27:111.

12. On the understanding of the *opus operatum* which is rejected here, compare Pfnür, *Einig*, pp. 45 ff.

13. *CT*, 7¹:296, ll. 37–41; 308, l. 31.

14. Cf. K. J. Becker, "Die Notwendigkeit des vollständigen Bekenntnisses in der Beichte nach dem Konzil von Trient," *Theol. u. Phil.* 47 (1972): 161–228; here, 204–5.

15. *BS*, 249:32–34; cf. 326:40–52.

16. Cf. Pfnür, *Einig*, pp. 264, 267–68.

17. See above, pp. 108–9.

18. *Confitendi ratio, WA*, 6:162; *LW*, 39:35.

19. *De Capt. Babyl., WA*, 6:546; *LW*, 36:86; cf. *Large Catechism, BS*, 732–33; Tappert, 459–60.

20. *Confitendi ratio, WA*, 6:162; *LW*, 39:35; cf. *WA*, 6:159; *LW*, 39:30.

21. *Small Catechism, BS*, 517:18; Tappert, 350:18; cf. *Unterricht der Visitatoren, WA*, 26:220; *LW*, 40:296.

22. *Schwabach Articles*, Art. 11, *BS*, 66:26.

23. *Small Catechism, BS*, 518:24; Tappert, 350:24.

24. *Confitendi ratio, WA*, 6:161; *LW*, 39:33.

25. Becker, "Notwendigkeit," esp. pp. 203–9. The quotation is from p. 205.

26. Ibid., p. 205.

27. H. Jedin, "La nécessité de la confession privée selon le Concile de Trente," *La Maison-Dieu* 104 (1970): 115.

28. Cf. *De Capt. Babyl.*, WA, 6:546; LW, 36:86.

29. Cf. *Defensio*, WA, 2:645; *De Capt. Babyl.*, WA, 6:546; LW, 36:86.

30. Cf. H. Jorissen, "Die Begründung der Eucharistie im nachösterlichen Offenbarungsgeschehen," in *Freispruch und Freiheit*, Festschrift W. L. Kreck, ed. by H. G. Geyer (Munich: Chr. Kaiser, 1973), pp. 206, 288.

31. Cf. Pfnür, *Einig*, pp. 14–27.

32. Becker, "Notwendigkeit," esp. pp. 221, 224.

33. Ibid., p. 219.

34. *Confitendi ratio*, WA, 6:161; LW, 39:33.

35. Cf. Pfnür, *Einig*, pp. 182, 193.

36. Cf. Peter Manns in *Amt und Eucharistie*, ed. P. Bläser (Paderborn: Bonifacius, 1973), p. 107, nn. 10–11, p. 126, n. 118; on lay confession cf. also Jorissen, "Beichte oder Busse?" pp. 224–25.

37. W. Pannenberg, p. 41 above.

38. Pfnür, *Einig*, pp. 264, 268.

39. Ibid., pp. 266–67.

40. *Large Catechism, BS,* 733; Tappert, 460–61.

What Would Catholic Recognition of the
Confessio Augustana Mean?

WALTER KASPER

As a result of the discussion which has taken place concerning the CA, one can today affirm two things:

(1) The CA, according to its own statement, is intended to be understood as a Catholic confession; as such it has never been rejected by an official Catholic decision.

(2) The studies of Vinzenz Pfnür, Wolfhart Pannenberg, Hans Jorissen, and others have convincingly shown that the CA can be interpreted in a fundamentally Catholic way, at least in the light of the post-Vatican II self-understanding of Catholic theology, and, to that extent, can be received as Catholic. This is a most gratifying result, and it justifies greater hope for the further progress of ecumenical efforts. The fundamental Lutheran confession need not be the basis for the separation of the churches; it could also bring about their unity!

In light of this positive result, the question arises: What does this theological reception of the CA imply, and what would an official recognition based on it mean? Harding Meyer has shown how unclear and ambiguous, but at the same time how open, this call for catholic recognition of the CA still is. Does it mean recognition/reception/acceptance by the Catholic Church, and would it be as Catholic, as a Roman Catholic confession, as a legitimate definition of Christian truth, as an independent expression of Catholic faith, or as a witness to the faith of all Christians? The differences between these abundant possibilities imply fundamental theological distinctions in which, finally, the goal of the ecumenical effort as such is at stake.

In what follows, an attempt will be made to clarify what recognition means in this context, or at least what it can mean. Perhaps the position taken here will disappoint many high expectations. Nevertheless the ecumenical discussion of the past years has shown that nothing is more detrimental to ecumenical progress than inflated and premature expectations which sooner or later have to be abandoned and which then produce a kind of ecumenical paralysis. If the discussion—progressing positively up to this point—of a Catholic recognition of the CA is not to lead into a blind alley but to a common future of the separated churches, then it is helpful to make the concept of recognition more precise in three ways.

1. Recognition belongs first and foremost to the sphere of interhuman relationships. The consciousness of man's personal worth is awakened any time when the person experiences himself as recognized and accepted as a person by another. The human freedom awakened to consciousness in this way can become concretely actualized only when a space for freedom is guaranteed by all others and when one's freedom is thus commonly recognized. Interpersonal recognition is therefore a basic anthropological datum and at the same time the foundation of the public order of law. It prescribes the recognition of common personal worth and therein, at the same time, recognition of the other as other. Recognition therefore implies commonality amid persisting diversity—a diversity which can only be maintained in the recognition of commonality. In this sense H. Fries, when discussing the memorandum on ministries put out by the ecumenical institutes at universities, has rightly emphasized that recognition means neither the resignation of one's own standpoint nor the pluralism of unconnected and perhaps contradictory standpoints. Recognition does not mean to reduce to the lowest common denominator but rather to heighten one's own standpoint. But this heightening does not lead to separatism; rather it recognizes a legitimate pluralism in expressing "that which is held in common."

In this sense Catholic recognition of the CA would be more than merely a theological reception; it would be an official act. On the other hand, such a recognition would not mean that the Catholic Church takes this confession as its own Roman Catholic confession; instead, on the basis of such an act, the CA would be allowed as *one* legitimate expression of the common catholic faith so that the ecclesiastical community which appeals to it would be given room within the unity of the Catholic Church. Nothing more, but also nothing less than this was intended by its presentation to Emperor Charles V at the Diet of Augsburg in 1530.

2. The concept of recognition is necessarily carried over from the interpersonal sphere into other kinds of relationships. Interpersonal relationships, and even the highest and most sublime form of interpersonal recognition—personal love, express themselves necessarily in words, gestures, gifts, and actions of this kind. Without such concrete symbolic expression, they would be neither serious nor real. The same goes for mutual recognition among the churches. It happens in a concrete way through the mutual recognition of confessions (symbols of faith), through eucharistic fellowship, through mutual recognition of ministries, and through common witness and common service. Such mutual recognition of "relationships" has meaning, of course, only as a symbolic expression for mutual personal recognition. Recognition of the CA ought not therefore to be considered as an isolated act. The text of the CA cannot be separated from the context of the CA's call for church unity; Lutheran theologians involved in the discussion have again and again pointed this out. For this reason J. Ratzinger has from the outset made it clear that such recognition involves neither a primarily historical question, nor a purely theoretical-theological question, nor is it entirely a matter to be handled through church politics, but rather it involves a spiritual-ecclesial process.

On this point there are, to be sure, very serious difficulties on the Catholic side as well as on the Lutheran side. On the Lutheran side, the CA cannot be separated from other confessional writings, such as the *Smalcald Articles*. Unlike the CA, the *Smalcald Articles* partially exclude expressly defined Catholic truths of faith and were partially placed under anathema by the Council of Trent. More important, according to Lutheran understanding, the CA must be regarded as the interpretation of Scripture; the binding force of the CA is thereby ultimately based on the binding force of Scripture as it is interpreted here. But who would dispute the fact that since 1530 very important changes have taken place in the understanding of Scripture through the rise of the historical-critical method in interpretation, and these changes raise the question of how the Lutheran churches first of all themselves stand today in relation to the CA. In any case, the CA cannot be the primary basis for the unification of the churches. Rather it must be the writings of the Old and New Testaments recognized by both churches as *norma normans non normata* ("the norm which norms but is not normed").

The difficulties on the Catholic side are no less important. Catholic recognition of the CA cannot be separated from the fact that the church carrying out this act is at the same time the church which appeals to the Council of Trent and the church which has created new dogmatic "facts" through Vatican I and through the mariological dogmas of 1854 and 1950, but it is also the church which, at Vatican II, placed these facts within a more inclusive perspective and to this extent reinterpreted them. An official recognition of the CA would once again put the above-mentioned dogmatic facts in a new light and thus reinterpret them anew. This would be the case above all because the Catholic Church would thereby recognize the "Reformation" impulse expressed in the CA as fundamentally legitimate today. On the other hand, the Lutheran churches' acceptance of such a recognition (for recognition is a two-sided phenomenon) would mean that these churches would, on the basis of the changed ecclesiastical and theological situation, assign a very precise meaning to the Reformation impulse, for it can be interpreted in numerous ways historically. They would interpret it as a corrective over against the concrete historical reality of what is Catholic, but they would not understand it as being intrinsically schismatic—an interpretation which fully and completely conforms to the original intentions of the Reformers.

The discussions concerning the recognition of the CA as well as the bilateral dialogues which have taken place in the meantime, plus the most recent talks on the Petrine ministry, have shown that possibilities for such reinterpretations on both sides exist. To be sure, it is impossible to say that theological agreement has already been achieved on all points, but there is no longer any question that at least the direction can be seen in which unity is possible. The joint commentary on the CA proposed by Heinz Schütte could clarify this situation and thus fulfill *one* prerequisite for recognition of the CA.[1]

Recognition of the CA, in view of all that has been said up to this point, would be quite different from simply a facile recognition of the status quo in both churches. It need not signify that today, after four hundred years of baneful doctrinal controversy, we have become "more sensible" and "more liberal" and can simply bury past controversies. It is neither a matter of giving up the Reformation concerns in the CA nor of giving up the question of truth; on the contrary, it is a matter of energetically taking up the question of truth once again in order to come to a renewed and deepened common spiritual understanding of one's own as well as a previously alien tradition and thereby to be authentic churches of Jesus Christ. Recognition of the CA would be an end and a beginning at the same time.

3. The mutual recognition of ecclesiastical communions by way of the recognition of confessions, sacraments, and ministers cannot and dare not be the final goal of ecumenical efforts. In contemporary ecumenical usage, recognition is understood as a very specific model of the visible unity to be striven for. This model goes beyond mere communal action and a mere federation of churches in which each retains its independence. When using recognition as a model, the partners, while remaining different, mutually understand each other without reservation as legitimate churches of Jesus Christ. They can celebrate the Eucharist with one another, and the ministers of both churches can also carry out their functions in both churches. The churches, while retaining their independence, would thereby constitute member churches of the one Church of Jesus Christ, whose unity, however, according to this model, takes on no structural form. Unlike this, the model of organic unity establishes a community with its own identity, and this leads to institutional structure, so that the Church can speak and act as the one Church. Such visible church unity is today no longer the desire of the Catholic side alone; since the last general assembly of the World Council of Churches at Nairobi (1975), it is the explicit constitutional goal of the entire ecumenical movement. Such organic union also implies oneness in pluriformity.

Nairobi speaks therefore of the unity of the Church in the sense of a conciliar community. This concept can be interpreted in various ways. In his book *Morgen wird Einheit sein*,[2] H. Mühlen has shown, in the most detailed way yet for the German world, how it could be taken up and realized on the Catholic side. The advocates of a Catholic recognition of the CA obviously also tend in this direction when they speak of a future corporate unity of the churches (thus J. Ratzinger).

Talk of recognizing the CA remains misleading unless it is expressly stated that such a recognition refers to a conciliar understanding of church community or to a corporate understanding of church unity. This means that the discussion of Catholic recognition of the CA must therefore clearly be placed within the total context of ecumenical efforts. Recognition would be an important step on the way to the ecumenical goal but not the attainment of the goal itself. In order to avoid such misunderstandings, it would probably suffice in the present situation—and correspond most nearly to the present state of ecumenical efforts—if the Catholic Church to begin with did not directly recognize the CA but rather officially recognized the way the CA has been theologically received up to this point, that is, if the Catholic Church would officially declare that the CA can be interpreted and received in a Catholic sense. Such an official step— perhaps at the occasion of the 450th anniversary of the CA in 1980— would lead beyond a purely theological reception of the CA and could signify an important turning point in the relationship between the Catholic and Lutheran churches.

As far as the real goal implied in such a step is concerned, there still remains a host of problems which have hardly been dealt with adequately. How is this corporate unity to be understood in the concrete? What does it mean for unity in the faith? Does it require the recognition of all the other church's articles of faith or only certain fundamental articles (practically speaking, the creeds of the ancient Church) together with an implied affirmation of, or perhaps only an agreement not to dispute, the remaining articles of faith? What does such a corporate unity mean on the institutional level? Concretely, what does it mean for the understanding and practice of the Petrine ministry as the servant of unity? These questions, which could easily be multiplied, can only be asked at this point. The answers, however, must be clear at least in outline form before a full recognition of the other church community as the Church of Jesus Christ is possible. The theological discussion of models for unity is still in its early stages. Its conclusion, according to Catholic understanding, could only occur at an ecumenical council. It would have to be ecumenical in both senses of the term: in the traditional Catholic sense of a gathering called and led by the pope and including all the bishops of the world (*oikumene*), and in the more recent sense of the word *ecumenical*, that is, as a council in which the leaders of other churches also took an active part in order in this way to reconcile all churches in one conciliar community. Such an ecumenical council is the great hope of the ecumenical movement; to work towards this is its explicit goal. It is to be hoped and desired that the discussion of a Catholic recognition of the CA can be an important step in this direction and that this discussion, and the theological reception of the CA which it has led to, can soon receive official recognition.

NOTES

1. See above, p. 63.
2. Paderborn: Schöningh, 1974.

The Augsburg Confession
and Contemporary Catholicism

AVERY DULLES, S. J.

The CA was not intended as an exclusively Lutheran statement. In its doctrinal section (Arts. 1–21), it aimed to serve the cause of Christian unity by stating positions on which Lutherans and Catholics of the papal party could agree. The second section (Arts. 22–28), dealing with questions of practice or discipline, sets forth "some few abuses which are new and have been adopted by the fault of the times although contrary to the intent of the canons." Everything in the CA was considered to be in agreement with the faith of the one catholic Church. The CA is therefore in principle an ecumenical document.

The ecumenical significance of the CA is not limited to Lutherans and Roman Catholics. Melanchthon later composed a variant form of the CA (the *confessio variata*) for the Swiss Reformers, and this was accepted by Calvin in 1541. At the Peace of Westphalia (1648), the Calvinist Reform was recognized as belonging to the family of the CA. In England Thomas Cranmer derived many of his Forty-two Articles from the CA, and in this way it became one of the major sources for the Thirty-nine Articles of the Church of England. Thus the three main branches of the Reformation are in different ways indebted to the CA.

In 1530 a commission of papal theologians, working in collaboration with the Emperor Charles V, found the CA in part unacceptable. The *Confutatio pontificia* (as the report of this commission has been misleadingly labeled) pointed out a number of ambiguities and omissions as well as some positive statements judged to be in conflict with the Catholic faith. Rejected by the Emperor, the CA failed to achieve its stated objective of bringing together the opposed parties on the basis of their common faith.

Periodically since the sixteenth century, there have been attempts to use the CA as a bridge to overcome the rift between Lutherans and Catholics. Since 1974 the question of Catholic recognition of the CA has been intensively discussed. Many distinguished Catholic theologians think that perhaps today the Catholic Church could at length extend some sort of recognition to the CA, but others, equally distinguished, continue to express doubts.

Four recurrent questions must be addressed:[1]

1. Can the CA be considered by itself alone?

The CA is intended to explain a phenomenon much larger than itself, namely, the character and aims of the reforming movement headed by Luther. The CA was evaluated by the Emperor and his theologians in the context of their perception of the movement it described. Subsequent Lutheranism has taken the CA as one of its confessional writings but has placed it alongside of others in *The Book of Concord*. Can the CA be rightly understood in isolation from the other writings of Melanchthon, and specifically from the Apology which he later wrote to explain and defend it? Can the writings of Melanchthon himself be understood in isolation from those of Luther, his theological mentor? Recognition of the CA alone, it is feared, would invite the charge that a single confessional document was being artificially torn out of its historical context and that the more irenic Melanchthon was being used to evade the more radical challenge of Luther.[2]

This difficulty is not by itself fatal. The CA does have unique status among the Lutheran confessional writings of the first generation, for it presents not the private opinions of a single theologian but a common statement of the tenets of the Lutheran Reform. Even though the other Reformation writings contribute to a better understanding of the CA, it is possible to address what is asserted in this document without simultaneously addressing all the assertions in all the confessional writings.

2. What is the force of the CA today?

Although the CA stands at the beginning of *The Book of Concord* (preceded only by the three "ecumenical" symbols of antiquity) and is rather universally accepted in churches which wish to be called Lutheran, it is not clear what authority it holds for Lutherans. Is it anything more than another piece of sixteenth-century theology, subject to correction in the light of the Bible, better interpreted? If so, is it really normative at all? And if Lutherans do not recognize it as having a binding character, what would be the point of any recognition by the Catholic Church?

The problem of the authority of the CA is intensified by the passage of time. Since it was written, new methods of exegesis have become common. New world views have gained adherence from Christians as well as non-Christians. The Catholic Church envisaged throughout the CA has shed many of its late scholastic and Renaissance trappings. For all these reasons, it seems anachronistic to canonize the CA in our time by a new act of recognition.

These difficulties, like the first set, admit of a partial answer. Since Lutherans, generally speaking, continue to regard the CA in the main as a correct interpretation of the word of God, it is scarcely necessary to specify, prior to recognition, how adequate or binding Lutherans now consider the CA to be. Even though it has far less authority than the Bible and the ancient creeds, it does enjoy a certain priority among the Lutheran confessional writings. Even though it might not be fully adequate for our times, Lutherans commonly regard it as acceptable in what it actually teaches. Can Catholics accord it the same status? Hence our third question:

3. Is the CA, in what it affirms and denies, compatible with Catholic teaching?

A Catholic today, in assessing the CA, will consider carefully the deficiencies noted by the *Confutatio*. The Roman theologians centered their objections on the last seven articles, which deal with what Melanchthon regarded as abuses in practice rather than strictly doctrinal matters. To a great extent, these practices have been so changed that the objections cannot be simply repeated today. The Latin Mass, private masses, the denial of the chalice to the laity, and the temporal power of bishops are no longer major issues of contention. The edge of the Lutheran protest against monastic vows and priestly celibacy is blunted, as Pannenberg points out,[3] by the relative ease with which dispensations from these obligations are granted in our day. The more lenient policy of the contemporary Catholic Church regarding the enumeration of sins in confession and the observance of fasts and holy days may mean that these practices are no longer subject to the objections made in the CA.

Nevertheless, the sweeping nature of the statements directed against many of these Catholic usages constitutes a difficulty against recognition. Can the Catholic Church today officially recognize a document that criticizes monastic vows and mandatory priestly celibacy with as few qualifications as the CA admits? Can it approve a confession which alleges that communion for the laity under the form of bread alone is contrary to Christ's command in the Scripture?

To this it must be added that the section dealing with abuses does not in fact deal only with questions of practice. Underlying the demands are certain doctrinal assumptions which here and there become explicit. In spite of the convergences reached in ecumenical dialogue during the past decade, it is not immediately apparent that the Catholic Church can endorse the formulations of the CA regarding the Mass as sacrifice and its restrictions on the power of bishops to impose obligations binding in conscience.

The first twenty-one articles, dealing with doctrinal matters, offer, on the whole, fewer problems. Some have proposed that Catholic recognition should extend to these articles alone. But would it be ecumenically useful to give such partial recognition to the CA? Would it even be possible in view of the fact that the earlier articles themselves condemn vows, holy days, and penitential works (Arts. 12, 15, 20), thus preparing the ground for the fuller polemic of the later articles?

In addition to these disciplinary questions (some of which are intimately bound up with doctrine), there is the fact that the CA, in its doctrinal section, apparently repudiates certain points of Catholic teaching. The Catholic theologians who composed the *Confutatio* read the CA as denying that sanctification and eternal life can be merited, even with the help of grace; they observed that it rejects the invocation of saints; and they feared that its description of the Church as the "assembly of saints and true believers" denied by implication that the wicked are, properly speaking, members. All these points were seen as unacceptable by the Catholic theologians in 1530. Recognition of the CA by the Catholic Church in our day could be interpreted as meaning that the Catholic Church in 1980 is prepared to reverse itself and accept these putative Lutheran positions.

Further, the CA omits all mention of certain Catholic beliefs which would seem to call for treatment. In view of the express denials in other Lutheran confessional writings, can Catholics accept as harmless the failure of the CA to speak of more than three sacraments, its omission of the papacy, and its incompleteness as to what constitutes a valid external call to the Ministry of word and sacrament?

These discrepancies between the CA and current Roman Catholic teaching raise very acutely the fourth question:

4. What would recognition mean?

In spite of the remarkable convergences reached in the ecumenical dialogues of the past few decades, it seems hardly likely that the Catholic Church in our time will be able to recognize the CA as an unexceptionable statement of Catholic doctrine. Even if in some way Catholics could see their way to saying that the formal statements of the CA could be acknowledged as in some sense true, still it can be argued that the CA contains, only slightly below the surface, fundamental differences that were to come into the open in more polemical writings, such as the *Smalcald Articles* of 1537.

Some have suggested that Catholic recognition of the CA need not mean that the Catholic Church accepts it as a properly Roman Catholic confession. Recognition might mean acceptance of the CA "as *one* legitimate expression of the common Catholic faith so that the ecclesiastical community which appeals to it would be given room within the unity of the Catholic Church."[4] Or it could mean that the CA "can be interpreted and received in a Catholic sense."[5]

Even these proposals are not free from difficulty. If the CA admits of a truly "Catholic interpretation," why could Roman Catholics not accept it as their own? In view of the historical context in which the CA originated, would such a Catholic interpretation be justified? Can the Catholic Church, while retaining its own beliefs regarding sacri-

135

fice, merit, vows, the invocation of the saints, and so on, admit the "legitimacy" of a Christianity which at least appears to deny these very tenets?

In this connection it is of interest that Cardinal Ratzinger, who initially expressed interest in the proposal of Catholic recognition of the CA, currently holds that the term *recognition* almost inevitably awakens false expectations and should be dropped, although he continues to be in favor of serious dialogue on the question whether "the theological and ecclesial structure of the Lutheran confessional writings is reconcilable with the teaching of the Catholic Church."[6]

Unless carefully nuanced, a Catholic "recognition" of the CA might be ecumenically counterproductive. This step would seem to endorse a "Catholic" reading of the CA and would thereby tend to obscure its distinctively Lutheran import. Ecumenists are increasingly disposed to recognize Lutheranism as an original expression of Christianity having a certain inner consistency which demands to be respected. As an ecclesial type, Lutheranism is morphologically distinct from Eastern Orthodoxy and from Western, or Roman, Catholicism. More than this, the Lutheran movement cannot easily be seen as a parallel expression of Christianity, peacefully taking its place alongside of Catholicism. From its inception, it was a reform movement, a prophetic protest. In this sense the CA may be seen as containing what Max Lackmann twenty years ago called "anti-Roman and anti-Catholic negatives."[7]

The Catholic Church, therefore, cannot properly domesticate the CA as being, without qualification, a Catholic confession (as it understands Catholicism). The Lutheran Confessions are dialectically related to the Catholicism which they criticize. Lutherans must continue to respect the Catholicism which they are attempting to renew and purify. Catholics, on the other hand, must continue to pay heed to the criticism coming from the Lutheran tradition. In the words of Lackmann: "To confront, as mother Church, these negatives without an a priori retreat behind the barricades of orthodox dogmatics is to make an indispensable contribution to healing the wounds of the torn Body of Christ."[8]

The CA, together with the other Lutheran confessional writings (and not separated from them), has had and can continue to have immense value by providing a far-reaching critique of the short-comings to which Roman Catholicism is subject. Granted the historical situation of the sixteenth century, it was perhaps necessary that this critique should come from a movement which broke with the Catholic Church. Even today we can find no easy synthesis between Luther's reforming critique and the Roman Catholic patrimony. But it seems certain that the two are inseparable. In the words of Lackmann: "The CA is a sign placed by God to remind us that Evangelical and Catholic Christians cannot escape each other, that the Reformation still awaits its fulfillment in a manner which will bring Evangelicals and Catholics together in one Church."[9]

As the dialogue proceeds, Lutherans and Catholics are coming closer to a mutual understanding that can respect the integrity of each. But they still remain separated and perhaps need to be for some time to come. Catholics must continue to ask themselves if they have fully heard the message of the Reformation, and Lutherans must continue to ask themselves whether their protest has not been in some respects too one-sided. Lutherans may well decide at some future time that even the CA, although perhaps more Catholic than general Lutheran belief and practice, is on some points insufficiently Catholic.

From a position within Catholicism, it is becoming evident that the Lutheran protest no longer comes only from outside. There is scarcely any position enunciated in the CA which is not at present defended by certain Roman Catholics. This does not necessarily mean that the Catholic Church is coming close to a recognition of the CA as a legitimate expression of its own faith. It means rather that dissent can no longer be kept out of the Church itself. The convictions of Christians no longer mirror exactly the official statements of their bishops and synods. For better or for worse, the collapse of authoritarianism is simply a fact of our times.

The churches have yet to face up to the ecumenical and ecclesiological implications of this new fact. A beginning was, however, made by the recognition in the Vatican II that "in Catholic teaching there exists an order or 'hierarchy' of truths since they vary in their relationship to the foundation of the Christian faith."[10] The fundamental affirmations of the Catholic faith, articulated in the classical creeds, remain part of the patrimony of both Lutherans and Catholics. In comparison with this immense common heritage, the discrepancies are relatively minor. Thus the time may not be far away when it will be possible for Catholics and Lutherans, without loss of their distinctive identities and without reaching full agreement on all doctrines, to recognize each other as belonging to the same ecclesial fellowship. Such a mutual recognition would be of vastly greater significance than a Catholic recognition of the CA. But if such recognition and ecclesial fellowship ever comes about, there is no doubt that the CA, thanks to its simultaneously Catholic and Lutheran character, will have prepared the way.

As a link between Rome and the Reformation, the CA may providentially perform for our age the unifying function for which it was initially intended. Even though a formal recognition of the CA by the Roman Catholic Church still appears remote and possibly undesirable, the joint effort by Lutherans and Catholics to see whether agreement can be reached on the import of the CA for our times is fraught with ecumenical promise.

NOTES

1. These questions, which seem to arise from the subject matter itself, correspond approximately to those asked by J. Ratzinger, "Anmerkungen zur Frage einer 'Anerkennung' der 'Confessio Augustana' durch die katholische Kirche," *Münchener theologische Zeitschrift* 29 (1978): 225–37.

2. See Peter Manns, "Zum Vorhaben einer 'katholischen Anerkennung der Confessio Augustana': Ökumene auf Kosten Martin Luthers?" *Ökumenische Rundschau* 35 (1977): 426–50. The same criticism has been made by the late Albert Brandenburg.

3. See p. 33 above.

4. Cf. Walter Kasper, pp. 124–25 above.

5. Ibid., p. 128.

6. Ratzinger, "Anmerkungen," p. 237.

7. M. Lackmann, *The Augsburg Confession and Catholic Unity* (New York: Herder and Herder, 1963), p. 85. The German original was published in 1959.

8. Ibid., p. 86.

9. Ibid., p. 142. For Lackmann "Evangelical" is a description of the Lutheran movement (p. 1).

10. Vatican II, *Decree on Ecumenism* (*Unitatis Redintegratio*), no. 11.

Catholic Recognition
of the *Confessio Augustana:*
Precedents, Problems, and Probabilities

HARRY McSORLEY

The effort to make Jesus Christ credible to the world by bringing Christians closer to God and to each other, an effort known as the ecumenical movement, gained wide publicity and increased momentum when the Roman Catholic Church officially endorsed the movement at the Second Vatican Council in 1964. One of the many effects of the *Decree on Ecumenism* was the unprecedented yet almost self-evident participation of Roman Catholics in various observances marking the 450th anniversary of the Reformation in 1967. On that occasion several theologians were able to speak some good news for the ecumenical movement by pointing to the growing consensus among Roman Catholic Luther scholars that Luther was not only a sincerely Christian person but also one who, in his central and original Reformation protest, was a Catholic reformer of the Church. Only through a complex set of tragic circumstances, they added, involving what Vatican II calls fault on both sides, did Luther's reform movement within the Catholic Church become a "Protestant" or "Lutheran" movement apart from full communion with the Church of which the Bishop of Rome is the chief earthly pastor.

Beginning in 1967 and continuing through 1979, there appeared a remarkable series of statements of consensus or convergence between officially appointed Lutheran / Roman Catholic dialogue groups at the national and international levels on such traditionally disputed themes as the Eucharist, the ordained Ministry, papal primacy, and teaching authority and infallibility in the Church.[1] Partly because these and similar convergences between other churches have received relatively little public attention, the reasons for which need not be discussed

139

here, a distinguished group of American ecumenists has recently called for "a celebrative event manifesting our growing oneness in Christ—to share what God has been doing in our midst, to further an effective mutuality of witness, to seek ways in service to others to be more obedient Christians together."[2]

Surely the 450th anniversary of the CA ought to be an occasion that signifies vividly how far the dialogue between Lutherans and Catholics has advanced since 1967. Encouraged by the deepening theological consensus emerging from the dialogues as well as by individual scholarly achievements such as Vinzenz Pfnür's *Einig in der Rechtfertigungslehre?*,[3] many Catholics, including the Secretariat for Promoting Christian Unity, are seriously entertaining the possibility that the Roman Catholic Church can in some ecumenically fruitful sense "receive the CA as a legitimate type of Christian truth."[4] I think two things ought to be said at the outset concerning this proposal. First, it is clear that such a reception or recognition of the CA cannot take place in 1980, given the fact that "a thorough consideration of all the problems" is a prerequisite for any official decision by the Roman Catholic Church.[5] Second, the very fact that this proposal is being seriously discussed in Europe and now in North America is certainly worth celebrating in 1980 by all Christians, not just Lutherans and Roman Catholics, who are praying and working for the healing of the wounds of division that mar the Body of Christ. That something even more positive ought to be said in this anniversary year will emerge in the course of this essay.

In what follows I wish, first of all, to draw attention to some of the findings of Pfnür's earlier work that do not come sufficiently to the fore in his present essay, findings which, in my opinion, necessitate a much more positive attitude on the part of Catholics to the CA than has traditionally been the case. Second, I will say something about recognition, and finally, a few words about some difficulties concerning recognition of the CA raised in a recent essay by Cardinal Ratzinger.

1. General accounts of the Diet of Augsburg by even the most distinguished Roman Catholic historians often give the impression that the discussions that took place during August 1530, after the Luth-

erans had refused to accept the *Confutation,* were not only fruitless but were doomed to failure from the start because of the dominating presence of the hard-line Catholic apologist, John Eck.[6] From Vinzenz Pfnür, however, we learn that an extraordinary degree of rapprochement was achieved not only on the core issue of the Reformation, the doctrine of justification, but also on virtually all issues of doctrine![7] Even before the "Committee of Fourteen" began to meet in mid-August, Melanchthon and Luther had already indicated that they saw a basic agreement between the doctrinal articles of the CA and of the *Confutation.*[8] Moreover, it is John Eck, among other participants in the negotiating committee, who informs us that, of the twenty-one doctrinal articles in the first part of the CA, agreement was reached on all but two of the nineteen articles that were discussed.[9] And of those two, CA, 20 and 21, there was considerable, though not full, agreement. In fact, of the nineteen doctrinal articles discussed in the committee, it would seem that the only doctrinal question left unresolved after Melanchthon had agreed to call the works of faith "meritorious" in Ap., 4:366 was the question of the legitimacy of invoking the saints![10]

On the basis of Pfnür's research, then, it is quite accurate to say that some of the original Catholic "confutors" of the CA, when they were able to engage in dialogue with the drafter of the CA and some of his colleagues, were inches away from recognizing the CA as Catholic, not just on the doctrine of justification but also on virtually every other doctrinal article of the CA. Surely that remarkable precedent of an "almost" Catholic recognition of the CA 450 years ago should both encourage and challenge Catholics to complete the task in this time of ecumenical grace.

2. Two questions may now be asked about recognition. The first is, Does it make ecumenical sense to work toward a recognition of only the first part of the CA, the doctrinal articles? I think a case can be made for this. It would be ideal, of course, if the Roman Catholic Church could find a way, consistent with truth, to recognize the entire document. This would be very difficult in terms of the complex and sometimes one-sided historical and theological arguments used in the second part of the CA.[11] Moreover, without denying that there are

doctrinal issues involved in the second part, especially christology and the doctrine of justification,[12] it would seem that the best way to deal with the practical reforms defended in the second part is through the kind of modification of discipline by the Catholic Church that had already been recommended by Cardinal Cajetan to Pope Clement VII in 1530 while the Diet of Augsburg was still in session. Cajetan recommended a married clergy for Germany along the lines of the Eastern churches, communion under both kinds, and a papal decree for the whole Church explaining that commandments of the Church regarding feast days, fasting, and the reception of the sacraments were not binding under grave sin.[13]

The very bipartite structuring of the CA and the different character of each part indicate that a recognition of the first part (CA, 1–21) might be acceptable to Lutherans.[14] The few passages in the first part likely to cause offense to Catholics could be dealt with in several ways: (1) by explaining in any official Roman Catholic declaration of recognition that already in 1530 representative Catholic theologians were able to reach agreement with Lutheran theologians on virtually all the originally controverted doctrinal articles; (2) by adding footnotes to the various articles, where appropriate, showing how they were originally "confuted" and then agreed to during the discussions that followed—these notes would include the various formulations of concord that were arrived at in 1530 or later in the sixteenth century, or in contemporary documents emanating from Lutheran/Catholic dialogues; (3) by appropriate Lutheran declarations analogous to that suggested, for example, by the recent statement on *Teaching Authority and Infallibility in the Church,* where the Lutherans recommended that their churches "officially declare that the Lutheran commitment to the Confessions does not involve the assertion that the pope or the papacy in our day is the antichrist";[15] (4) if none of the former means was found to be effective in dealing with the difficulty for Catholics posed by CA, 15: 3–4 concerning vows and laws of fast and abstinence,[16] the Roman Catholic Church could simply withhold recognition pending a dialogue on the question. One could see an analogy here to Rome's nonacceptance of Canon 28 of the Council of Chalcedon, but a more appropriate precedent, as we saw above, is the fact that the Lutheran/Catholic committee at Augsburg agreed to discuss this article along with two others in the context of Articles 22–28.

Recognition of the first part of the CA commends itself not only by reason of its simplicity but also because it carries with it great promise for deeper concord. It would be relatively simple to achieve, given the fact that full agreement was almost reached in 1530; our much more propitious situation today would surely enable full agreement to be reached in the very near future. It would also be promising because if Lutherans and Catholics can agree on the doctrinal articles—on the gospel—they would thereby lay a solid foundation for discussion of such residual issues as the papacy. "Laying foundations" is actually an understatement in view of Luther's assertion that he *would* accept the papacy if the pope would only teach the gospel.[17]

The second question which may now be asked about recognition is, What would Catholic recognition of the CA mean? Aligning myself with the remarks of Kasper and Pfnür on this question, I would simply add these five observations:

At the very least, the Roman Catholic Church, in recognizing or receiving the CA, would be saying: We recognize that the CA contains a confession of the faith of the Catholic Church. Moreover, the CA rejects ancient and medieval doctrines and practices which the Roman Catholic Church also rejects.

Recognition could also mean that the Roman Catholic Church acknowledges new experiences and insights which belong to the whole catholic Church and which might be appropriated by Roman Catholics.[18]

It goes without saying that Catholic recognition of the CA would not retroactively immunize it from the effects of time. In the light of our present historical and exegetical knowledge, it must be said that in the CA, as in the teaching of the Council of Trent, there are inadequacies and even inaccuracies.[19] This is by no means to deny that the gospel comes to expression in these documents. Nor is it to deny a properly understood doctrine of infallibility.[20]

Nor would Catholic recognition mean that the CA represents what Roman Catholics would regard as a full confession of the Catholic faith. It must immediately be said, however, that not even the Apostles' Creed or the Nicene Creed are full expressions of the faith from the standpoint of the sacraments, the Ministry, and so on. Yet these confessions are rightly used and revered by both churches as expressing the very core of the faith.

Finally, and again positively, recognition of the CA by the Roman Catholic Church would mean that the CA is an authentic expression of the Catholic faith which has served to nurture faith and good works (!) in the lives of many. Recognition would thus surely imply that Roman Catholics should study the CA carefully as a means of deepening their own faith and their own understanding of the Christian message.

3. As recently as 1976, Cardinal Ratzinger was able to add his support to the movement toward recognition of the CA as Catholic.[21] In a more recent essay,[22] however, Ratzinger, who was an examiner of Pfnür's doctoral thesis, continues to say that Pfnür's proposal is pointing in the right direction but lists several difficulties that cause him to draw back somewhat from his earlier endorsement. These are: (a) the place of the CA in the totality of the Lutheran Confessions, (b) the problem of the authority of the Confessions, (c) the question of the reconcilability of the content of the CA with the Catholic faith, and (d) the concept of recognition.

Even though these problems are set forth by Ratzinger as observations and not as a carefully worked out position, they require a fuller response than can be given here both because of Ratzinger's standing as a theologian and his position in the church. My sometimes indirect remarks may be more appropriate than a direct reply inasmuch as Ratzinger himself seems to suggest that he is writing as a theologian-pastor rather than a theologian's theologian in setting forth the misgivings about the proposal which he has picked up in discussion with others, presumably educated laity, clergy, and perhaps even some theologians.

(a) Ratzinger asks: How is the CA related to the other confessional books, and how strong is the inner unity of *The Book of Concord?* These are intrinsically interesting questions, but Catholic recognition of the CA does not depend on an answer to them. In any case, Meyer's remarks above offer a good response to these questions.

Ratzinger asserts that, for the Reformation, doctrinal statements by the church can be in principle no different qualitatively than statements made by theologians. He repeats this charge in (b) and (c), where he calls it "the really central question." Here I would cite Edmund Schlink: "Surely the Confessions as the *voice of the church* are important enough to be heard out first . . . before the individual Christian lifts his own voice to speak."[23]

Whether Luther is to be interpreted more as a "churchly" person or as "fundamentally critical of the Church" (Ratzinger thinks the latter is more likely, over against Schlink, Althaus, Kinder, Meinhold, Joest, Lortz, Manns, and Iserloh) is not relevant to the question of Catholic recognition of the CA, especially in view of Luther's approval of the CA.

(b) Ratzinger thinks Luther's *sola scriptura* principle leads to the view that doctrinal statements of the Church can be revised in the light of a deeper understanding of Scripture. He seems to forget that the *Decree on Ecumenism* (par. 6) calls for the reformation of church doctrine when that is shown to be deficient. He also overlooks the fact that Luther insists on being guided by the articles of faith in interpreting Scripture.[24] For Luther, moreover, the custom of the church in such matters as infant baptism and belief in the real presence is not only authoritative but inerrant.[25]

(c) Ratzinger points out that the polemic of the *Smalcald Articles* contradicts the claim of the CA that "the whole dissension is concerned with a certain few abuses." However, Catholics are not being asked to recognize the *Smalcald Articles,* and there are plenty of good Lutherans who do not.

To claim that, according to CA, 24, the liturgy of the Church is subsumed under the category of "ceremony" and that this is measured solely by its pedagogical effects is not only to disregard CA, 24: 30, where the Mass is *not* reduced to the consolation of consciences, but also the fuller context of the CA's sacramental teaching as seen in CA, 9, 10, 11 and 13. Careful reading of the CA, moreover, starting with CA, 6, does not allow the divinely instituted sacraments to be equated with human ceremonies.

CA, 28: 55 is incorrectly adduced to support Ratzinger's claim that for the CA "church doctrine can only be an 'ordinance for the sake of love and peace.'" This passage is not speaking of the doctrinal authority of bishops but of their disciplinary enactments. When CA, 28 does speak about doctrine, it says: "By divine right" bishops have the jurisdiction "to reject doctrine which is contrary to the Gospel" and "churches are therefore bound by divine law to be obedient to the bishops" (CA, 28:20–22).

(d) Recognition of the CA, says Cardinal Ratzinger, certainly cannot mean that "through historical analysis of the text, this document could be proven to be a correct, or, in any case, a dogmatically unexceptionable, reliable rendering of Catholic doctrine." This is not a rejection of the view taken by Pfnür, myself, and others. None of us contends that the text of the CA can be taken in isolation from the intentions behind it, which can only be discovered by studying the context. That includes the dialogues about the meaning of the text which were held in 1530. The productive theological dialogues of the past fifteen years are also part of the context which the Roman Catholic Church must consider if it is to make a positive decision about recognizing the CA.

Nor is Cardinal Ratzinger at odds with the contributors to this volume who favor recognition of the CA when he warns against premature actions such as trying to rush to a decision by 25 June 1980.

His proposal, however, that the very concept of recognition be abandoned because it "almost necessarily awakens false ideas" will, I think, respectfully be declined not only on the question of fact but also on the principle that abuse does not take away use. The "use" here is that responsible efforts toward recognition of the CA in a properly nuanced manner such as we have tried to outline above can, should, and do awaken true ideas about unity between Catholics and Lutherans.

Barring a miracle, Lutheran/Catholic unity will not be realized in 1980, nor will that important symbolic step toward it: recognition of the CA as Catholic. There is, however, good reason for hoping that 1980 will be a year in which commitment to both the proximate and the ultimate goal will be deepened. One very good reason, it seems to me, is that 450 years ago, John Eck, a man who "rejected every compromise at the expense of truth,"[26] could write to the Archbishop of Mainz of the doctrinal articles of the CA *after* the *Confutation*: If we could have discussions with them, "I believe concord would immediately take place on the other 22 articles."[27] Surely Catholics and Lutherans should hope for nothing less when they gather for prayer and dialogue in Augsburg and elsewhere in 1980.

NOTES

1. For bibliography, see above, p. 93, n. 1–p. 94, n. 3.

2. See Gerald M. Moede and John A. Radano, "Seton Hall Consultation on Christian Unity Issues Call," *Journal of Ecumenical Studies* 15 (1978): 602.

3. Vinzenz Pfnür, *Einig in der Rechtfertigungslehre?* (Wiesbaden: Franz Steiner, 1970). This work must be consulted to appreciate fully the firm grounds supporting Pfnür's essay above, pp. 1–26.

4. See the Foreword by Cardinal Willebrands, p. vii above. For an understanding of the technical term *type*, see "Cardinal Willebrands' Address in Cambridge, England, January 18, 1970," *Documents on Anglican / Roman Catholic Relations* (Washington: United States Catholic Conference, 1972), pp. 32–41. A *typos* of the Church is present, according to Willebrands, "where there is a long coherent tradition commanding men's love and loyalty, creating and sustaining a harmonious and organic whole of complementary elements, each of which supports and strengthens the other." In this view there can be "a plurality of *typoi* within the communion of the one and only Church of Christ" (pp. 38–39).

5. See the Foreword by Willebrands, p. vii above.

6. Cf. Hubert Jedin, *A History of the Council of Trent,* vol. 1, trans. Ernest Graf (St. Louis: B. Herder, 1957), pp. 257–59; Karl Bihlmeier and Hermann Tüchle, *Church History,* vol. 3 (Westminster, Md.: Newman, 1966), pp. 39–41. On Eck's hatred for Luther and his allegedly irreconcilable attitude see Jedin, *A History,* 1: 380, 381, 390, 393, 396.

7. *Einig,* pp. 251–71.

8. Cf. *CR,* 2: 269: "Von der Lahr acht ich werde der Kaiser nicht disputiren. *So sind unsre Artikel an ihnen selb alle concedirt in der Confutatio,* allein sind etliche viele calumniae daran gehangt" (italics mine); *WA Br,* 5: 590. Pfnür provides these references in his review of Klaus Rischar's book on John Eck in *Theologische Revue* 67 (1971): 64.

9. Pfnür, *Einig,* pp. 268–69. CA, 11 and 15 were reserved for discussion with the articles of the second part of the CA.

10. Pfnür, *Einig,* p. 267. This issue can hardly be deemed a church-dividing one. CA, 21 says: "The Scriptures do not teach us to pray to the saints or seek their help, for the only mediator . . . and intercessor whom the Scriptures set before us is Christ." Trent (DS, 1821) simply rejects the view that the invocation of the saints "contradicts the word of God

and is opposed to the honor of the 'one mediator of God and man, Jesus Christ.'" Trent does not command the invocation of the saints but teaches that it is a "good and useful" practice.

11. I think especially of the overstated defence of communion under both forms in CA, 22 as well as the argumentation in CA, 27 on vows. In *Einig* Pfnür does not analyze the second part of the CA (nor CA, 11, 14, and 15, which were discussed with CA, 22–28), since he was mainly concerned with the doctrine of justification. A thorough study of the way the Committee of Fourteen dealt with these other articles is surely needed.

12. This is especially true concerning CA, 24 on the Mass. It must be noted, however, that the contemporary dialogues on the Eucharist (see Lindbeck/Vajta, pp. 89–91 above) as well as the liturgical reforms of Vatican II have clearly met the main concern of this article.

13. See Jedin, *A History*, 1:274.

14. Pannenberg says as much in his essay, pp. 31–32, 34 above.

15. *Theological Studies* 40(1979): 165. A similar strategy was followed in the Leuenberg Concord with respect to past mutual condemnations of doctrine. See part III, especially nn. 20, 23, 26, 27; *Ecumenical Review* 25 (1973): 357–58. The great difference between the situation addressed by Leuenberg and that of the CA, of course, is that the CA was in no sense conscious of condemning any doctrine of the Roman Catholic Church.

16. Luther regarded the matter of "human traditions" as "the most difficult question of all" (*WA Br*, 5: 529, l. 1).

17. *WA*, 40^{I}: 357; *LW*, 26:225.

18. In these first two points, I have adopted suggestions made by Max Lackmann, *The Augsburg Confession and Catholic Unity* (New York: Herder and Herder, 1963), pp. 43, 65, 75–85. I take seriously but do not subscribe to Lackmann's further thesis that "the CA clearly adduces anti-Roman and anti-Catholic negatives which dispute and structurally alter the doctrine and form of the Western Church" (p. 85). Written over twenty years ago, this thesis has to be overhauled in the light of more recent historical and theological work, up to and including that which can be found in this volume.

19. See the several hundred searching questions concerning the exegetical adequacy of the Lutheran Confessions raised by that most loyal expositor of those Confessions, Edmund Schlink, *The Theology of the Lutheran Confessions*, trans. Paul F. Koehneke and Herbert J. A. Bouman (Philadelphia: Fortress Press, 1961), pp. 299–314.

20. See my essay, "Some Forgotten Truths About the Petrine Ministry," *Journal of Ecumenical Studies* 11 (1974): 208–36, 225–27.

21. J. Ratzinger, "Prognosen für die Zukunft des Ökumenismus," *Bausteine* 17, no. 65 (1977): 6–14.

22. "Anmerkungen zur Frage einer 'Anerkennung' der Confessio Augus-

tana durch die katholische Kirche," *Münchener Theologische Zeitschrift* 29 (1978): 225–37.

23. Schlink, *Theology,* pp. xxii–xxiii; the entire paragraph should be read.

24. For some references see Paul Althaus, *The Theology of Martin Luther,* trans. Robert C. Schultz (Philadelphia: Fortress Press, 1966), p. 386.

25. Ibid., pp. 334, 359–61, 363; cf. *WA,* 51: 510–18; *LW,* 41:212–17; *WA,* 38:216; *LW,* 38:171.

26. Erwin Iserloh, "Eck, Johannes," *LThK²* 3: 644.

27. *Credo statim fieret concordia in aliis XXII articulis;* cited by Pfnür, *Einig,* p. 256, n. 273. The other articles of which Eck is speaking are CA, 1–20, 25, and 28.

On Recognizing
the Augsburg Confession

ROBERT JENSON

I.

That the search for rapprochement between the Roman Catholic and
Lutheran communions takes the form of a proposal for Roman Catholic recognition of the CA is to be greeted with joy. It puts the ball in
the right court.

The Lutheran reformers, beginning with observed "abuses" in the
life of the medieval church, proposed new doctrinal regulations to
safeguard that character of the gospel which they believed was
abused by the abuses. The Church's proclamation, they said, must
be such as to open the sort of righteousness that faith grasps and is,
rather than the sort constituted by works. Their advocacy of this
proposal, polemic as it was against dominant practice, was found
intolerable by most of the contemporary church and by nearly all its
officialdom; very quickly the Reformers were expelled for their unwill-
ingness to refrain. The separation was practically sealed at the Diet
of Augsburg; it is the Lutheran statement presented in the course of
those proceedings whose reception is now, most appropriately, again
weighed.

It was this rejection—and it alone!—which made the Lutheran
concerns "church divisive." Insofar, therefore, as the ecclesiastical in-
stitutions descended from the parties then divided acknowledge their
origins, it is for Roman Catholicism to decide whether what was then
done was well or ill done—not necessarily who was to blame—and
what course is now to be taken in the consequent situation. Lutherans
can only stand anxiously ready to assist the decision in any way they
can. On their own behalf, Lutherans continue to wait for their insight
to be acknowledged as needed within the whole Church or to be

convinced of its illegitimacy. Lutherans should not—it must promptly be noted—wait for all the Church to agree on one or another formulation of any one doctrine but should only ask to be allowed to pursue a specific reforming activity in those parts of the empirical church now closed to them. If, of course, Lutherans no longer are a reforming group, their existence is passé, and the sooner this is admitted the better.

Just by these dialectics of the situation, there are ways in which Roman Catholic recognition of the CA could be carried out that would rob it of its great hope. The threat is not remote; two such errors seem to appear in the arguments of the very persons who have most powerfully promoted recognition's possibility: Wolfhart Pannenberg, in this volume, and Vinzenz Pfnür, in this volume and in the remarkable book[1] that has provided the scholarly basis of the current discussion. It is not the office of a Lutheran writer to decide whether recognition is possible for Roman Catholic authorities, but it may be his office to warn against arguments for its possibility that could render the venture nugatory.

II.

Wolfhart Pannenberg argues that the CA can be accepted by Roman Catholicism because it never intended to describe any disagreements at the dogmatic level and thus can be church-divisive only if self-deceived. If, he says, we take the CA at its own self-evaluation, we find it saying that the whole quarrel is only about "certain abuses that have . . . come in with time" and locating such doctrines as justification or original sin—in which later Lutherans have supposed a church-divisive controversy with Rome to lie—in the section of "chief articles of faith" (1–21), which contain "nothing contrary to the catholic or even Roman churches."[2] Thus the Lutheran confessors did not think there was any quarrel about matters of dogmatic status, and as for the "actual matters of conflict" at the level of practice (22–28), most of those are no longer problems.

We should now, according to Pannenberg, govern our understanding of the CA by this, its original self-understanding; then the only question will be whether the CA's claim not to differ from Roman Catholicism is correct. The latter portion of Pannenberg's paper argues that the claim is in fact so near to being correct that it makes no difference; we will come back to this. Our first concern is the hermeneutic proposal just sketched—which seems astonishingly ahistorical.

Of course, it was "abuses" that were the initial target of reforming polemic; reformations are not made about university theology but about churchly proclamation, liturgy, and order. Vice versa, it was the attack on abuses that initially offended those who regarded the controversial practices as right and necessary; the Lutherans were seen as intolerable precisely because they objected, for example, to private masses. But if we wish to understand any of this, the obvious and essential question is: What did the Reformers think was being abused? And of the CA's answer to this question there can be no doubt: abused was that essential character of the gospel which the Wittenberg theology evoked with the slogan "justification by faith alone."

The organization of the CA is set by the three-article creeds, following an established pattern of expansion.[3] Article 1 gives the "first article," expanded by the trinitarian identification of God. Article 2 discusses original sin as the condition for the saving history to follow. Article 3, despite its title, covers both the second and third creedal articles. Son and Spirit appear in one article because the systematic heart of the CA is a rigorously christological determination of the doctrine of the works of the Spirit, that is, in the medieval scheme, of grace: it is the risen Lord who from God's right hand rules all creatures and "through the Holy Spirit sanctifies, purifies," and so on "those who believe." All the remaining eighteen articles of the CA's dogmatic part follow as commentary on the third creedal article's statement of the Spirit's work, enforcing at every point an interpretation by the polar reality of Christ and faith.

So Article 4 says explicitly that the things the Spirit gives he gives not to works but *gratis . . . propter Christum per fidem*. Article 5 founds the Church's ministry in the necessity of preachers if this is to happen. Article 6 stipulates the structure of life under such preaching: that we obey God's law just because it is God's and "receive forgiveness of sin" not by this obedience but "through faith in Christ." Article 7 arrives at the Church as the assembly gathered by the preaching stipulated in 5 and 6. Article 8 deals with a misunderstand-

ing to which this way of deriving the Church had exposed the Reformers. Articles 9–11 stipulate the necessarily sacramental—and not
merely verbal—character of the preaching that justifies. Article 12
states the Reformers' position on that one of the sacraments about
which the whole controversy had first broken out: the works of "confession and satisfaction" are replaced as components of penance by
faith in the preaching of Christ, in its extreme form as absolution.
In Article 13 this principle is extended to all the sacraments: the
communication of God's saving will, to be apprehended by faith, is
their function. Articles 14–15 affirm standing church order insofar as
it does not fall to the critique generated by "not by works." In Article
16 this critique is put actually in course, knocking down the special
status of churchly works over against civil works. Article 17 finishes
where the creedal third article finishes, with the Final Judgment, and
makes faith or its absence the criterion. Finally, Articles 18–21 treat
already-standing theological controversies between the Reformers and
their critics, making justification by faith alone the matter at issue in
each. In fact, the whole section of "chief articles of catholic faith" is
one long treatise on justification by faith apart from works.

As for the abuses, argued in Articles 22–28, the first two are merely
carry-overs from previous reform movements. In each of the other
cases, what is deplored is the abuse of "justification by faith alone,"
as is explicit at every step of the arguments establishing that the
reprobated practices are indeed abuses, for example: "Thus Saint
Paul teaches that we . . . receive grace through faith and not through
works. This is manifestly contradicted by this abuse of the Mass."[4]

Pannenberg's assertion, "In general, it is true of the disputed questions named in the second part of the CA that, in the self-understanding of the CA, they do not touch the agreement in basic articles of
faith,"[5] is incorrect. The abuses are discussed insofar as they touch
the matter of justification, which in turn is the entire content of the
CA's discussion of basic articles of faith.

The CA was an irenic document in a precise sense: it was written
in the desperate hope that a conflict with the manifest potential to
divide the Church would not in fact divide it. To this irenic end,
Melanchthon described the immediate occasions of controversy as
"only" recent abuses. He could do so without deception because the

practices in question were not practices to which the Roman authorities or the late medieval church generally had yet irrevocably committed themselves; reform could be carried out without official recantation. Justification by faith alone and its most immediate corollaries—that is, that which was at issue in the abuses—appeared in the earlier articles of catholic faith simply because the Reformers thought they *were* part of catholic faith, not because they thought these doctrines were certainly part of the *opponents'* faith. But there was no need, in view of the CA's irenic purpose, for the Reformers to state their fear that their opponents did not share this catholic faith and thus surely divide the Church by giving dogmatic status to matters of simple disagreement, since again no party was as yet committed. Thus the general structure of the CA is: "Justification by faith alone is a chief article of common faith—is it not?—from which we can together go on to regulate the controverted practices."

The confessors at Augsburg did not think they had no dispute of dogmatic rank with their Roman critics. They thought they had no such dispute with catholic Christians, among whom they still claimed to hope to find their critics. The key passage that Pannenberg gives in his notes does not say quite what Pannenberg attributes to it in his text.[6] Melanchthon's formulation is very careful. That the first twenty-one articles, of dogmatic weight, do not teach anything against "the catholic, and even Roman Church" is carefully insured against being misunderstood as Pannenberg does, as a general declaration of dogmatic peace, by the immediate qualification, "insofar as this can be determined by the writings of the Fathers." As to the place of the Reformers' opponents in this consensus, Melanchthon carefully does not say that *in fact* the opponents agree in these chief articles of faith, or even that he thinks they *will* agree, but precisely that they *must* agree: "And so we also suppose that our opponents cannot disagree with us in the above articles."[7] Melanchthon could not be more precise: the opponents constitute a group in possible distinction from the catholic consensus in which the Reformers assert their membership, who the Reformers "suppose" will—despite suspected disinclination—be compelled to adhere to the consensus by the weight of mutually acknowledged tradition.

That the above indeed states the CA's self-understanding is clear

from—besides the CA's own text—what happened when the opponents did in fact formally disagree about "justification by faith alone,"
in—as Melanchthon says—"Articles 4, 5, 6, and 11"[8] of the *Confutation*. Although the rejection was cautious and less emphasized than
several other matters, Melanchthon devoted one-third of the total
bulk of the Apology to his Article 4 in defense of the CA's Article 4,
and in actual fact he devoted most of the rest of the Apology to the
same rebuttal, although on the face of it he seems to be defending
other CA articles. In the *Confutation*, the Roman delegates formally
said, for example, in Article 20: When it is said "of good works that
they do not merit the remission of sins, . . . this is rejected." This was
all that was needed for the Reformers to certify a dissension in fundamental doctrine.

Now the controversy was no longer about abuses but directly about
that which the Reformers thought to be abused—which Melanchthon
now labels "the chief locus of Christian doctrine."[9] Now he can no
longer speak of Christians attempting together to settle contrary eval-
uations of practice; now he speaks of Lutheran confessors and their
"adversaries," who have no "knowledge of Christ."[10] By dividing on
this issue, the opponents have definitely divided the Church: "Therefore, even if they successfully claim the name *church* for themselves,
we know that Christ's Church itself is among us."[11]

In the self-understanding of the CA, the matter at issue between
the confessors and their critics is "justification by faith alone" and
nothing else of independent importance. And where this dogmatic
proposal was actually rejected, there the confessors could not recognize the true Church. Pfnür is quite right that the object of Roman
Catholic consideration and of Lutheran advocacy must be the CA
and not the theology of Luther as such.[12] If both sides of ecumenical
discussions could keep this rigorously in mind, much would be gained.
But just so, it is vital to remember with equal rigor how radical a
document the CA is. It was an ecumenical statement and claim, but
that does not mean that it was or is a list of existing agreements. It is
a proposal to subject all churchly teaching and practice to the critique
formulated by the proposition that we are justified by faith alone.
Recognition of the CA—by whomever—is recognition of the need and
biblical-traditional legitimacy of this critical enterprise.

III.

There is a second sort of argument for recognition that could render its own conclusion vain. It is a very traditional sort of argument and has created a long series of ecumenical disasters, from incidents at the Diet of Augsburg itself to the present day. This argument treats theological propositions as if they were meaningful independently of their critical and creative function in the life of the Church and so negotiates them directly and for their own sake. In the present case, this form of discussion sets the formula "justification by faith alone," and various propositions from the CA, between the parties and sets out to inquire whether they cannot be so interpreted as to be acceptable by all. But of course, with sufficient dialectical skill, any formulas can be so interpreted for any set of parties, and little is usually thereby accomplished. Moreover, in that "justification by faith alone" is—as we shall see—a hermeneutical slogan for a whole reformation of churchly discourse; the procedure is even more futile in its case than in some others.

When the above is forgotten, discussion of justification eludes reality; its center will not hold. We will certainly find that the Reformers' formula can be made acceptable to all hands. And after the agreement, we will approve one another's actual proclamation of the gospel and sacramental practice as little as before. The classic case is none other than the negotiations of the Committee of Fourteen, at the Diet of Augsburg itself, hoping to reconcile the CA and its *Confutation*.[13] Melanchthon reported to Luther: "I compelled Eck to confess that righteousness is correctly assigned by us to faith. But he wanted us to write 'that we are justified through grace and faith.' I had no objection—but then, that fool didn't understand the word *grace*."[14]

It would be unfair to suggest that Vinzenz Pfnür's work runs neatly in this track, but it perhaps does not altogether avoid it. And Pannenberg's—for the rest, tendentious[15]—use of Pfnür's results avoids it less. In Pfnür's major work, his chief contention is (1) that the Reformers' polemic was directed against only one version of medieval teaching about justification, that of the Franciscans and nominalists; (2) that their Roman opponents' polemic was directed against a misunderstood version of the Reformers' teaching, occasioned by incautious formulations from the earliest period of the Reformation; and (3) that if this talking past each other is cured, mutually satisfactory formulations are possible.[16] Pfnür's observations are of great value in themselves; whether they eliminate "justification" as an occasion of controversy between Rome and Wittenberg is another matter.

From the Committee of Fourteen[17] to Pfnür[18] and now others, the most tempting enterprise of formula-negotiation has been the adjusting to each other of the Reformers' "faith" and the scholastics' key formula "faith formed by love" (*fides caritate formata*). Each side regularly comes to see how it *could* say what the other says—"properly interpreted." Since the Reformers teach that the faith which justifies is not "mere historical faith" but "living faith," why should not love be understood as the required liveliness? And if the reforming movement can accept that interpretation, why could not Roman Catholics agree that we are saved "only by" *such* "faith"? Just as regularly, each side remains obscurely uneasy with the slogan of the other. So why not move to a new, more comprehensive formula? The Committee of Fourteen agreed on "justification by faith," with the latter understood as *gratia gratum faciens* (the grace that makes graced); here *gratum faciens* stands for that element of real occurrence in the life of the believer that the Reformers' critics missed in the sheer word *faith*. And Pfnür regards that agreement as the great sign of hope for the present.[19]

What can be wrong with the above proceedings? They are undoubtedly attractive on the page or in the conference room. Nor may we say that the dialectic possibilities they disclose are entirely unworthy of attention. Yet by them we have lost hold of the Reformers' whole point. Indeed, if we attend to more than the sheer terminology of the two initial formulas, they direct us not to a third mediating formula but to where the real theological difference was.

"Mere historical faith" and "unformed faith" refer doubtless to the same phenomenon: the possession of true information about Christ such as the damned have and still perish. What more is needed for justification?

The formula *fides caritate formata* adds[20] an additional quality in the believer: love. *Fides caritate formata* is the formula for a pattern of churchly exhortation a la Saint James: "You believe. That is good.

Now produce appropriate works of love." This is the whole message of the *Confutation* itself, which explicitly identifies the demand for works other than faith, and for their recognition as meritorious, with the position that it is not faith "by itself" that justifies, but only faith "which works through love," that the gift of grace is faith and "also" hope and love.[21]

There is of course nothing wrong with the exhortation to love, even to love because we would be faithful. But if its slogan, *fides caritate formata*, is made the formula for what justifies, then in its churchly function it becomes a slogan for precisely what the Reformers attacked: a proclamation of Christ that itself turns into new exhortation and directs people back to their own fulfillment of—in themselves, necessary—moral and religious standards, to find therein the ground of their confidence before God.

If we turn now to the Reformers' distinction between historical and living faith, we perhaps expect to find a similar pattern, with some personal quality—though perhaps, for example, sincerity instead of love—stipulated as a needed supplement to historical faith. But in fact the CA makes a wholly different kind of distinction: "historical faith" is apprehension of the mere "history" of Christ; "living faith" is apprehension of the promise made by those histories when proclaimed as done for us.[22] If my faith is merely historical, the problem is not that I lack a personal quality but that the essential point of the gospel has not gotten through to me—perhaps because the Church did not make it. And thus we come to the true function of the Reformers' distinction. The difference between historical and living faiths is not between two responses to one message, but between the responses to two different messages: "Christ died for the world, and now this is how you get into the result of his death" versus "Christ died and now lives for you."

"We are justified by faith alone" is not a stipulation about the anthropological conditions of justification, but about the special hermeneutical character of the gospel as a mode of discourse: that it must be promise and not exhortation if it is to be the creative word from God that sets lives right. The Reformers' complaint is that such authentic proclamation occurs too rarely in the Church and that this is no accident but is made inevitable by entrenched patterns of practice and interpretation. Their proposal is to set new doctrinal regulation against such practice and interpretation. It is all this churchly reality that is not seen[23] when we stare too hard at mere formulas.

That the above is the correct interpretation of the CA's intention is proven by Article 4 of Melanchthon's Apology, in which the CA's author lays out what the Roman delegates rejected in rejecting it. Faced with the denial of "justification by faith alone," he does not proceed immediately to the defense of the proposition as such. He rather undertakes to describe the "generative starting points"[24] of the Reformers' and their opponents' antagonistic modes of practice and proclamation.[25] These he discovers not in scholastic differences but in what we would now call hermeneutics: the Reformers acknowledge and practice two necessary modes of discourse in the Church, their opponents but one. The Reformers preach, verbally and sacramentally, both law and promise,[26] their opponents—contrary perhaps to their subjective intention[27]—only law.[28]

The "abuse" of the medieval church is that remission and justification enter the Church's discourse as if they, at least in part, depended on conditions controllable by us, that is, as if they were matters of law.[29] Discourse about Christ then becomes the provision of information that some other conditions, those beyond our fulfilling, have objectively been satisfied—that is, hermeneutically, the Church's discourse about Christ becomes merely historical speech about him, lacking any unique existential function,[30] a transfer from one head to another of information which can be possessed without personal transformation.[31]

The adversaries' teaching, by its legal hermeneutic, is done as description of a process leading to salvation: *a* must happen for *b* to be possible, then *b* must happen for *c* to be possible, and so on.[32] When salvation is described as a process, God will—by any Christian —be named as Chief Mover, but the creature must be given *some* conditions of the process's completion to fulfill or he will be left out of the event of his own salvation. At some *b* or *c*, the process must— so far as my *concern* is concerned—be up to me. The demand that the creature's "doing what lies in him" in *some* way "merits" remission, and so on,[33] is then inevitable and indeed—within this scheme!— justified. Moreover, knowing historical information about Christ can be some of the creature's part, but implausibly the whole of it; *this* faith must indeed be completed by other, more substantial works.[34]

As propositions on the page or in a suitably isolated classroom, this sort of theology can be so developed as to avoid the appearance of Pelagianism; all we need do is adopt the anti-Pelagian codicil that if some step "b" is my contribution to the salvation process's completion, it too is, at the level of primary causality, to be attributed to God. But Melanchthon is concerned with his opponents' whole style of churchly discourse, and when this theology determines the discourse of the confessional or of preaching or catechetics, when it functions for hearers, the anti-Pelagian codicil is no help. If I understand my final relation to God as the outcome of a process which can at certain points stop if my contribution fails, and precisely if I am assured of God's grace, that is, that his contribution can be relied upon, my contribution or its failure makes the whole difference in my life.[35]

For actual hearers of this theology, Melanchthon thus sees only a choice of damnations.[36] If the hearer "remains unconcerned," that is, is unbroken in his alienated assumption that the reasonable conditions of the salvation process's completion are in his control, spiritually empty works-righteousness is the result.[37] If, alternatively, this teaching encounters a "troubled conscience," it works damnation.[38] If the law enters that realm of endlessly uncontrolled ambiguity called the heart and so demands not this or that civil work but love and hope, the hearer's situation is desperate and can be saved only by promise. For the heart's law cannot be obeyed by one who in any way already is and knows himself a sinner: all lawlike talk "accuses his conscience and terrifies him," and the flight from God thus imposed is the opposite of loving obedience, even when the flight takes the form of religiosity. If then the teachers of the Church bring no different kind of message from God, if also their talk about Christ is legal in its logic, all is lost.[39]

I have developed these last paragraphs somewhat more fully than the immediate point about the CA's interpretation might have required in order to make a chief point of this paper more plastic. "Justification by faith alone" is a slogan for precisely the sort of critique developed in the Apology's Article 4; I have wanted to provide a brief sample. Recognition of the CA would be recognition that such critique, when it finds an object, is legitimate, and that in fact it is needed. Therewith we also see the relative importance of such researches as Pfnür's. If indeed the Lutheran polemic touches only preaching and teaching instructed by Biel and his like, we may rejoice—and look about all denominations to see if Biel is really gone. If, as seems clear to me, it touches pretty well all Western Christianity after Augustine—including even Thomas[40]—the work to be done is more daunting. The main question, however, is whether the polemic had and has any legitimate object at all. For Roman Catholics to join Lutherans in affirming the CA would be for them to agree that it did and does also on their side of denominational lines.

Having described the two opposing modes of teaching and attacked the one's legitimacy, Melanchthon in the remainder of the Apology's Article 4 argues—on this basis—for the controversial slogan itself. The form of his arguments is most instructive, but there is no room to analyze them here. It is, however, in place to wonder why he bothers at all. Challenged by the *Confutation,* he begins with the hermeneutic of law and promise. Why not leave it at that instead of deriving from this hermeneutic a defense of the slippery slogan about justification? Much misunderstanding might have been avoided.

The explanation most pertinent here is also the simplest: history had cast the discussion as a discussion about the grace that makes graced, about that in us which corresponds to the grace of God, and that is how the argument was then pursued by all parties to the discussion. The same assertion is made by the active-voice sentence "Only God, by speaking promise, justifies us" and by the passive "We are justified only by hearing God's promise." The first form of expression is the plainer hermeneutical statement, but history picked the second form and for the hearing provided the word *faith.* The Reformers' use of *faith* presumes, and sometimes makes explicit, a logical analysis: hearing is not a univocal notion; there are modes of hearing, distinguished as response to the modes of address. Faith is a way of knowing, formally determined by its object, promise.[41] The mode is specified: to apprehend a promise and to "oppose the promise" to guilt and anxiety are exactly the same thing.[42]

So much for the exegesis of the Apology. It is time to return to the main line of argument and draw the conclusions.

IV.

Fundamentally, to recognize the CA must be to recognize that a specific critique of all churchly discourse is a needed activity in the whole Church. Just so, it is an act of dogmatic significance.

If we understand this, the question of recognition wears a different aspect than is often supposed. Above all, it loses its denominational onus. It is not fundamentally a question of Roman Catholic approval of the Lutheran denomination. The Lutheran ferment is alive in Roman Catholicism itself; indeed, it probably is now livelier there than in the Lutheran denomination. First and foremost, meaningful Roman Catholic recognition of the CA would be a word for this reality within Roman Catholicism's own life. Why should that word not now be spoken?

Secondarily, recognition would be a word spoken together with those who already—however feebly!—so speak, and therefore a great ecumenical act. The CA has of course become in the meantime the charter of a denomination.

Ecumenically, one aim would surely be that clearing of the road which Pfnür and others analyze and advocate: if the descendants of the Reformers and their critics can agree about the CA, what can permanently separate them? To what has been so well said on this point, I have nothing to add. But I do want to add a second ecumenical aim: Roman Catholic recognition of the CA might even recall official Lutherans to the CA's actual meaning.

In that Lutherans necessarily now take the CA as the charter of our denomination, we are tempted to forget its intent in a yet more disastrous way than any so far analyzed in this paper. We are tempted to take it as a listing of what we believe that others may not—and, just so, *not* as the charter of a reforming movement. As long as we are alone with our document, the temptation is apparently irresistible. But what if the CA were no longer only ours?

For all that I have—rightly—called Roman Catholicism and Lutheranism alike denominations, Roman Catholicism is the bulk of Western Christianity, from which all other groups willy-nilly take their cues. What if *Rome* said, "The critique of churchly discourse represented by 'justification by faith alone' is something we all need?"

Perhaps the Lutheran denomination might be shocked into rereading the CA and examining its own life thereby. Perhaps the Lutheran denomination might even be shocked into its own sole authenticity and again nurture and release into the Church a few actual Lutheran reformers. There is no saying what might happen then, *ubi et quando visum est spiritu* ("when and where the Spirit pleases"; cf. CA, 5:2).

NOTES

1. Vinzenz Pfnür, *Einig in der Rechtfertigungslehre? Die Rechtfertigungslehre der "Confessio Augustana" (1530) und die Stellungnahme der katholischen Kontroverstheologie zwischen 1530 und 1535* (Wiesbaden: Franz Steiner, 1970).

2. CA, foreword to Arts. 22 ff.

3. All of this is now neatly laid out by Pfnür, *Einig*, pp. 98 ff.

4. CA, 24:28–29.

5. See p. 34 above.

6. Ibid., p. 28.

7. CA, foreword to part 2.

8. Ap., 4: 1.

9. Ibid., 2.

10. Ibid., 398.

11. Ibid., 400.

12. The theology of Melanchthon is also not the object—a point which Pfnür does not always keep clearly in mind. As to whether the differences between Luther and the CA represent corrections of overstatements, as Pfnür maintains throughout, or the inevitable and appropriate differences between a theological genius and the spokesman for the church party, this is outside our present concern.

13. For a report of these, see now Pfnür, *Einig*, pp. 251 ff.

14. *WA Br*, 5: 555.

15. "Tendentious" is unfortunately not too strong. Appealing to Pfnür, Pannenberg writes: "Eck found it possible to speak of a consensus 'on the thing itself,' and Melanchthon was able in the Apology to connect the concept of faith with the *gratia gratum faciens* (the grace which makes graced) on the grounds that love is the effect of faith" (see p. 35 above). We have just seen what Melanchthon thought of Eck's agreement. And the passage of the Apology to which Pannenberg refers, 4: 116, turns out, to one's astonishment, to read: "And because this faith by itself (*sola haec fides*) receives remission of sins, makes us acceptable to God, and brings the Holy Spirit, it could more correctly be called 'grace which makes

164

graced' than can its subsequent effect, that is, love (*rectius vocari gratia gratum faciens poterat, quam effectus sequens, videlicet dilectio*)." There is indeed "reference to" love, but negatively, in order to attach the tag *gratia gratum faciens* to faith as to something *other* than love.

16. Summarizing Pfnür, *Einig*, pp. 385, 397.

17. See the account, ibid., pp. 251 ff.

18. Esp. in the essay in this volume, pp. 13–15. But see also *Einig*, pp. 193 ff., 379 ff.

19. See pp. 14, 19 above.

20. There will be protests at my use of *adds*. *Fides caritate formata*, it will be said, is in proper Aristotelian language and should not be taken to name two phenomena, one of which could be added to the other; rather faith and love are named as matter and form of one reality, which without either would not be. Certainly, modern theologians who wish to use the formula following proper Aristotelian canons may do so, but that is not how the formula has heretofore in fact been used, except in classrooms. It is already bad Aristotelese that matter and form are named by words that in ordinary use pick out two actual phenomena of the same ontological sort. And if we note how the formula has functioned in the life of the Church, we see that this Aristotelian barbarism is no accident but dictated by the practical intention, which indeed wishes to establish an additive relation between faith and love. So, for example, no less a person than Seripando at no less a place than Trent (*CT*, 5: 522, l. 1 ff.): "Through sins that are against love, love itself is in such fashion removed that unformed faith (sic!) remains." Here unformed faith is itself an actual phenomenon—even if that is an Aristotelian oddity—produced by the subtraction of love and to be cured by love's return. The council itself agreed and explicitly stipulated that this unformed faith is a real phenomenon and properly called faith (*Decree on Justification*, canon 28). Or one may consider the Roman polemicists described by Pfnür, for example, Johannes Mensing, as quoted by Pfnür, *Einig*, pp. 341–42: "What good did it do them (biblical figures such as Ananias and Sapphira) . . . that they believed and were baptized? . . . Why did they not live through this faith? Something must be missing, and that is love, the reliable virtue that gives its power to faith and all other virtues."

21. *Confutation*, 5, 20.

22. For example, CA, 20: 26.

23. Assuredly not by Pfnür.

24. Ap., 4: 4: *fons*.

25. This task occupies Ap., 4: 5–47.

26. Ibid., 5: *locos*.

27. Ibid., 17.

28. Ibid., 7.

29. Ibid., 9, 22–23, 34, 130–131, etc.

30. Ibid., 17.

31. Ibid., 48, 240, 303, etc.

32. Ibid., 7, 17, 19.

33. Ibid., 7, 9.

34. Ibid., 17, 48.

35. This analysis, assumed throughout Ap., 4, appears explicitly in such arguments as that in 109.

36. Ibid., 21, 34.

37. Ibid., 9, 10, 12–16, 212, 258, etc.

38. Ibid., 20, 167, 221, 285, 289, 301, 319, etc.

39. Ibid., 33–35, 38.

40. The *even* is sincerely meant; Thomas is doubtless the ecumenical dogmatician of the Western Church—though that compliment may be double-edged. Nevertheless, no more compendious statement of what the CA and the Apology finally attack could be made than Thomas's definition (ST, 1–2, q. 113, a. 5): "The justification of the ungodly is a certain process (*motus*) in which the human person (*mens*) is moved from a state of sin to a state of justice."

41. Ap., 4: 50–51, 55–56, 67, 70, 83–84, 86, 98, 101, 212, 297, etc.

42. Ibid., 247, 304.

The Augsburg Confession*

*A Confession of Faith Presented in Augsburg
by certain Princes and Cities to His
Imperial Majesty Charles V
in the Year 1530*

PREFACE

(1) Most serene, most mighty, invincible Emperor, most gracious Lord:

A short time ago Your Imperial Majesty graciously summoned a diet of the empire to convene here in Augsburg. In the summons Your Majesty indicated an earnest desire to deliberate concerning matters pertaining to the Turk, that traditional foe of ours and of the Christian religion, and how with continuing help he might effectively be resisted. (2) The desire was also expressed for deliberation on what might be done about the dissension concerning our holy faith and the Christian religion, and to this end it was proposed to employ all diligence amicably and charitably to hear, understand, and weigh the judgments, opinions, and beliefs of the several parties among us, to unite the same in agreement on one Christian truth, (3) to put aside whatever may not have been rightly interpreted or treated by either side in the writings of either party, (4) to have all of us embrace and adhere to a single, true religion and live together in unity and in one fellowship and church, even as we are all enlisted under one Christ. (5) Inasmuch as we, the undersigned elector and princes and our associates, have been summoned for these purposes, together with other electors, princes, and estates, we have complied with the command and can say without boasting that we were among the first to arrive.

(6) In connection with the matter pertaining to the faith and in conformity with the imperial summons, Your Imperial Majesty also

*According to the translation of the Latin text in Tappert, 23–96.

167

graciously and earnestly requested that each of the electors, princes, and estates should commit to writing and present, in German and Latin, his judgments, opinions, and beliefs with reference to the said errors, dissensions, and abuses. (7) Accordingly, after due deliberation and counsel, it was decided last Wednesday that, in keeping with Your Majesty's wish, we should present our case in German and Latin today (Friday). (8) Wherefore, in dutiful obedience to Your Imperial Majesty, we offer and present a confession of our pastors' and preachers' teaching and of our own faith, setting forth how and in what manner, on the basis of the Holy Scriptures, these things are preached, taught, communicated, and embraced in our lands, principalities, dominions, cities, and territories.

(9) If the other electors, princes, and estates also submit a similar written statement of their judgments and opinions, in Latin and German, (10) we are prepared, in obedience to Your Imperial Majesty, our most gracious lord, to discuss with them and their associates, in so far as this can honorably be done, such practical and equitable ways as may restore unity. Thus the matters at issue between us may be presented in writing on both sides, they may be discussed amicably and charitably, our differences may be reconciled, and we may be united in one, true religion, (11) even as we are all under one Christ and should confess and contend for Christ. All of this is in accord with Your Imperial Majesty's aforementioned summons. That it may be done according to divine truth we invoke almighty God in deepest humility and implore him to bestow his grace to this end. Amen.

(12) If, however, our lords, friends, and associates who represent the electors, princes, and estates of the other party do not comply with the procedure intended by Your Imperial Majesty's summons, if no amicable and charitable negotiations take place between us, (13) and if no results are attained, nevertheless we on our part shall not omit doing anything, in so far as God and conscience allow, that may serve the cause of Christian unity. (14) Of this Your Imperial Majesty, our aforementioned friends (the electors, princes, and estates), and every lover of the Christian religion who is concerned about these questions will be graciously and sufficiently assured from what follows in the confession which we and our associates submit.

(15) In the past, not only once, but many times, Your Imperial Majesty graciously gave assurance to the electors, princes, and estates of the empire, especially in a public instruction at the diet in Spires in 1526, (16) that for reasons there stated Your Imperial Majesty was not disposed to render decisions in matters pertaining to our holy faith but would diligently urge it upon the pope to call a council. (17) Again, by means of a written instruction at the last diet in Spires a year ago, (18) the electors, princes, and estates of the empire were, among other things, informed and notified by Your Imperial Majesty's viceroy (His Royal Majesty of Hungary and Bohemia, etc.) and by Your Imperial Majesty's orator and appointed commissioners, that Your Imperial Majesty's viceroy, administrators, and councilors of the imperial government (together with the absent electors, princes, and representatives of the estates) who were assembled at the diet convened in Ratisbon had considered the proposal concerning a general council (19) and acknowledged that it would be profitable to have such a council called. Since the relations between Your Imperial Majesty and the pope were improving and were progressing toward a good, Christian understanding, Your Imperial Majesty was sure that the pope would not refuse to call a general council, (20) and so Your Imperial Majesty graciously offered to promote and bring about the calling of such a general council by the pope, along with Your Imperial Majesty, at the earliest opportunity and to allow no hindrance to be put in the way.

(21) If the outcome should be such that these differences between us and the other party should not be amicably settled, we offer in full obedience, even beyond what is required, to participate in such a general, free, and Christian council as the electors, princes and estates have with the highest and best motives requested in all the diets of the empire which have been held during Your Imperial Majesty's reign. (22) We have at various times made our protestations and appeals concerning these most weighty matters, and have done so in legal form and procedure. (23) To these we declare our continuing adherence, and we shall not be turned aside from our position by these or any following negotiations (unless the matters in dissension are finally heard, amicably weighed, charitably settled, and brought

169

to Christian concord in accordance with Your Imperial Majesty's summons) as we herewith publicly witness and assert. (24) This is our confession and that of our associates, and it is specifically stated, article by article, in what follows.

ARTICLES OF FAITH AND DOCTRINE

1. God

(1) Our churches teach with great unanimity that the decree of the Council of Nicaea concerning the unity of the divine essence and concerning the three persons is true and should be believed without any doubting. (2) That is to say, there is one divine essence, which is called and which is God, eternal, incorporeal, indivisible, of infinite power, wisdom, and goodness, the maker and preserver of all things, visible and invisible. (3) Yet there are three persons, of the same essence and power, who are also coeternal: the Father, the Son, and the Holy Spirit. (4) And the term "person" is used, as the ancient Fathers employed it in this connection, to signify not a part or a quality in another but that which subsists of itself.

(5) Our churches condemn all heresies which have sprung up against this article, such as that of the Manichaeans, who posited two principles, one good and the other evil, and also those of the Valentinians, Arians, Eunomians, Mohammedans, and all others like these. (6) They also condemn the Samosatenes, old and new, who contend that there is only one person and craftily and impiously argue that the Word and the Holy Spirit are not distinct persons since "Word" signifies a spoken word and "Spirit" signifies a movement which is produced in things.

2. Original Sin

(1) Our churches also teach that since the fall of Adam all men who are propagated according to nature are born in sin. That is to say, they are without fear of God, are without trust in God, and are concupiscent. (2) And this disease or vice of origin is truly sin, which even now damns and brings eternal death on those who are not born again through Baptism and the Holy Spirit.

(3) Our churches condemn the Pelagians and others who deny that the vice of origin is sin and who obscure the glory of Christ's

170

merit and benefits by contending that man can be justified before God by his own strength and reason.

3. The Son of God

(1) Our churches also teach that the Word—that is, the Son of God—took on man's nature in the womb of the blessed virgin Mary. (2) So there are two natures, divine and human, inseparably conjoined in the unity of his person, one Christ, true God and true man, who was born of the virgin Mary, truly suffered, was crucified, dead, and buried, (3) that he might reconcile the Father to us and be a sacrifice not only for original guilt but also for all actual sins of men. (4) He also descended into hell, and on the third day truly rose again. Afterward he ascended into heaven to sit on the right hand of the Father, forever reign and have dominion over all creatures, and sanctify those who believe in him (5) by sending the Holy Spirit into their hearts to rule, comfort, and quicken them and defend them against the devil and the power of sin. (6) The same Christ will openly come again to judge the living and the dead, etc., according to the Apostles' Creed.

4. Justification

(1) Our churches also teach that men cannot be justified before God by their own strength, merits, or works but are freely justified for Christ's sake through faith (2) when they believe that they are received into favor and that their sins are forgiven on account of Christ, who by his death made satisfaction for our sins. (3) This faith God imputes for righteousness in his sight (Rom. 3, 4).

5. The Ministry of the Church

(1) In order that we may obtain this faith, the ministry of teaching the Gospel and administering the sacraments was instituted. (2) For through the Word and the sacraments, as through instruments, the Holy Spirit is given, and the Holy Spirit produces faith, where and when it pleases God, in those who hear the Gospel. (3) That is to say, it is not on account of our own merits but on account of Christ that God justifies those who believe that they are received into favor for

Christ's sake. Gal. 3:14, "That we might receive the promise of the Spirit through faith."

(4) Our churches condemn the Anabaptists and others who think that the Holy Spirit comes to men without the external Word, through their own preparations and works.

6. The New Obedience

(1) Our churches also teach that this faith is bound to bring forth good fruits and that it is necessary to do the good works commanded by God. We must do so because it is God's will and not because we rely on such works to merit justification before God, (2) for forgiveness of sins and justification are apprehended by faith, as Christ himself also testifies, "When you have done all these things, say, 'We are unprofitable servants'" (Luke 17:10). (3) The same is also taught by the Fathers of the ancient church, for Ambrose says, "It is ordained of God that whoever believes in Christ shall be saved, not through works but through faith alone, and he shall receive forgiveness of sins by grace."

7. The Church

(1) Our churches also teach that one holy church is to continue forever. The church is the assembly of saints in which the Gospel is taught purely and the sacraments are administered rightly. (2) For the true unity of the church it is enough to agree concerning the teaching of the Gospel and the administration of the sacraments. (3) It is not necessary that human traditions or rites and ceremonies, instituted by men, should be alike everywhere. (4) It is as Paul says, "One faith, one baptism, one God and Father of all," etc. (Eph. 4:5, 6).

8. What is the Church?

(1) Properly speaking, the church is the assembly of saints and true believers. However, since in this life many hypocrites and evil persons are mingled with believers, it is allowable to use the sacraments even when they are administered by evil men, according to the saying of Christ, "The scribes and Pharisees sit on Moses' seat," etc. (Matt. 23:2). (2) Both the sacraments and the Word are effectual by

reason of the institution and commandment of Christ even if they are administered by evil men.

(3) Our churches condemn the Donatists and others like them who have denied that the ministry of evil men may be used in the church and who have thought the ministry of evil men to be unprofitable and without effect.

9. Baptism

(1) Our churches teach that Baptism is necessary for salvation, that the grace of God is offered through Baptism, (2) and that children should be baptized, for being offered to God through Baptism they are received into his grace.

(3) Our churches condemn the Anabaptists who reject the Baptism of children and declare that children are saved without Baptism.

10. Lord's Supper

(1) Our churches teach that the body and blood of Christ are truly present and are distributed to those who eat in the Supper of the Lord. (2) They disapprove of those who teach otherwise.

11. Confession

(1) Our churches teach that private absolution should be retained in the churches. However, in confession an enumeration of all sins is not necessary, (2) for this is not possible according to the Psalm, "Who can discern his errors?" (Ps. 19:12).

12. Repentance

(1) Our churches teach that those who have fallen after Baptism can receive forgiveness of sins whenever they are converted, (2) and that the church ought to impart absolution to those who return to repentance. (3) Properly speaking, repentance consists of these two parts: (4) one is contrition, that is, terror smiting the conscience with a knowledge of sin, (5) and the other is faith, which is born of the Gospel, or of absolution, believes that sins are forgiven for Christ's sake, comforts the conscience, and delivers it from terror. (6) Then good works, which are the fruits of repentance, are bound to follow.

(7) Our churches condemn the Anabaptists who deny that those

who have once been justified can lose the Holy Spirit, (8) and also those who contend that some may attain such perfection in this life that they cannot sin. (9) Also condemned are the Novatians who were unwilling to absolve those who had fallen after Baptism although they returned to repentance. (10) Rejected also are those who do not teach that remission of sins comes through faith but command us to merit grace through satisfactions of our own.

13. The Use of the Sacraments

(1) Our churches teach that the sacraments were instituted not merely to be marks of profession among men but especially to be signs and testimonies of the will of God toward us, intended to awaken and confirm faith in those who use them. (2) Consequently the sacraments should be so used that faith, which believes the promises that are set forth and offered, is added.

14. Ecclesiastical Order

Our churches teach that nobody should preach publicly in the church or administer the sacraments unless he is regularly called.

15. Ecclesiastical Rites

(1) Our churches teach that those rites should be observed which can be observed without sin and which contribute to peace and good order in the church. Such are certain holy days, festivals, and the like.

(2) Nevertheless, men are admonished not to burden consciences with such things, as if observances of this kind were necessary for salvation. (3) They are also admonished that human traditions which are instituted to propitiate God, merit grace, and make satisfaction for sins are opposed to the Gospel and the teaching about faith. (4) Wherefore vows and traditions about foods and days, etc., instituted to merit grace and make satisfaction for sins, are useless and contrary to the Gospel.

16. Civil Affairs

(1) Our churches teach that lawful civil ordinances are good works of God (2) and that it is right for Christians to hold civil office, to sit as judges, to decide matters by the imperial and other existing laws,

174

to award just punishments, to engage in just wars, to serve as soldiers, to make legal contracts, to hold property, to swear oaths when required by magistrates, to marry, to be given in marriage.

(3) Our churches condemn the Anabaptists who forbid Christians to engage in these civil functions. (4) They also condemn those who place the perfection of the Gospel not in the fear of God and in faith but in forsaking civil duties. The Gospel teaches an eternal righteousness of the heart, but it does not destroy the state or the family. (5) On the contrary, it especially requires their preservation as ordinances of God and the exercise of love in these ordinances. (6) Therefore Christians are necessarily bound to obey their magistrates and laws except when commanded to sin, (7) for then they ought to obey God rather than men (Acts 5:29).

17. The Return of Christ for Judgment

(1) Our churches also teach that at the consummation of the world Christ will appear for judgment and will raise up all the dead. (2) To the godly and elect he will give eternal life and endless joy, (3) but ungodly men and devils he will condemn to be tormented without end.

(4) Our churches condemn the Anabaptists who think that there will be an end to the punishments of condemned men and devils. (5) They also condemn others who are now spreading Jewish opinions to the effect that before the resurrection of the dead the godly will take possession of the kingdom of the world, the ungodly being suppressed everywhere.

18. Free Will

(1) Our churches teach that man's will has some liberty for the attainment of civil righteousness and for the choice of things subject to reason. (2) However, it does not have the power, without the Holy Spirit, to attain the righteousness of God—that is, spiritual righteousness—because natural man does not perceive the gifts of the Spirit of God (I Cor. 2:14); (3) but this righteousness is wrought in the heart when the Holy Spirit is received through the Word. (4) In Book III of his *Hypognosticon* Augustine said these things in so many words: "We concede that all men have a free will which enables them to

175

make judgments according to reason. However, this does not enable them, without God, to begin or (much less) to accomplish anything in those things which pertain to God, for it is only in acts of this life that they have freedom to choose good or evil. (5) By 'good' I mean the acts which spring from the good in nature, that is, to will to labor in the field, will to eat and drink, will to have a friend, will to clothe oneself, will to build a house, will to marry, will to keep cattle, will to learn various useful arts, or will to do whatever good pertains to this life. (6) None of these exists without the providence of God; indeed, it is from and through him that all these things come into being and are. (7) On the other hand, by 'evil' I mean such things as to will to worship an idol, will to commit murder," etc.

19. The Cause of Sin

Our churches teach that although God creates and preserves nature, the cause of sin is the will of the wicked, that is, of the devil and ungodly men. If not aided by God, the will of the wicked turns away from God, as Christ says in John 8:44, "When the devil lies, he speaks according to his own nature."

20. Faith and Good Works

(1) Our teachers are falsely accused of forbidding good works. (2) Their publications on the Ten Commandments and others of like import bear witness that they have taught to good purpose about all stations and duties of life, indicating what manners of life and what kinds of work are pleasing to God in the several callings. (3) Concerning such things preachers used to teach little. Instead, they urged childish and needless works, such as particular holy days, prescribed fasts, brotherhoods, pilgrimages, services in honor of saints, rosaries, monasticism, and the like. (4) Since our adversaries have been admonished about these things, they are now unlearning them and do not preach about such unprofitable works as much as formerly. (5) They are even beginning to mention faith, about which there used to be marvelous silence. (6) They teach that we are justified not by works only, but conjoining faith with works they say that we are justified by faith and works. (7) This teaching is more tolerable than

176

the former one, and it can afford more consolation than their old teaching.

(8) Inasmuch, then, as the teaching about faith, which ought to be the chief teaching in the church, has so long been neglected (for everybody must grant that there has been profound silence concerning the righteousness of faith in sermons while only the teaching about works has been treated in the church), our teachers have instructed our churches concerning faith as follows:

(9) We begin by teaching that our works cannot reconcile God or merit forgiveness of sins and grace but that we obtain forgiveness and grace only by faith when we believe that we are received into favor for Christ's sake, who alone has been ordained to be the mediator and propitiation through whom the Father is reconciled. (10) Consequently whoever trusts that he merits grace by works despises the merit and grace of Christ and seeks a way to God without Christ, by human strength, although Christ has said of himself, "I am the way, and the truth, and the life" (John 14:6).

(11) This teaching concerning faith is everywhere treated in Paul, as in Eph. 2:8, "For by grace you have been saved through faith; and this is not because of works," etc.

(12) Lest anyone should captiously object that we have invented a new interpretation of Paul, this whole matter is supported by testimonies of the Fathers. (13) In many volumes Augustine defends grace and the righteousness of faith against the merits of works. (14) Ambrose teaches similarly in *De vocatione gentium* and elsewhere, for in his *De vocatione gentium* he says: "Redemption by the blood of Christ would become of little value and the preeminence of human works would not be superseded by the mercy of God if justification, which is accomplished by grace, were due to antecedent merits, for then it would be a reward for works rather than a free gift."

(15) Although this teaching is despised by inexperienced men, God-fearing and anxious consciences find by experience that it offers the greatest consolation because the consciences of men cannot be pacified by any work but only by faith when they are sure that for Christ's sake they have a gracious God. (16) It is as Paul teaches in Rom. 5:1, "Since we are justified by faith, we have peace with God."

(17) This whole teaching is to be referred to that conflict of the terrified conscience, nor can it be understood apart from that conflict. (18) Accordingly inexperienced and profane men, who dream that Christian righteousness is nothing else than civil or philosophical righteousness, have bad judgment concerning this teaching.

(19) Consciences used to be plagued by the doctrine of works when consolation from the Gospel was not heard. (20) Some persons were by their consciences driven into the desert, into monasteries, in the hope that there they might merit grace by monastic life. (21) Others invented works of another kind to merit grace and make satisfaction for sins. (22) Hence there was very great need to treat of and to restore this teaching concerning faith in Christ in order that anxious consciences should not be deprived of consolation but know that grace and forgiveness of sins are apprehended by faith in Christ.

(23) Men are also admonished that here the term "faith" does not signify merely knowledge of the history (such as is in the ungodly and the devil), but it signifies faith which believes not only the history but also the effect of the history, namely, this article of the forgiveness of sins—that is, that we have grace, righteousness, and forgiveness of sins through Christ.

(24) Whoever knows that he has a Father reconciled to him through Christ truly knows God, knows that God cares for him, and calls upon God. (25) He is not without God, as are the heathen, for devils and ungodly men are not able to believe this article of the forgiveness of sins; hence they hate God as an enemy, do not call upon him, and expect no good from him. (26) Augustine, too, admonishes his readers in this way concerning the word "faith" when he teaches that in the Scriptures the word "faith" is to be understood not as knowledge, such as is in the ungodly, but as confidence which consoles and lifts up terrified hearts.

(27) Our teachers teach in addition that it is necessary to do good works, not that we should trust to merit grace by them but because it is the will of God. (28) It is only by faith that forgiveness of sins and grace are apprehended, (29) and because through faith the Holy Spirit is received, hearts are so renewed and endowed with new affections as to be able to bring forth good works. (30) Ambrose says, "Faith is the mother of the good will and the right deed." (31) For

without the Holy Spirit man's powers are full of ungodly affections and are too weak to do works which are good in God's sight. (32) Besides, they are in the power of the devil, who impels men to various sins, impious opinions, and manifest crimes. (33) This we may see in the philosophers, who, although they tried to live honest lives, were not able to do so but were defiled by many manifest crimes. (34) Such is the feebleness of man when he governs himself by human strength alone without faith and without the Holy Spirit.

(35) Hence it may readily be seen that this teaching is not to be charged with forbidding works. On the contrary, it should rather be commended for showing how we are enabled to do good works. (36) For without faith human nature cannot possibly do the works of the First or Second Commandments. (37) Without faith it does not call upon God, expect anything of God, or bear the cross, but it seeks and trusts in man's help. (38) Accordingly, when there is no faith and trust in God, all manner of lusts and human devices rule in the heart. (39) Wherefore Christ said, "Apart from me you can do nothing" (John 15:5), (40) and the church sings,

> "Where Thou art not, man hath naught,
> Nothing good in deed or thought,
> Nothing free from taint of ill."

21. The Cult of Saints

(1) Our churches teach that the remembrance of saints may be commended to us so that we imitate their faith and good works according to our calling. Thus the emperor may follow the example of David in waging war to drive the Turk out of his country, for like David the emperor is a king. (2) However, the Scriptures do not teach us to pray to the saints or seek their help, for the only mediator, propitiation, highpriest, and intercessor whom the Scriptures set before us is Christ. (3) He is to be prayed to, and he has promised to hear our prayers. Such worship Christ especially approves, namely, that in all afflictions he be called upon. (4) "If anyone sins, we have an advocate with the Father," etc. (I John 2:1).

(1) This is about the sum of our teaching. As can be seen, there is nothing here that departs from the Scriptures or the catholic church

or the church of Rome, in so far as the ancient church is known to us from its writers. Since this is so, those who insist that our teachers are to be regarded as heretics judge too harshly. (2) The whole dissension is concerned with a certain few abuses which have crept into the churches without proper authority. Even if there were some difference in these, the bishops should have been so lenient as to bear with us on account of the confession which we have now drawn up, for even the canons are not so severe as to demand that rites should be the same everywhere, (3) nor have the rites of all the churches ever been the same. (4) Among us the ancient rites are for the most part diligently observed, for it is false and malicious to charge that all ceremonies and all old ordinances are abolished in our churches. (5) But it has been a common complaint that certain abuses were connected with ordinary rites. Because these could not be approved with a good conscience, they have to some extent been corrected.

ARTICLES IN WHICH AN ACCOUNT IS GIVEN OF THE ABUSES WHICH HAVE BEEN CORRECTED

(1) Inasmuch as our churches dissent from the church catholic in no article of faith but only omit some few abuses which are new and have been adopted by the fault of the times although contrary to the intent of the canons, we pray that Your Imperial Majesty will graciously hear both what has been changed and what our reasons for such changes are in order that the people may not be compelled to observe these abuses against their conscience.

(2) Your Imperial Majesty should not believe those who disseminate astonishing slanders among the people in order to inflame the hatred of men against us. (3) By thus exciting the minds of good men, they first gave occasion to this controversy, and now they are trying by the same method to increase the discord. (4) Your Imperial Majesty will undoubtedly discover that the forms of teaching and of ceremonies observed among us are not so intolerable as those ungodly and malicious men represent. (5) The truth cannot be gathered from common rumors or the accusations of our enemies. (6) However, it can readily be judged that nothing contributes so much to the maintenance of dignity in public worship and the cultivation of reverence

and devotion among the people as the proper observance of ceremonies in the churches.

22. Both Kinds

(1) In the sacrament of the Lord's Supper both kinds are given to
laymen because this usage has the command of the Lord in Matt.
26:27, "Drink of it, all of you." (2) Christ has here manifestly commanded with reference to the cup that all should drink of it.

(3) Lest anybody should captiously object that this refers only to
the priests, Paul in I Cor. 11:20 ff. cites an example from which it
appears that a whole congregation used both kinds. (4) This usage
continued in the church for a long time. It is not known when or by
whom it was changed, although Cardinal Cusanus mentions when the
change was approved. (5) Cyprian in several places testifies that the
blood was given to the people. (6) The same is testified by Jerome,
who said, "The priests administer the Eucharist and distribute the
blood of Christ to the people." (7) In fact, Pope Gelasius commanded
that the sacrament should not be divided. (8) It is only a custom of
quite recent times that holds otherwise. (9) But it is evident that a
custom introduced contrary to the commands of God is not to be
approved, as the canons testify (Dist. 3, chap. "Veritate" and the
following chapters). (10) This custom has been adopted not only in
defiance of the Scriptures but also in contradiction to ancient canons
and the example of the church. (11) Consequently, if any people preferred to use both kinds of sacrament, they should not have been
compelled, with offense to their consciences, to do otherwise. (12)
Because the division of the sacrament does not agree with the institution of Christ, the processions which were hitherto held are also
omitted among us.

23. The Marriage of Priests

(1) There has been common complaint concerning priests who have
not been continent. (2) On this account Pope Pius is reported to have
said that there were some reasons why priests were forbidden to marry
but that there are now far weightier reasons why this right should be
restored. Platina writes to this effect. (3) Since priests among us

desired to avoid such open scandals, they took wives and taught that it was lawful for them to contract matrimony. (4) In the first place, this was done because Paul says, "Because of the temptation to immorality each man should have his own wife" (I Cor. 7:2), and again, "It is better to marry than to be aflame with passion" (I Cor. 7:9). (5) In the second place, Christ said, "Not all men can receive this precept" (Matt. 19:11), by which he declared that all men are not suited for celibacy because God created man for procreation (Gen. 1:28). (6) Moreover, it is not in man's power to alter his creation without a singular gift and work of God. (7) Therefore those who are not suited for celibacy ought to marry, (8) for no law of man and no vow can nullify a commandment of God and an institution of God. (9) For these reasons our priests teach that it is lawful for them to have wives.

(10) It is also evident that in the ancient church priests were married men. (11) Paul said that a married man should be chosen to be bishop (I Tim. 3:2), (12) and not until four hundred years ago were priests in Germany compelled by force to live in celibacy. In fact, they offered such resistance that the archbishop of Mayence, when about to publish the Roman pontiff's edict on this matter, was almost killed by the enraged priests in an uprising. (13) In such a harsh manner was the edict carried out that not only were future marriages prohibited but existing marriages were also dissolved, although this was contrary to all laws, divine and human, and contrary even to the canons, both those made by the popes and those made by the most celebrated councils.

(14) Inasmuch as the world is growing old and man's nature is becoming weaker, it is also well to take precautions against the introduction into Germany of more vices.

(15) Besides, God instituted marriage to be a remedy against human infirmity. (16) The canons themselves state that in later times the old rigor should be relaxed now and then on account of man's weakness, and it is devoutly to be desired that this be done in the case of sacerdotal marriage. (17) And it seems that the churches will soon be lacking in pastors if marriage continues to be forbidden.

(18) Although the commandment of God is in force, although the custom of the church is well known, and although impure celibacy

causes may scandals, adulteries, and other crimes which deserve the punishments of just magistrates, yet it is a marvelous thing that nowhere is greater cruelty exercised than in opposition to the marriage of priests. (19) God has commanded that marriage be held in honor. (20) The laws of all well-ordered states, even among the heathen, have adorned marriage with the greatest praise. (21) But now men, and even priests, are cruelly put to death, contrary to the intent of the canons, for no other cause than marriage. (22) To prohibit marriage is called a doctrine of demons by Paul in I Tim. 4:3. (23) This can be readily understood now that the prohibition of marriage is maintained by means of such penalties.

(24) Just as no human law can nullify a command of God, so no vow can do so. (25) Accordingly Cyprian advised that women who did not keep the chastity which they had promised should marry. His words in the first book of his letters, Epistle XI, are these: "If they are unwilling or unable to persevere, it is better for them to marry than to fall into the fire through their lusts; at least they should give no offense to their brothers and sisters."

(26) The canons show some consideration toward those who have made vows before attaining a proper age, and as a rule vows used to be so made in former times.

24. The Mass

(1) Our churches are falsely accused of abolishing the Mass. Actually, the Mass is retained among us and is celebrated with the greatest reverence. (2) Almost all the customary ceremonies are also retained, except that German hymns are interspersed here and there among the parts sung in Latin. These are added for the instruction of the people, (3) for ceremonies are needed especially in order that the unlearned may be taught. (4) Paul prescribed that in church a language should be used which is understood by the people. (5) The people are accustomed to receive the sacrament together, in so far as they are fit to do so. (6) This likewise increases the reverence and devotion of public worship, for none are admitted unless they are first heard and examined. (7) The people are also admonished concerning the value and use of the sacrament and the great consolation it offers to anxious consciences, that they may learn to believe in God and ask for and

expect whatever is good from God. (8) Such worship pleases God, and such use of the sacrament nourishes devotion to God. (9) Accordingly it does not appear that the Mass is observed with more devotion among our adversaries than among us.

(10) However, it is evident that for a long time there has been open and very grievous complaint by all good men that Masses were being shamefully profaned and applied to purposes of gain. (11) It is also well known how widely this abuse extends in all the churches, by what manner of men Masses are celebrated only for revenues or stipends, and how many celebrate Masses contrary to the canons. (12) But Paul severely threatened those who dealt unworthily with the Eucharist when he said, "Whoever eats the bread or drinks the cup of the Lord in an unworthy manner will be guilty of profaning the body and blood of the Lord." (13) Accordingly when our priests were admonished concerning this sin, private Masses were discontinued among us inasmuch as hardly any private Masses were held except for the sake of gain.

(14) The bishops were not ignorant of these abuses. If they had corrected them in time, there would now have been less dissension. (15) By their own negligence they let many corruptions creep into the church. (16) Now when it is too late they are beginning to complain about the troubles of the church, although the disturbance was brought about by nothing else than those abuses which had become so manifest that they could no longer be borne. (17) Great dissensions have arisen concerning the Mass, concerning the sacrament. (18) Perhaps the world is being punished for such long continued profanations of the Mass as have been tolerated in the church for many centuries by the very men who were able to correct them and were under obligation to do so. (19) For in the Decalogue it is written, "The Lord will not hold him guiltless who takes his name in vain." (20) Since the beginning of the world nothing of the divine institution seems ever to have been so abused for the sake of gain as the Mass.

(21) To all this was added an opinion which infinitely increased private Masses, namely, that Christ had by his passion made satisfaction for original sin and had instituted the Mass in which an oblation should be made for daily sins, mortal and venial. (22) From this has come the common opinion that the Mass is a work which by its per-

formance takes away the sins of the living and the dead. (23) Thus was introduced a debate on whether one Mass said for many people is worth as much as special Masses said for individuals, and this produced that infinite proliferation of Masses to which reference has been made.

(24) Concerning these opinions our teachers have warned that they depart from the Holy Scriptures and diminish the glory of Christ's passion, (25) for the passion of Christ was an oblation and satisfaction not only for original guilt but also for other sins. (26) So it is written in the Epistle to the Hebrews, "We have been sanctified through the offering of the body of Jesus Christ once for all," (27) and again, "By a single offering he has perfected for all time those who are sanctified."

(28) The Scriptures also teach that we are justified before God through faith in Christ. (29) Now, if the Mass takes away the sins of the living and the dead by a performance of the outward act, justification comes from the work of the Mass and not from faith. But the Scriptures do not allow this.

(30) Christ commands us to do this in remembrance of him. Therefore the Mass was instituted that faith on the part of those who use the sacrament should remember what benefits are received through Christ and should cheer and comfort anxious consciences. (31) For to remember Christ is to remember his benefits and realize that they are truly offered to us; (32) and it is not enough to remember the history, for the Jews and the ungodly can also remember this. (33) Consequently the Mass is to be used to this end, that the sacrament is administered to those who have need of consolation. Ambrose said, "Because I always sin, I ought always take the medicine."

(34) Inasmuch as the Mass is such a giving of the sacrament, one common Mass is observed among us on every holy day, and on the other days, if any desire the sacrament, it is also administered to those who ask for it. (35) Nor is this custom new in the church, but before the time of Gregory the ancients do not mention private Masses but speak often of the common Mass. (36) Chrysostom says that the priest stands daily at the altar, inviting some to Communion and keeping others away. (37) And it appears from the ancient canons that some one person or other celebrated Mass and the rest of the presbyters and

deacons received the body of the Lord from him, (38) for the words of the Nicene canon read, "In order, after the presbyters, let the deacons receive Holy Communion from the bishop or from a presbyter." (39) Paul also commands concerning Communion that one wait for another in order that there may be a common participation.

(40) Since, therefore, the Mass among us is supported by the example of the church as seen from the Scriptures and the Fathers, we are confident that it cannot be disapproved, especially since the customary public ceremonies are for the most part retained. Only the number of Masses is different, and on account of the great and manifest abuses it would certainly be of advantage to reduce the number. (41) In former times, even in churches most frequented, Mass was not held every day; as the Tripartite History testifies in Book 9, "Again, in Alexandria, the Scriptures are read and the doctors expound them on Wednesday and Friday, and all things are done except for the solemn remembrance of the sacrifice."

25. Confession

(1) Confession has not been abolished in our churches, for it is not customary to administer the body of Christ except to those who have previously been examined and absolved. (2) The people are very diligently taught concerning faith in connection with absolution, a matter about which there has been profound silence before this time. (3) Our people are taught to esteem absolution highly because it is the voice of God and is pronounced by God's command. (4) The power of keys is praised, and people are reminded of the great consolation it brings to terrified consciences, are told that God requires faith to believe such absolution as God's own voice heard from heaven, and are assured that such faith truly obtains and receives the forgiveness of sins. (5) In former times satisfactions were immoderately extolled, but nothing was said about faith. Accordingly no fault is to be found with our churches on this point, (6) for even our adversaries are forced to concede to us that our teachers have shed light on the doctrine of repentance and have treated it with great care.

(7) Concerning confession they teach that an enumeration of sins is not necessary and that consciences should not be burdened with a scrupulous enumeration of all sins because it is impossible to recount

all of them. So the Psalm testifies, "Who can discern his errors?" (8) Jeremiah also says, "The heart of man is corrupt and inscrutable." (9) But if no sins were forgiven except those which are recounted, our consciences would never find peace, for many sins can neither be perceived nor remembered. (10) The ancient writers also testify that such an enumeration is not necessary, (11) for Chrysostom is quoted in the canons as saying, "I do not say that you should expose yourself in public or should accuse yourself before others, but I wish you to obey the prophet who says, 'Show your way to the Lord.' Therefore, confess your sins to God, the true judge, in your prayer. Tell him of your sins not with your tongue but with the memory of your conscience." (12) The marginal note in *De poenitentia*, Dist. 5, in the chapter "Consideret," admits that such confession is of human right. (13) Nevertheless, confession is retained among us on account of the great benefit of absolution and because it is otherwise useful to consciences.

26. The Distinction of Foods

(1) It has been the common opinion not only of the people but also of those who teach in the churches that distinction among foods and similar human traditions are works which are profitable to merit grace and make satisfaction for sins. (2) That the world thought so is evident from the fact that new ceremonies, new orders, new holy days, and new fasts were daily instituted, and the learned men in the churches exacted these works as a service necessary to merit grace and sorely terrified the consciences of those who omitted any of them. (3) From this opinion concerning traditions much harm has resulted in the church.

(4) In the first place, it has obscured the doctrine concerning grace and the righteousness of faith, which is the chief part of the Gospel and ought above all else to be in the church, and to be prominent in it, so that the merit of Christ may be well known and that faith which believes that sins are forgiven for Christ's sake may be exalted far above works and above all other acts of worship. (5) Paul therefore lays the greatest weight on this article and puts aside the law and human traditions in order to show that the righteousness of a Christian is something other than works of this sort; it is faith which believes

that for Christ's sake we are received into grace. (6) This teaching of Paul has been almost wholly smothered by traditions which have produced the opinion that it is necessary to merit grace and righteousness by distinctions among foods and similar acts of worship. (7) In treating of repentance no mention was made of faith; only works of satisfaction were proposed, and the whole of repentance was thought to consist of these.

(8) In the second place, these precepts obscured the commands of of God, for traditions were exalted far above the commands of God. Christianity was thought to consist wholly in the observance of certain holy days, rites, fasts, and vestments. (9) Such observances claimed for themselves the glamorous title of comprising the spiritual life and the perfect life. (10) Meanwhile the commands of God pertaining to callings were without honor—for example, that a father should bring up his children, that a mother should bear children, that a prince should govern his country. These were regarded as secular and imperfect works, far inferior to those glittering observances. (11) This error greatly tormented the consciences of devout people who grieved that they were bound to an imperfect kind of life—in marriage, in the magistracy, or in other civil occupations—and admired the monks and others like them, falsely imagining that the observances of such men were more pleasing to God.

(12) In the third place, traditions brought great dangers to consciences, for it was impossible to keep all traditions, and yet men judged these observances to be necessary acts of worship. (13) Gerson writes that many fell into despair, and some even took their own lives, because they felt that they could not keep the traditions and, meanwhile, they had never heard the consolation of grace and of the righteousness of faith. (14) We see that the summists and theologians gathered the traditions together and sought mitigations to relieve the consciences; yet they did not altogether succeed in releasing them but rather entangled consciences even more. (15) Schools and sermons were so preoccupied with gathering traditions that they have had no time to treat the Scriptures and seek for the more profitable teachings concerning faith, the cross, hope, the importance of civil affairs, and the consolation of sorely tried consciences. (16) Hence Gerson and certain other theologians greatly lamented that they were so hindered

by these bickerings about traditions that they were unable to devote their attention to a better kind of teaching. (17) Augustine also forbids the burdening of consciences with such observances and prudently admonishes Januarius that he should know that they are to be as things indifferent, for these are his words.

(18) Our teachers, therefore, must not be looked upon as having taken up this matter rashly or out of hatred for the bishops, as some wrongly suspect. (19) There was great need to warn the churches of these errors which had arisen from misunderstanding of traditions. (20) For the Gospel compels us to insist in the church on the teaching concerning grace and the righteouness of faith, and this cannot be understood if men suppose that they merit grace by observances of their own choice.

(21) Accordingly our teachers have taught that we cannot merit grace or make satisfaction for sins by the observance of human traditions. Hence observances of this kind are not to be thought of as necessary acts of worship. (22) Our teachers add testimonies from the Scriptures. In Matt. 15:1–20 Christ defends the apostles for not observing the customary tradition, a tradition which was seen to be legalistic and to have a relationship with the purifications of the law, and he says, "In vain do they worship me with the precepts of men." (23) So he does not require an unprofitable act of worship. Shortly afterward Christ says, "Not what goes into the mouth defiles a man." (24) It is also written in Rom. 14:17, "The kingdom of God is not food and drink," (25) and in Col. 2:16, "Let no one pass judgment on you in questions of food and drink or with regard to a festival or a sabbath."* (27) In Acts 15:10, 11 Peter says, "Why do you make trial of God by putting a yoke upon the neck of the disciples which neither our fathers nor we have been able to bear? But we believe that we shall be saved through the grace of the Lord Jesus, just as they will." (28) Here Peter forbids the burdening of consciences with numerous rites, whether of Moses or of others. (29) And in I Tim. 4:1, 3 Paul calls the prohibition of foods a doctrine of demons, for it is in conflict with the Gospel to institute or practice such works for the purpose of meriting grace through them or with the notion that Christian righteousness cannot exist without such acts of worship.

*The so-called *editio princeps* at this point cites Col. 2:20–21 as (26).

(30) Here our adversaries charge that our teachers, like Jovinian, forbid discipline and mortification of the flesh. But something different may be perceived in the writings of our teachers, (31) for they have always taught concerning the cross that Christians are obliged to suffer afflictions. (32) To be harassed by various afflictions and to be crucified with Christ is true and real, rather than invented, mortification.

(33) Besides, they teach that every Christian ought so to control and curb himself with bodily discipline, or bodily exercises and labors, that neither plenty nor idleness may tempt him to sin, but not in order to merit forgiveness of sins or satisfaction for sins by means of such exercises. (34) Such bodily discipline ought to be encouraged at all times, and not merely on a few prescribed days. (35) So Christ commands, "Take heed to yourselves lest your hearts be weighed down with dissipation," (36) and again, "This kind of demon cannot be driven out by anything but fasting and prayer." (37) Paul also said, "I pommel my body and subdue it." (38) By this he clearly shows that he pommeled his body not to merit forgiveness of sins by that discipline but to keep his body in subjection and fit for spiritual things and for discharging his duty according to his calling. (39) Condemned therefore is not fasting in itself, but traditions which with peril to conscience prescribe certain days and certain foods as if works of this sort were necessary acts of worship.

(40) Many traditions are nevertheless kept among us (such as the order of lessons in the Mass, holy days, etc.) which are profitable for maintaining good order in the church. (41) At the same time men are warned that such observances do not justify before God and that no sin is committed if they are omitted without scandal. (42) Such liberty in human rites was not unknown to the Fathers,' (43) for Easter was kept in the East at a time different from that in Rome, and when on account of this difference the Romans accused the East of schism, they were admonished by others that such customs need not be alike everywhere. (44) Irenaeus says, "Disagreement about fasting does not destroy unity in faith," and Pope Gregory indicates in Dist. 12 that such diversity does not violate the unity of the church. (45) In the Tripartite History, Book 9, many examples of dissimilar rites are gathered,

and this statement is made: "It was not the intention of the apostles to enact binding laws with respect to holy days but to preach piety toward God and good conversation among men."

27. Monastic Vows

(1) What is taught among us concerning monastic vows will be better understood if it is recalled what the condition of monasteries was and how many things were done in these monasteries every day that were contrary to the canons. (2) In Augustine's time they were voluntary associations. Afterward, when discipline fell into decay, vows were added for the purpose of restoring discipline, as in a carefully planned prison. (3) Many other observances were gradually added in addition to vows. (4) These fetters were laid on many, contrary to the canons, before they had attained a lawful age. (5) Many entered this kind of life through ignorance, for although they were not wanting in years, they were unable to judge their own strength. (6) Those who were thus ensnared were compelled to remain, though some could have been freed by appealing to the canons. (7) This was the case in convents of women more than in those of men, although more consideration should have been given to the weaker sex. (8) Such rigor displeased many good men before our time when they saw that girls and boys were thrust into monasteries for their maintenance and saw what unfortunately resulted from this arrangement, what scandals were created, what snares were placed on consciences. (9) They regretted that in such a momentous matter the authority of the canons was utterly ignored and despised. (10) To these evils was added the fact that vows had such a reputation that it was clearly displeasing to those monks in former times who had a little more understanding.

(11) They said that vows were equal to Baptism, and they taught that they merited forgiveness of sins and justification before God by this kind of life. (12) What is more, they added that monastic life merited not only righteousness before God but even more, for it was an observance not only of the precepts but also of the counsels of the Gospel. (13) Thus they made men believe that the monastic profession was far better than Baptism, and that monastic life was more meritorious than the life of magistrates, pastors, and the like who,

191

without man-made observances, serve their calling in accordance with God's commands. (14) None of these things can be denied, for they appear in their own books.

(15) What happened after such people had entered monasteries? Formerly there had been schools of the Holy Scriptures and other branches of learning which were profitable to the church, and pastors and bishops were taken from them. Now everything is different, and it is needless to rehearse what is well known. (16) Formerly people came together in monasteries to learn. Now they pretend that this kind of life was instituted to merit grace and righteousness. In fact, they assert that it is a state of perfection, and they put it far above all other kinds of life instituted by God. (17) We have rehearsed these things without odious exaggeration in order that our teaching on this topic may better be understood.

(18) In the first place, we teach concerning those who contract matrimony that it is lawful for all who are not suited for celibacy to marry, for vows can not nullify that command and institution of God. (19) This is the command of God, "Because of fornication let every man have his own wife." (20) Nor is it the command only, but God's creation and institution also compel those to marry who are not excepted by a singular work of God. This is according to the text in Gen. 2:18, "It is not good that the man should be alone." (21) Therefore those who obey this command and institution of God do not sin.

(22) What objection can be raised to this? Exaggerate the obligation of a vow as much as one pleases, it cannot be brought about that a vow abrogates the command of God. (23) The canons state that every vow is subject to the right of a superior. How much less are those vows valid which are made contrary to God's commands!

(24) If the obligation of vows could not be changed for any reason at all, the Roman pontiffs would not have granted dispensations, for it is not lawful for a man to annul an obligation which is plainly derived from divine law. (25) But the Roman pontiffs have prudently judged that leniency should be observed in connection with this obligation. Therefore, we read that they often granted dispensation from vows. (26) Well known is the case of the king of Aragon, who was recalled from a monastery, and there is no want of examples in our time.

(27) In the second place, why do our adversaries exaggerate the obligation or effect of a vow while they remain silent concerning the nature of a vow, which ought to be voluntary and chosen freely and deliberately? (28) Yet it is not unknown to what an extent perpetual chastity lies in man's power. (29) How few there are who have taken the vow spontaneously and deliberately! Before they are able to judge, boys and girls are persuaded, and sometimes even compelled, to take the vow. (30) Accordingly it is not fair to argue so insistently about the obligation inasmuch as it is conceded by all that it is contrary to the nature of a vow to make a promise which is not spontaneous and deliberate.

(31) Many canons annul vows made before the age of fifteen on the ground that before that age a person does not seem to have sufficient judgment to make a decision involving the rest of his life. (32) Another canon, making a greater concession to human weakness, adds a few years and forbids making a vow before the eighteenth year. (33) Whether we follow one canon or the other, most monastics have an excuse for leaving the monastery because a majority of them took vows before they reached such an age.

(34) Finally, although the violation of vows might be rebuked, yet it seems not to follow of necessity that the marriages of persons who violated them ought to be dissolved. (35) For Augustine denies that they should be dissolved in *Nuptiarum,* Question 27, Chapter I, and his authority is not inconsiderable, although others have subsequently differed from him.

(36) Although it appears that God's command concerning marriage frees many from their vows, our teachers offer still another reason to show that vows are void. Every service of God that is instituted and chosen by men to merit justification and grace without the command of God is wicked, for Christ says, "In vain do they worship me with the precepts of men." (37) Paul also teaches everywhere that righteousness is not to be sought for in observances and services devised by men but that it comes through faith to those who believe that they are received by God into favor for Christ's sake.

(38) It is evident that the monks have taught that their invented observances make satisfaction for sins and merit grace and justification. What is this but to detract from the glory of Christ and obscure

and deny the righteousness of faith? (39) It follows, therefore, that the vows thus customarily taken were wicked services and on this account were void, (40) for a wicked vow, taken contrary to the commands of God, is invalid. As the canon says, no vow ought to bind men to iniquity.

(41) Paul says, "You are severed from Christ, you who would be justified by the law; you have fallen away from grace." (42) Therefore those who would be justified by vows are severed from Christ and fall away from grace, (43) for those who ascribe justification to their vows ascribe to their own works what properly belongs to the glory of Christ.

(44) It cannot be denied that the monks taught that they were justified and merited forgiveness of sins by their vows and observances. In fact, they invented greater absurdities when they claimed that they could transfer their works to others. (45) If out of hatred anybody should be inclined to enlarge on these claims, how many things could be collected of which even the monks are now ashamed! (46) Besides all this, they persuaded men that their invented observances were a state of Christian perfection. (47) Is not this attributing justification to works? (48) It is no light offense in the church to recommend to the people a certain service invented by men without the command of God and to teach that such service justifies men. For righteousness of faith, which ought especially to be taught in the church, is obscured when the eyes of men are blinded by these remarkable angelic observances and this pretense of poverty, humility, and chastity.

(49) Furthermore, the commands of God and true service of God are obscured when men hear that only monks are in a state of perfection. For this is Christian perfection: honestly to fear God and at the same time to have great faith and to trust that for Christ's sake we have a gracious God; to ask of God, and assuredly to expect from him, help in all things which are to be borne in connection with our callings; meanwhile to be diligent in the performance of good works for others and to attend to our calling. (50) True perfection and true service of God consist of these things and not of celibacy, mendicancy, or humble attire. (51) The people draw many pernicious conclusions from such false commendations of monastic life. (52) They hear celibacy praised above measure, and therefore they engage in their married life

with a troubled conscience. (53) They hear that only mendicants are perfect, and therefore they have a troubled conscience when they keep their possessions or engage in business. (54) They hear that it is an evangelical counsel not to take revenge, and therefore some are not afraid to take vengeance in their private life since they are told that this is prohibited by a counsel and not by a precept. (55) Others err still more, for they judge that all magistracy and all civil offices are unworthy of Christians and in conflict with the evangelical counsel.

(56) Cases can be read of men who, forsaking marriage and the administration of the state, withdrew into a monastery. (57) They called this "fleeing from the world" and "seeking a holy kind of life." They did not perceive that God is to be served by observing the commands he has given and not by keeping the commands invented by men. (58) A good and perfect kind of life is one which has God's command in its favor. (59) Concerning such things it was necessary to admonish men.

(60) Before our times Gerson rebuked the error of the monks concerning perfection and testified that it was a novelty in his day to say that monastic life is a state of perfection.

(61) So there are many impious opinions which are associated with vows: that they justify, that they constitute Christian perfection, that the monks observe both the counsels and the precepts, and that monks do works of supererogation. (62) All these things, since they are false and useless, make vows null and void.

28. Ecclesiastical Power

(1) In former times there has been great controversy about the power of bishops, and some have improperly confused the power of the church with the power of the sword. (2) From this confusion great wars and tumults have resulted, while the pontiffs, relying on the power of keys, not only have instituted new forms of worship and burdened consciences with reservation of cases and violent excommunications but also have undertaken to transfer kingdoms of this world and take away the imperial power. (3) These wrongs have long since been rebuked in the church by devout and learned men. (4) Accordingly our teachers have been compelled, for the sake of instructing consciences, to show the difference between the power of the

church and the power of the sword, and they have taught that on account of God's command both are to be held in reverence and honor as the chief gifts of God on earth.

(5) Our teachers hold that according to the Gospel the power of keys or the power of bishops is a power or command of God to preach the Gospel, to remit and retain sins, and to administer the sacraments. (6) For Christ sent out the apostles with this command. "As the Father has sent me, even so I send you. Receive the Holy Spirit. If you forgive the sins of any, they are forgiven; if you retain the sins of any, they are retained." (7) According to Mark 16:15 he also said, "Go and preach the gospel to the whole creation."

(8) This power is exercised only by teaching or preaching the Gospel and by administering the sacraments either to many or to individuals, depending on one's calling. For it is not bodily things that are thus given, but rather such eternal things as eternal righteousness, the Holy Spirit, and eternal life. (9) These things cannot come about except through the ministry of Word and sacraments, for Paul says, "The gospel is the power of God for salvation to everyone who has faith," and Ps. 119:50 states, "Thy Word gives me life." (10) Inasmuch as the power of the church bestows eternal things and is exercised only through the ministry of the Word, it interferes with civil government as little as the art of singing interferes with civil government. (11) For civil government is concerned with other things than the Gospel. The state protects not souls but bodies and goods from manifest harm, and constrains men with the sword and physical penalties, while the Gospel protects souls from heresies, the devil, and eternal death.

(12) Therefore, ecclesiastical and civil power are not to be confused. The power of the church has its own commission to preach the Gospel and administer the sacraments. (13) Let it not invade the other's function, nor transfer the kingdoms of the world, nor abrogate the laws of civil rulers, nor abolish lawful obedience, nor interfere with judgments concerning any civil ordinances or contracts, nor prescribe to civil rulers laws about the forms of government that should be established. (14) Christ says, "My kingdom is not of this world," (15) and again, "Who made me a judge or divider over you?" (16) Paul also wrote in Phil. 3:20, "Our commonwealth is in heaven," (17)

and in II Cor. 10:4, 5, "The weapons of our warfare are not worldly but have divine power to destroy arguments," etc.

(18) In this way our teachers distinguish the functions of the two powers, and they command that both be held in honor and acknowledged as gifts and blessings of God.

(19) If bishops have any power of the sword, they have this not as bishops under a commission of the Gospel, but by human right granted by kings and emperors for the civil administration of their lands. This, however, is a function other than the ministry of the Gospel.

(20) When one inquires about the jurisdiction of bishops, therefore, civil authority must be distinguished from ecclesiastical jurisdiction. (21) Hence according to the Gospel (or, as they say, by divine right) no jurisdiction belongs to the bishops as bishops (that is, to those to whom has been committed the ministry of Word and sacraments) except to forgive sins, to reject doctrine which is contrary to the Gospel, and to exclude from the fellowship of the church ungodly persons whose wickedness is known, doing all this without human power, simply by the Word. (22) Churches are therefore bound by divine law to be obedient to the bishops according to the text, "He who hears you hears me."

(23) However, when bishops teach or ordain anything contrary to the Gospel, churches have a command of God that forbids obedience: "Beware of false prophets" (Matt. 7:15), (24) "If an angel from heaven should preach any other Gospel, let him be accursed" (Gal. 1:8), (25) "We cannot do anything against the truth, but only for the truth" (II Cor. 13:8), (26) and also, "Given to me is the authority for building up and not for tearing down." (27) The canons require the same thing (II, question 7, in chapters "Sacerdotes" and "Oves"). (28) Augustine also says in reply to the letters of Petilian that not even catholic bishops are to be obeyed if they should happen to err or hold anything contrary to the canonical Scriptures of God.

(29) If they have any other power or jurisdiction to decide legal cases (for example, pertaining to matrimony, tithes, etc.), bishops have this by human right. When the bishops are negligent in their performance of their duties, princes are bound, even against their will, to administer justice to their subjects for the sake of maintaining public peace.

(30) Besides, it is disputed whether bishops or pastors have the right to introduce ceremonies in the church and make laws concerning foods, holy days, grades or orders of ministers, etc. (31) Those who attribute this right to bishops cite as evidence the passage, "I have yet many things to say to you, but you cannot bear them now. When the Spirit of truth comes, he will guide you into all the truth." (32) They also cite the example of the apostles who commanded men to abstain from blood and from what is strangled. (33) Besides, they cite the change from the Sabbath to the Lord's Day—contrary to the Decalogue, it appears. No case is made more of than this change of the Sabbath. Great, they say, is the power of the church, for it dispensed from one of the Ten Commandments!

(34) Concerning this question our teachers assert, as has been pointed out above, that bishops do not have power to institute anything contrary to the Gospel. The canons concede this throughout the whole of Dist. 9. (35) Besides, it is against Scripture to require the observance of traditions for the purpose of making satisfaction for sins or meriting justification, (36) for the glory of Christ's merit is dishonored when we suppose that we are justified by such observances. (37) It is also evident that as a result of this notion traditions have multiplied in the church almost beyond calculation, while the teaching concerning faith and the righteousness of faith has been suppressed, for from time to time more holy days were appointed, more fasts prescribed, and new ceremonies and new orders instituted because the authors of these things thought that they would merit grace by these works. (38) So the penitential canons formerly increased, and we can still see some traces of these in the satisfactions.

(39) Again, the authors of traditions act contrary to the command of God when they attach sin to foods, days, and similar things and burden the church with the bondage of the law, as if in order to merit justification there had to be a service among Christians similar to the Levitical, and as if God had commissioned the apostles and bishops to institute it. (40) For thus some have written, and the pontiffs seem in some measure to have been misled by the example of the law of Moses. (41) This is the origin of such burdens as this, that it is a mortal sin to do manual work on holy days, even when it gives no offense to others, that certain foods defile the conscience, that fasting

which is privative and not natural is a work that appeases God, that it is a mortal sin to omit the canonical hours, that in a reserved case a sin cannot be forgiven except by the authority of the person who reserved the case, although the canons themselves speak only of reserving ecclesiastical penalties and not of reserving guilt.

(42) Where did the bishops get the right to impose such traditions on the churches and thus ensnare consciences when Peter forbids putting a yoke on the disciples and Paul says that authority was given for building up and not for tearing down? Why do they multiply sin with such traditions?

(43) Yet there are clear testimonies which prohibit the making of traditions for the purpose of appeasing God or as if they were necessary for salvation. (44) In Col. 2 Paul says, "Let no one pass judgment on you in questions of food and drink or with regard to a festival or a new moon or a sabbath." (45) Again, "If with Christ you died to the elemental spirits of the universe, why do you live as if you still belonged to the world? Why do you submit to regulations, 'Do not handle, Do not taste, Do not touch' (referring to things which all perish as they are used), according to human precepts and doctrines? These have an appearance of wisdom." (46) In Tit. 1 Paul also says, "Not giving heed to Jewish myths or to commands of men who reject the truth."

(47) In Matt. 15 Christ says concerning those who require traditions, "Let them alone; they are blind and leaders of the blind." (48) He rebukes such services and says, "Every plant which my heavenly Father has not planted will be rooted up."

(49) If bishops have the right to burden consciences with such traditions, why does Scripture so often prohibit the making of traditions? Why does it call them doctrines of demons? Was it in vain that the Holy Spirit warned against these?

(50) Inasmuch as ordinances which have been instituted as necessary or instituted with the intention of meriting justification are in conflict with the Gospel, it follows that it is not lawful for bishops to institute such services or require them as necessary. (51) It is necessary to preserve the doctrine of Christian liberty in the churches, namely, that bondage to the law is not necessary for justification, (52) as it is written in the Epistle to the Galatians, "Do not submit

again to a yoke of slavery." It is necessary to preserve the chief article of the Gospel, namely, that we obtain grace through faith in Christ and not through certain observances or acts of worship instituted by men.

(53) What, then, are we to think about Sunday and about similar rites in our churches? To this our teachers reply that it is lawful for bishops or pastors to make regulations so that things in the church may be done in good order, but not that by means of these we make satisfaction for sins, nor that consciences are bound so as to regard these as necessary services. (54) So Paul ordained that women should cover their heads in the assembly and that interpreters in the church should be heard one after another.

(55) It is proper that the churches comply with such ordinances for the sake of love and tranquility and that they keep them, in so far as one does not offend another, so that everything in the churches may be done in order and without confusion. (56) However, consciences should not be burdened by suggesting that they are necessary for salvation or by judging that those who omit them without offense to others commit a sin, any more than one would say that a woman sins by going out in public with her head uncovered, provided no offense is given.

(57) Of the same sort is the observance of Sunday, Easter, Pentecost, and similar festivals and rites. (58) Those who hold that the observance of the Lord's Day in place of the Sabbath was instituted by the church's authority as a necessary thing are mistaken. (59) The Scriptures, not the church, abrogated the Sabbath, for after the revelation of the Gospel all ceremonies of the Mosaic law can be omitted. (60) Nevertheless, because it was necessary to appoint a certain day so that the people may know when they ought to assemble, it appears that the church designated the Lord's Day for this purpose and it seems that the church was the more pleased to do this for the additional reason that men would have an example of Christian liberty and would know that the keeping neither of the Sabbath nor of any other day is necessary.

(61) There are monstrous discussions concerning the mutation of the law, concerning ceremonies of the new law, concerning the change of the Sabbath, all of which have arisen from the false notion that

there must be a service in the church like the Levitical service and that Christ commissioned the apostles and bishops to devise new ceremonies which would be necessary for salvation. (62) These errors crept into the church when the righteousness of faith was not taught with sufficient clarity. (63) Some argue that the observance of the Lord's Day is not *indeed* of divine obligation but is *as it were* of divine obligation, and they prescribe the extent to which one is allowed to work on holy days. (64) What are discussions of this kind but snares of conscience? Although they try to mitigate the traditions, moderation can never be achieved as long as the opinion remains that their observance is necessary. And this opinion must remain where there is no understanding of the righteousness of faith and Christian liberty.

(65) The apostles commanded that one should abstain from blood, etc. Who observes this prohibition now? Those who do not observe it commit no sin, for the apostles did not wish to burden consciences with such bondage but forbade such eating for a time to avoid offense. (66) In connection with the decree one must consider what the perpetual aim of the Gospel is.

(67) Scarcely any of the canons are observed according to the letter, and many of them become obsolete from day to day even among those who favor traditions. (68) It is not possible to counsel consciences unless this mitigation is practiced, that one recognizes that canons are kept without holding them to be necessary and that no harm is done to consciences even if the usage of men changes in such matters.

(69) The bishops might easily retain the lawful obedience of men if they did not insist on the observance of traditions which cannot be kept with a good conscience. (70) But now they demand celibacy and will admit no one to the ministry unless he swears that he will not teach the pure doctrine of the Gospel. (71) Our churches do not ask that the bishops restore concord at the expense of their honor (which, however, good pastors ought to do), (72) but ask only that they relax unjust burdens which are new and were introduced contrary to the custom of the church catholic. (73) Perhaps there were acceptable reasons for these ordinances when they were introduced, but they are not adapted to later times. (74) It is also apparent that some were adopted out of misunderstanding. It would therefore befit the clem-

ency of the bishops to mitigate these regulations now, for such change does not impair the unity of the church inasmuch as many human traditions have been changed with the passing of time, as the canons themselves show. (75) However, if it is impossible to obtain a relaxation of observances which cannot be kept without sin, we are bound to follow the apostolic injunction which commands us to obey God rather than men.

(76) Peter forbids the bishops to be domineering and to coerce the churches. (77) It is not our intention that the bishops give up their power to govern, but we ask for this one thing, that they allow the Gospel to be taught purely and that they relax some few observances which cannot be kept without sin. (78) If they do not do this, they must see to it how they will answer for it before God that by their obstinacy they offer occasion for schism.

Conclusion

(1) We have now reviewed the chief articles that are regarded as controversial. Although more abuses could be mentioned, to avoid undue length we have discussed only the principal ones. (2) There have been grave complaints about indulgences, pilgrimages, and misuse of excommunication. Parishes have been troubled in many ways by indulgence sellers. There have been endless quarrels between parish ministers and monks about parochial rights, confessions, burials, and countless other things. (3) We have passed over matters of this sort so that the chief points at issue, being briefly set forth, may more readily be understood.

(4) Nothing has here been said or related for the purpose of injuring anybody. (5) Only those things have been recounted which it seemed necessary to say in order that it may be understood that nothing has been received among us, in doctrine or in ceremonies, that is contrary to Scripture or to the church catholic. For it is manifest that we have guarded diligently against the introduction into our churches of any new and ungodly doctrines.

(6) In keeping with the edict of Your Imperial Majesty, we have desired to present the above articles in order that our confession may be exhibited in them and that a summary of the doctrine taught among us may be discerned. (7) If anything is found to be lacking in this

confession, we are ready, God willing, to present ampler information according to the Scriptures.

Your Imperial Majesty's faithful subjects:

> JOHN, duke of Saxony, elector
> GEORGE, margrave of Brandenburg
> ERNEST, with his own hand
> PHILIP, landgrave of Hesse, subscribes
> JOHN FREDERICK, duke of Saxony
> FRANCIS, duke of Lüneburg
> WOLFGANG, prince of Anhalt
> Senate and magistrate of Nuremberg
> Senate of Reutlingen